DATE DUE	
2 3 1997	

D1792114

LIBRARY
COLLEGE of the REDWOODS
EUREKA
7351 Tompkins Hill Road
Eureka, California 95501

OVERSIZE
LB1032.M424 1988   102933

The nurturing classroom: developing self-esteem, thinking...

THE NURTURING CLASSROOM

developing self-esteem, thinking skills and responsibility
through simple cooperation

Margaret E. McCabe, Ed.D. & Jacqueline Rhoades, M.S.

ITA Publications, Willits, California 95490

Copyright © 1988, 1989, 1990 by Margaret E. McCabe and Jacqueline Rhoades.
(Revised to include cooperative student study teams.)

All rights reserved. No part of this book may be reproduced or utilized in any form or by any means, electronic or mechanical, including photocopying, recording or by any information storage and retrieval system, without permission in writing from the authors.

Simple Cooperation™ and ITA™ are Trademarks belonging to Jacqueline Rhoades and Margaret E. McCabe.

For information on publications write or phone:

ITA Publications
1500 W. El Camino, Suite 350
Sacramento, CA 95833
1-916-922-1615

For information on workshops write to the above address or phone:
1-707-459-6100

Printed in the United States of America

Printing: 10, 9, 8

Library of Congress Cataloguing-in-Publication Data
McCabe, Margaret E.
    The Nurturing Classroom: developing self-esteem, thinking skills and responsibility through simple cooperation.
    Forward by David and Roger Johnson
    References & Resources; Index; Appendices
    1. Cooperative Learning
    2. Education
    3. Thinking Skills Development
    4. Communication
    5. Problem Solving
    6. Teaching Social Responsibility
    7. Student Group Learning
    8. Leadership Development
    9. Self-Esteem
  I. Rhoades, Jacqueline, Joint Author
  II. Title

Library of Congress Catalog Card Number: 88-81501

This book is dedicated to:

Margaret E. McCabe, my mother, my friend, who created a safe and caring home environment in which I could learn and grow.
                              Peggy

Renee Herman who taught me how to teach.
                              Jacquie

ACKNOWLEDGEMENTS

A very special "thank you" to three international leaders in education for taking time from their hectic schedules.

- **Dr. David Johnson** and **Dr. Roger Johnson** from the University of Minnesota for reviewing our manuscript and writing the Forward.

- **Dr. Arthur Costa** from California State University, Sacramento for reviewing and giving us valuable feedback and suggestions for Chapter 9: "Thinking Skills and the Cooperative Classroom."

We are indebted to four busy and exceptional educators: **Dana Lovitt**, first grade; **Starla Warburton**, special education; **Mary Rose**, secondary, and **Elaine Skeete**, County Office Instructional Services Coordinator, who read and contributed to this manuscript. And to **Jack Ward**, SELPA Director, who also took time from his busy schedule to read and comment on the manuscript.

To **Cindy Thompson** who saw us through the final stages of the "desk top publishing" system, in fact, we couldn't have completed this edition without Cindy. (And to **Bob Whitney** who helped us get started with "desk-top publishing.") And to **Cindy Kreeger** who proofed the final manuscript

Our appreciation also goes **to the teachers who allowed us to print** their lesson plans and other activities.

Finally, "thank you" to **all our workshop and class participants** who continually teach us.

TABLE OF CONTENTS

List of Figures xi
Forward: Dr. David Johnson xiii
Notes From Peggy and Jacquie xv

1. Welcome To Simple Cooperation 1
What is Simple Cooperation? 3
Goal Structures 4
Why Bother? 6
Integrating Academic and Social Skills 7
Conflict 9
Groups and Group Roles 10
Grades and Rewards 10
Teaching Thinking Skills 11
Teachers and Simple Cooperation 11
Laying the Foundation 13
Before you Begin 13

2. Creating A Cohesive Classroom Group 15
Setting Standards 17
Sample Standards 20
Getting Acquainted 21
Students Setting Standards 23
Completing the Task 25
Breaking Up 26
Conflict 27
Group Growth and Maturity 28
Summary 30
Quiz 31
Supplemental Information and Activities 32
Implementation Activities 34
Lesson/Activity Analysis 35
Sample Activities 36

3. Successful Communication 47
What is Successful Communication 50
Sending Messages - The "Speaker" 53
  (Get listener's attention; Establish eye contact; Claim own thoughts,
  ideas, feelings; The 3 C's; Expressing and Naming feelings;
  Frame of Reference; Conflict Situations; "I-Messages")
Receiving the Message -- The "Listener 58
  (Focus on Speaker; Clarify; Check your Perceptions;)
Nonverbal Communication 62
  (Proximity; Watching Yourself; Chcking Perceptions)
Congruence and Incongruence 67
Powerful Listening 68
Teaching Efective Communication 69
Feedback 69
Communication Continuum 71
Quiz 73
Supplemental Information and Activities 74
Sample Activities 79

4. Problem Solving And Conflict Management 95
Problem Solving Steps 99
Brainstorming 102
Decision Making Models 103
Summary 111
Quiz 112
Supplemental Information and Activities 113
Activity to Practice Before Teaching Problem Solving 114
Sample Activities 115

5. The Classroom As A Meeting: Helping Students Develop Responsibility And Dependability 117
The Group Member 121
The Facilitator as Monitor 123
The Beginning Recorder 124
The Praiser 125
The Time-Keeper 129
Checker 130
The Observer 130
The Advanced Recorder for Problem Solving and Brainstorming 135
The Advanced Facilitator 138
Summary 139
Quiz 141
Supplemental Information 142
Implementation Activities 145
Lesson Analysis Form 147

6. Grouping Students For Success 149
About Group Roles 152
Duration of Groups 152
Group Size 153
Academic Groups 154
Methods of Teacher Group Selection 155
Methods of Random Group Selection 158
Summary 162
Quiz 164
Supplemental Information 165
Implementation Acitivites 166

7. Monitoring Student Progress 167
Teacher Observation 169
Wrap-Up 173
Summary 176
Quiz 177
Supplemental Information 178
Sample Activities 180

8. Grades And Rewards 185
Group Rewards 188
Individual Rewards 190
Group Grades 190
Summary 193
Quiz 194
Implementation Activities 195

9. Thinking Skills And The Cooperative Classroom 199
Thinking Paths/Patterns 203
Internal Dialogue 204
Mediation 204
Developing Thinking Skills Vicariously 206
  (Group Process; Wrap-Up; Teacher-Student Observation)
Effective Thinking Behaviors 210-212
Infusing Higher-Level Questioning into Lessons 213
Direct Instruction Using a Published Program 215
Summary 215
Quiz 216
Supplemental Information and Sample Activities 217
Sample Acitivites 223
Self-Analysis of Questioning Strategies Used in Your Classroom 226
Self-Analysis of Your Own Thinking Strategies 227
Selected list of Publixhed Thinking Skills Programs 228
Bonus: Organizing for Success 230

10. Putting It All Together 233
Room Arrangement 235
Designing a Lesson 236
Planning Your Lesson 241
Lesson Plan Form 245
Summary 250
Quiz 251

Appendix I: Introducing Simple Cooperation to your Students 253

Appendix II: Sample Implementation Schedule 257

Appendix III: Sample Lesson Plans 277

Appendix IV: Cooperative Student Study Teams 319

Glossary 337

References & Resources 351

Index 343

LIST OF FIGURES

1. Major Components of Simple Cooperation 8
2. Stages of Group Development 18
3. Getting Acquainted Card 40
4. Focus Worksheet 44
5. Communication Process 51
6. Major Components of Effective Communication 70
7. Communication Continuum 71
8. Geometric Design Samples 83
9. Sample Tangrams 90
10. Brainstormed Ideas vs Constraints Charts .... 104 - 106
11. Problem Solving Examples .... 109 - 110
12. Group Roles 120
13. Group Roles Continuum 122
14. Praise, Compliment, Appreciation Forms .... 128 - 129
15. Observation Forms .... 133 - 135
16. Wall Chart 156
17. Teacher Observation Form 171
18. Wrap-Up Sheets 183
19. Achievement Certificates .... 195 - 197
20. Examples of Thinking Paths/Patterns 205
21. Preparing Higher-Level Questions 225
22. Organizing for Success Worksheet 231
23. Major Components of Simple Cooperation 237
24. Social Skills Components 238
25. Academic Components 239
26. Lesson Design 240
27. Integration of Social and Academic Objectives 242
28. Social Skills Continuum 243
29. Group Roles Continuum 244
30. Lesson Plan Form 245

Forward

This book will help you teach better and it will help students live better. Students will achieve more, use higher level reasoning strategies more frequently, think more critically, and gain more creative insights into the material being studied. Any classroom will benefit from the increased amount and depth of learning promoted by cooperation among students.

Higher achievement is not the only reason for using cooperative learning. The quality of life within classrooms improves when cooperative learning dominates over competitive and individualistic learning. Students care about each other and become committed to each other's success and well-being. Each day, students enter the classroom knowing that there are peers within the room who will be glad to see them, who care about them as persons, and who will help and assist them learn. Every student develops friends. And this is true regardless of ethnic and cultural differences, differences in primary languages, and whether they are handicapped or nonhandicapped. The joint success and the commitment to each other's well-being results in positive relationships regardless of how heterogeneous the students are. The caring and committed relationships fostered within cooperative classrooms can literally change lives.

The benefits of cooperative learning do not end at the close of the school day or school year. Cooperative learning provides an arena in which basic life survival skills are mastered. There is some evidence that grades in school are not correlated with career success or with quality of life as an adult. What is related to getting and keeping a job, and the quality of personal and family life, is social skills. The more skilled individuals are in working together to complete a task, the more likely they are to succeed in their careers and to build meaningful and satisfying personal relationships. Using cooperative learning makes the classroom more realistic in terms of the real world of work and family life and gives students a push toward success and happiness.

Of all the books on cooperative learning, this is one of the best. Jacquie Rhoades and Peggy McCabe are two very talented classroom teachers who have had the persistence, courage, and commitment to gain real expertise in using cooperative learning. They are also very talented and creative teacher trainers who have spent considerable time helping and supporting other teachers master cooperative learning. There are many insights into cooperative learning that only may be obtained by working side-by-side with a wide variety of classroom teachers, helping them solve the implementation problems unique to their classroom situations. Four of these insights are that (1) teachers need a clear conceptual understanding of cooperative learning in order to use it effectively, (2) conceptual understanding goes hand-in-hand with applying practical procedures in one's own classroom, (3) the power of cooperative learning springs from the personal commitment students feel toward each other and toward helping each other learn, and (4) students gain both short- and long-term when they are instructed in the basic interpersonal and small group skills they need to work effectively with each other to get the job done.

The Nurturing Classroom brings these four insights to life. After reading this book you will understand what cooperative learning is and you will have numerous practical applications that you may immediately use in your classrooms. The importance of building cohesive learning groups in which students care about each other is emphasized. And the teaching of social skills is highlighted. The combination of descriptions of what to do as a teacher and practical materials to help you use cooperative learning in your classroom makes this book invaluable. Reading it carefully, and applying what you learn in your classroom, will help you be more successful as a teacher, and it will help students live more productive and happy lives.

David W. Johnson
Roger T. Johnson
Cooperative Learning Center
University of Minnesota

NOTES FROM JACQUIE AND PEGGY

This book is about cooperative learning and how to teach your students the social skills they need for success in school and life.

ABOUT COOPERATIVE LEARNING

The concept of cooperative learning and students working together in groups is not a new idea. Its "formal" origin can be found in the works of pioneer sociologists and psychologists such as: John Dewey; Kurt Lewin; George Herbert Mead; Harry Stack Sullivan; Morton Deutsch; and others. "Formal" beginnings are usually founded on "informal" beginnings and cooperative learning is no exception. Throughout the history of education, teachers have used student groups, both cooperative and competitive, in their classrooms.

Cooperative Learning as a formal instructional model has gained a great deal of attention since the mid-sixties, mostly as a result of the work of David Johnson, Roger Johnson and Frank Johnson, The Johns Hopkins University, Elliot Aronson and Robert Slavin. And, although not as well known in the United States, Shlomo Sharan has conducted extensive research on the effect of cooperative learning in Israel. During the last seven or eight years, numerous other theorists and educational practiners have contributed volumes of work on using cooperative groups.

Research studies consistently reveal students learn more when cooperative learning techniques are used in the classroom. Their academic achievement increases; their self-concept improves; they become more enthusiastic learners; and they have fewer discipline problems.

The research says...

Thousands and thousands of teachers across the world are turning to cooperation. Their students no longer feel all alone without support nor do they feel they must try to overpower their classmates, intellectually or physically, in order to get needed attention. These students feel good about themselves, their learning, their peers, their teachers and their schools.

How students feel

ABOUT THIS BOOK

This book is about incorporating social skills as a regular part of the curriculum and how to teach those skills using cooperative groups. It explains the components of cooperation in the classroom, the steps in the group development process, how to develop a cohesive class, how to develop each student's sense of responsibility for his or her own actions, how to enhance thinking skills and how to integrate academic and social skills objectives in your lesson plan.

Sample activities are provided for each of the components. Using these samples as models you will no doubt create numerous other activities. We look forward to receiving your ideas and activities; we'll include as many as possible in our next edition.

Before attending one of our trainings, teachers sometimes ask us what's different about our "model?" Actually, when we first began presenting this information in Cooperative Learning workshops, we didn't think about it in terms of a "model." In our minds, we enhanced the workshops by stressing the importance of including direct instruction of the social skills that research has identified as necessary for future success.

Use continuums with caution.

We were also addressing the questions many workshop participants had asked: "What social skills do I begin teaching first?" and "Exactly, how do I teach them?" Our response was to identify the social skills necessary for success in and out of school, to describe and explain each of those skills, and to create a social skills continuum. (Caution: *Continuums should always be used with caution. All people do not learn in the same sequence.*)

The classroom is a meeting

Because we view the classroom as a meeting and the teacher and students as co-leaders and co-managers of that meeting, we added certain meeting management techniques that we knew to be successful in the classroom.

Learning social skills cannot be left to chance.

We also strongly believe that social skills should be taught like any other subject area in the curriculum — these skills cannot be left to chance, osmosis or occasional instruction. Developing successful social and human interaction skills is a long-term endeavor. Learning and using effective communication techniques, for instance, is a very intricate, complex process. (If effective communication were easy to achieve, we wouldn't have so much conflict in our world!) Our goal was, and is, to make the process of teaching and learning these skills simple, thus the term, "*Simple Cooperation.*" Based on the book reviews we have received and, more importantly, on comments teachers have made to us, we have succeeded in doing just that — we made it simple.

This book is much like a manual — the teacher new to cooperative learning strategies will find the step by step process relatively easy to follow; the experienced cooperative teacher will gain new insight and new ideas for teaching social skills. The book is designed to be self-instructional. A self-evaluation quiz follows most chapters (there is no answer key; the correct responses are clearly presented in the text). Most chapters include supplemental information, implementation suggestions, and sample activities to use when teaching the techniques in the chapter. There are also sample lesson plans written by some of the teachers who participated in workshops (Appendix III).

Both the experienced and inexperienced co-operative teacher can gain from this book.

A sample implementation schedule is offered in Appendix II. It covers six weeks. This is meant only as a guide for you — to help you while you gain confidence. You will no doubt break away from the sample long before the six weeks have passed.

Appendix II

It might be helpful to read Appendix I: "Introducing Cooperation to Your Students" before you initiate cooperative strategies in your classroom.

Read Appendix I first

About Implementing Simple Cooperation

Simple Cooperation is a model of teaching social skills, in other words, social responsibility, while teaching the academic content. It is a fluid, evolving process which takes time.

Move at your own pace. Take the time necessary for you and your students to master each step before moving on. If you follow this suggestion, the pangs of anxiety you (and your students) might feel when changing your instructional processes will soon be replaced with confidence and great success. Remember that change does not occur overnight — for you or your students, but if you "hang in there" and don't give up, you'll be amazed with the results.

Take your time

Your students will learn more in a shorter period of time, they'll be more enthusiastic and they'll have fewer problems interacting with each other in and out of the classroom. Your job as a teacher will be easier, you'll feel better about what you're doing, and you and your students will enjoy school a whole lot more.

If, when first implementing cooperative lessons, your lesson is not a raving success, don't let it scare you and don't immediately decide that "this is never going to work!" This just happens occasionally. Sometimes we can determine what went wrong, sometimes we can't. The important thing is that you (and your students) attempt to analyze what has happened, revise your process and try again.

Don't give up!

Cooperative strategies **do** work — give them, yourself and your students multiple chances to experience that success.

There is no "one right way"

> **IMPORTANT: It is our opinion that within certain parameters, the only correct method of implementing cooperation in your classroom is what works for you and your students.**

GIVING CREDIT

We have made a sincere attempt to give credit to the originators of activities and concepts presented in the following pages. We found this was not as easy as we thought it would be. Activities and information have been duplicated in workshops and lectures and books and articles have been written throughout the years without credit being given to the originators. We have, whenever possible, given appropriate credit. If we have given credit to someone other than the originator of a concept or an activity, or if we have not given credit where credit is due, it is definitely unintentional.

ABOUT GENDER

To avoid the awkwardness of "he/she, him/her," etc. we have simply rotated genders throughout the text.

We'd like to hear from you. If you have any comments, questions, or ideas for activities, please address them to:

> Peggy and Jacquie
> ITA Publications
> Drawer 1599
> Willits, CA 95490-1599
> (707)459-6100

Chapter 1

WELCOME TO SIMPLE COOPERATION

OVERVIEW: This chapter will introduce you to Simple Cooperation, an instructional method for teaching social skills and academic content simultaneously in heterogeneous and homogeneous student groups.

TOPICS INCLUDE:

1. What is Simple Cooperation.
2. Components of Simple Cooperation.
3. Goal Structures -- What are they?
4. Group Development.
5. Thinking Skills.
6. What to do before you begin.

Chapter 1: Welcome To Simple Cooperation

When you enter a Simple Cooperation classroom, the first thing you will notice is that students are clustered in small groups at workplaces around the room. As you watch, you will begin to notice an unusual level of concentration in the groups with students focusing on the assignment and materials. You'll become aware of the lack of distracting behavior. Instead, students will be discussing their work, speaking one at a time, listening to each other and encouraging each other to share their thoughts and ideas. The teacher will be walking around the room, stopping at groups here and there to observe and offer guidance where needed. An atmosphere of support and friendliness pervades the entire room.

Students focus on their assignment

Mutual support is apparent in cooperative classrooms

The groups of students might be discussing the best way to approach a problem or they may be studying spelling, history, math, literature or any of the other subjects normally taught in the classroom. And, in spite of the unusually high level of relaxed concentration, the students are the usual mix of skill levels and emotional development found in any classroom.

The Simple Cooperation method works with any age or grade level, with any ability level and with most curriculums.

It can work for you and your students, too, regardless of the subject matter or age level you teach.

WHAT IS SIMPLE COOPERATION ?

> *Simple Cooperation focuses on the instruction of social skills in heterogeneous and homogeneous student groups while maintaining an emphasis on academic content..*

Definition

In other words, you will teach your students the social skills necessary to get along in life.

Using this methodology, you will provide direct instruction in effective communication techniques, problem solving and conflict management, group dynamics, thinking skills and leadership. Students will practice these skills in cooperative groups while studying and completing academic assignments.

Students develop responsibility and dependability

Tangentially, students develop a sense of responsibility and dependability. They learn how to cooperate rather than compete and, as a result, they achieve greater success.

GOAL STRUCTURES

A "goal structure" is the manner in which a task is structured. In 1949, Morton Deutsch identified three goal structures: individualistic, competitive, and cooperative. David and Roger Johnson of the University of Minnesota have expanded on Deutsch's research and found that there is a significant increase in learning when teachers provide a cooperative environment.

The three goal structures are defined in the following manner:

1. INDIVIDUALISTIC GOAL STRUCTURE - "I'M ALL ALONE IN THIS." Each student is on his own and works alone to attain a specific goal. Each individual's achievement is in no way related to any other student's achievement. For example, when working in a programmed learning kit, a student moves from one level to another regardless of what any other student does.

2. COMPETITIVE GOAL STRUCTURE - "IT'S ME AGAINST YOU; SOMEONE WINS AND SOMEONE LOSES." Success is dependent upon others failing to reach the goal. Grading on a strict bell curve is an example of a competitive structure. Only two percent of the class population can earn "A's" regardless of how many points a student gets on the test.

   In a competitive environment, students have no incentive to help each other, in fact, quite the opposite. The incentive is to "best" the others, to attempt to put others at a disadvantage, sometimes by withholding necessary information, giving wrong information or whatever else can be done to get ahead of competitors.

3. **COOPERATIVE GOAL STRUCTURE** - "WE'RE IN THIS TOGETHER; WE CAN ONLY SUCCEED IF WE DO IT TOGETHER." In a cooperative group, students work together toward the completion of an assignment; they work together to achieve a common goal. Their success is dependent upon all group members doing an equal share of the work and helping other group members learn the material. In fact, the group's study is not completed until each and every member of the group knows and understands the lesson content. These parameters lead to a sense of group, or social, responsibility while developing group cohesion.

This is **not** a situation where students are haphazardly grouped at tables, each doing the same or similar work, with permission to talk or socialize while completing assignments. The learning environment becomes cooperative only when students are working together towards a common goal.

Not haphazard grouping

A cooperative environment supports and encourages students helping other students.

Each of the goal structures can play an important role in a well-rounded educational program. An individualistic goal structure is needed to be sure each student has mastered specific knowledge and skills. Students will likely encounter competitive situations outside of school and need to learn how to function constructively within that type environment. Also, competitive activities such as spelling bees where prizes or special recognition are offered can be fun occasionally.

The cooperatively structured classroom provides students the opportunity to develop leadership, self-confidence, self-esteem and responsibility and to learn academic content more quickly.

It's time for a change

WHY BOTHER?

To understand the need for cooperation and the teaching of social skills, it is necessary to look at what is happening in our society today. It is also necessary to review the forecasts for our future society.

Study after study has indicated that our graduates are leaving high school ill-prepared for the immediate future, whether that be work or higher education.

Employers complain that high school students and graduates cannot apply the basic skills to the everyday tasks of the "work world" such as completing application forms correctly or answering the phone in a courteous and friendly manner.

Employers also complain that these young people have little or no initiative, are not dependable, and cannot get along with their fellow workers, supervisors or consumers.

During the last several years, major studies have consistently concluded that human interaction skills such as effective communication, problem solving and conflict management; a knowledge of and ability to function effectively within small and large groups and an ability to identify and utilize resources whether they be intellectual, informational or recreational are the skills we need for a successful future society. Our citizens must possess a sense of responsibility for self and others; they must be dependable and they must be able to use their own initiative if they are to be successful.

If we accept the premise that our task as teachers is to help our students learn what is needed to live a happy and successful life, and to provide a learning environment in which they can use their potential then, we must provide instruction and experience in the skills identified as necessary for success in our future society.

Social skills are essential in almost every aspect of life. Since there are few, if any, jobs where an individual is completely isolated from all contact with others, our students will be required to interact with others throughout their lives. Yet, the social skills required for good group and interpersonal functioning are rarely taught. It seems to be assumed that students will somehow just "pick up" these skills or absorb them from the air. Some do. Most don't.

Social skills are the most basic of basic skills

Cooperative learning not only teaches our young people social skills, research studies by Johnson and Johnson and Slavin reveal that academic learning is enhanced and accelerated in a cooperative classroom.

Cooperative learning accelerates academic achievement

Cooperative approaches can be used with any age group and in any curriculum area. Because there is an emphasis on social skills as well as academics, it is also a near-perfect vehicle for mainstreaming identified special education students into the regular education program.

Simple Cooperation helps you develop socially responsible young people.

INTEGRATING ACADEMIC AND SOCIAL SKILLS

Simple Cooperation integrates academic and social skills instruction with group development and meeting management techniques. See Figure 1.

This model takes seriously the student's need to learn good communication skills; not just reading and writing, but speaking and listening as well. Also included are group techniques and activities to use in making a collection of individuals, your class, a unified, cooperative group with a shared purpose. You will learn how a group works and how to direct its working to increase the level of academic and social skills of its members.

Begin by establishing a secure environment

The group development process begins with activities and techniques to establish a secure, supportive environment in the classroom. The first step is to *Set Standards* of expected behaviors for your students. Students then

Figure 1: Major Components of Simple Cooperation

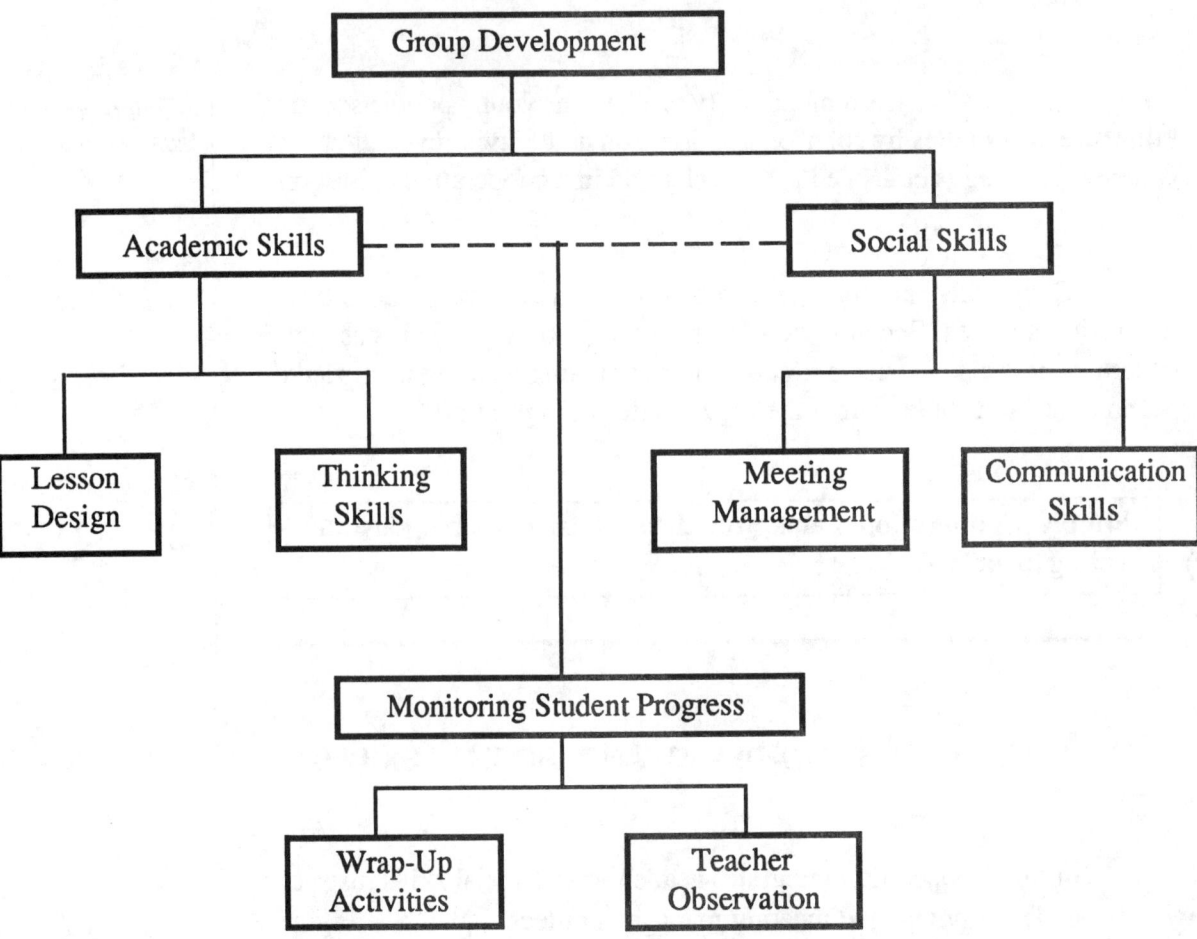

have the opportunity to get to know you and each other through *Getting Acquainted* activities. Their attention and energies are refocused at the beginning of each day and after lunch, recess or breaks with *Transition* and *Energizing* activities which are extensions of Getting Acquainted activities.

As students progress in group skills, they participate in *Student Setting Standards* activities and are introduced to practices which teach *Completing The Task*. Because Simple Cooperation classes develop such a high degree of trust and support, the anxiety of ending the class is eased with *Breaking Up* activities. These are all part of the group development process and will be explained later in greater detail.

CONFLICT

Conflict in the classroom is typically viewed as a negative and frightening event. It means trouble with a capital "T" and many people shudder at the thought of having to deal with conflict. Teachers sometimes envision a loss of authority and classroom control, resulting in utter chaos.

The truth is that conflict occurs in most classrooms at some time or other. The Simple Cooperation classroom is no exception. Conflict is part of the group development process and it can erupt at any time

Conflict is part of the group development process.

In reality, conflict, in and of itself, is neither negative nor positive. How you approach and deal with a conflict situation makes it negative or positive.

Later, in the section on Group Development, we'll demonstrate how to approach conflict situations so they become positive experiences. We'll explain how to use conflict to teach students basic problem solving and brainstorming skills.

GROUPS AND GROUP ROLES

Simple Cooperation uses small cooperative groups in which students study and complete assignments together.

Each Simple Cooperation lesson has both an academic and a social skill objective, very simple ones at first, progressing only as each level is mastered.

Group roles help students develop responsibility

Within this small group framework, students learn group roles. These roles help the group stay on task, give feedback, complete the group assignment and measure achievement while teaching each member the skills needed to succeed in school and life. These skills include:

Group roles also teach students numerous social skills

- getting your message across;
- attentive listening;
- giving and receiving praise and compliments;
- clarifying information;
- self-evaluation of skills and effort;
- developing responsibility and dependability;
- enhancing thinking skills; and
- increasing one's self-esteem and confidence level.

GRADES AND REWARDS

Each student may be given an individual grade or reward for each lesson and/or the group as a whole may be graded or rewarded for working together successfully.

Individual or group

Group grades are a valuable but very controversial aspect of cooperative learning. They provide a clear and definite incentive for students to work together. You can also use group bonus points or rewards as an incentive for students to cooperate with each other.

In either case, students must receive a strong and clear message that to succeed they must work together with each group member doing his or her share of the work..

TEACHING THINKING SKILLS

Enhancing thinking skills is an inherent element in a cooperative lesson. As students share their thoughts and ideas, they provide each other with new ways of approaching problems and completing tasks.

Students learn that there are other ways of viewing the world, of approaching assignments and of meeting life's challenges.

Simple Cooperation activities empower each student by providing the opportunity to develop the thinking skills necessary to function better in and out of school.

Specific methods for infusing thinking skills activities into cooperative lessons are discussed in a later chapter.

TEACHERS AND SIMPLE COOPERATION

At the core of the Simple Cooperation model is that you, the teacher, become a facilitator of learning rather than an "expert" who stands in front of the class disseminating facts and information. As a facilitator, you become a guide, provide direction and help draw out the strengths of each student to accomplish the group objectives. Being a teacher-facilitator will give you the time to become more directly involved with your students.

Teacher as facilitator

While the concept of teacher-as-facilitator is fundamental to the Simple Cooperation model, it does not take the place of direct teaching. New information must always be taught. There are always times when the "teacher as expert" role is necessary. Relying exclusively on this role, however, robs your students of the chance to think for themselves; to discover information on their own, make connections, share knowledge and ideas and

The Nurturing Classroom

formulate questions. By combining the traditional and facilitation roles, you will vastly increase your effectiveness as a teacher, and your students' abilities as learners.

Start slow

It is not necessary to immediately change your whole teaching approach to begin realizing the benefits of Simple Cooperation. In fact, we recommend choosing just one academic area at first. If you're an elementary teacher, choose a subject area that traditionally lends itself to group activities, such as science or social studies. Secondary teachers might choose to begin Simple Cooperation in one class period only.

As with any new process, when you first begin implementing cooperation, it will take longer to prepare your lessons and more class time to complete a given assignment. There may even be times in the first few weeks when you wonder why you ever got into this! After a while, though, the frustration will dissolve. Designing a Simple Cooperation lesson will become second nature, and you will be rewarded by seeing your students exhibiting a high degree of on-task behavior and group skills.

As the process of Simple Cooperation becomes part of the regular classroom routine, learning will accelerate markedly. There seem to be three major reasons for the significant burst of academic achievement:

Mulltimodality approach

* ***First,*** a multi-modality approach to instruction is built into each Simple Cooperation lesson. Students are talking and listening to each other as well as reading and writing lesson material. In most cases, it is no longer necessary to design special lessons to meet individual student modality strengths.

Active involvement in learning

* ***Second,*** the time that students are actively involved in learning is extremely high. Each student not only has a vested interest in completing the task, each also has a commitment to the group.

Thinking skills are enhanced

* ***Third,*** Simple Cooperation brings another crucial element into the learning process—enhancing thinking skills.

LAYING THE FOUNDATION

The following chapters discuss and explain aspects of communication and group development (which can easily be ignored in the context of classrooms) and how to teach these skills. The sample activities and lessons provided for each of the major components of Simple Cooperation will help you implement cooperation in your classroom immediately. . .

You may already know some of the concepts presented on the following pages; others may be brand new to you. If you find yourself somewhat confused at first, be patient; it will come together in time, and it will be well worth your efforts.

BEFORE YOU BEGIN

It's a good idea to let your principal know that you're going to be changing your instructional methodology before you actually implement Simple Cooperation in your classroom. You'll want his or her support and encouragement.

Tell your site administrator

It's also a good idea to let your students' parents know about your new methods of instructing. The best introduction for parents is through a meeting where you can demonstrate and have them participate in cooperative activities. If a meeting isn't possible, then a letter will do. Tell them their children will be gaining new skills and they will most likely see a change in their child's sense of responsibility as well as an increase in academic performance.

Meet with parents

IF YOU PLAN TO USE GROUP GRADES......

It is especially important to talk with your supervisor and to notify parents if you decide to use group grades, group rewards, and/or bonus points based on group work.

The Nurturing Classroom

> **Group grades? Caution**

Parents of high achieving students often don't want their children's grades, rewards, or bonus points based on group work. Parents fear their high achieving children's grades will be lowered when their children must depend on lower achieving students. It's important to point out that all students benefit from cooperative activities and that in the work-world their children will be involved in team work with individuals of different ability levels.

High achievers also benefit from cooperative approaches

High achievers benefit from cooperative classrooms in many ways:

1. They learn how to analyze how they arrive at the correct response.

2. They gain more effective communication skills such as paraphrasing and encouraging others to share their thoughts.

3. Rather than using assumptions and educated guesses as a response mode, they become aware of their thinking processes.

4. They gain a greater understanding of how to solve different problems.

5. They also gain insight into group dynamics and how to get along with diverse populations.

After explaining the benefits to parents, ask them to support the process for three or four months and see what results are produced.

Consider starting with bonus points

We personally discourage using group grades for reporting purposes when first implementing Simple Cooperation. The political and community problems are just too great to overcome. Later, when students and parents are familiar with the benefits of cooperation and when everyone has seen that this model benefits **all** students, it may be possible to use group grades as part of the report card grade. Before then, the group grade can be used as bonus points or you can use a group reward for successful completion of the assignment.

Chapter 2

DEVELOPING A COHESIVE CLASSROOM GROUP

OVERVIEW: This chapter discusses, in sequence, the various stages necessary for the development of a cohesive, productive group.

TOPICS INCLUDE:
1. Each of the six stages of group development is discussed in depth.
2. How a group matures.
3. Implementation and sample activities to help guide your students through the group development process.

Chapter 2: Creating A Cohesive Classroom Group

When people come together, whether it is a faculty, a scout troop or a class, a group is formed. Some groups come together as a cohesive unit almost immediately. Others do not; they remain just a collection of individuals in the same space, never seeming to agree on anything, never establishing supportive relationships, and usually failing to accomplish their goal.

The students gathered in your classroom form a group. With your guidance and direction, your students will become a cohesive group. Your students will care about each other; they will help and respect each other; they'll learn to be responsible; and they will achieve at greater levels than in the past. To create the type of environment that fosters these characteristics will take some time, effort and energy **but** it will be well worth it. Your students will be recognized in the school as the kids who cooperate and who have the fewest discipline problems. And you will be recognized as an exceptional teacher.

Be recognized as an exceptional teacher

There are six stages in the group development process (see Figure 2). Each will be discussed separately.

SETTING STANDARDS

Any group of people that meets on a regular basis has certain expected standards of behavior. If these standards, or rules, are not established by the leader, the group members will develop their own standards, usually through a trial and error process. Members "try on" different behaviors to see what works and what doesn't, what's accepted and what isn't. Behaviors are then modified according to the response of the other group members.

Each group develops standards of behavior.

The pattern of trying out and modifying behaviors will be repeated many times until the group has developed what is considered the norm, i.e., a repertoire of acceptable behaviors.

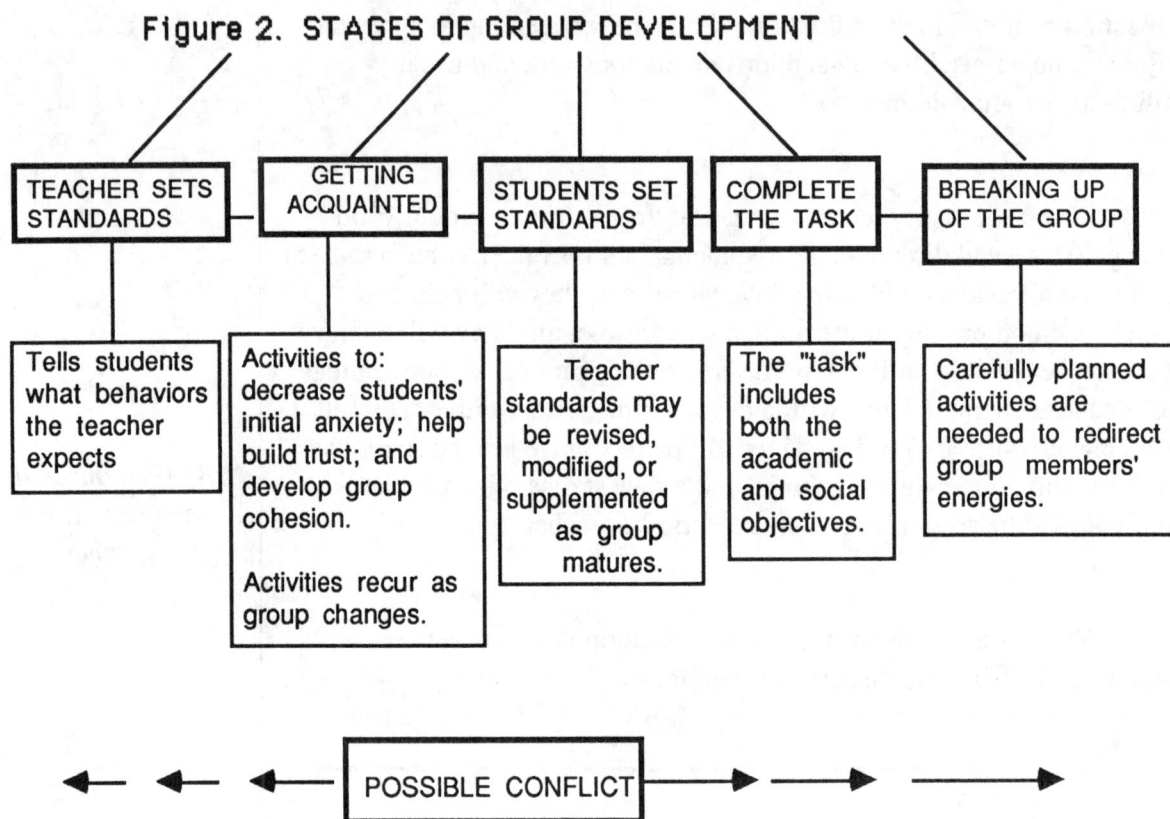

The teacher unwittingly participates in this trial and error process when he or she does not initiate standards of behavior. This laissez-faire leadership style does **not** produce a cohesive, productive group.

The first step, then, in creating a cohesive, effective group is for you, the teacher, to take the initiative and set standards in a conscious, directed manner. It's easy to come up with a list of rules for the classroom but if you intend to create a comfortable, safe and cooperative environment, you will need to give serious thought to what your beginning standards will be.

Step 1: Set Standards

To set standards, you need to consider community norms and values as well as district and school rules because your classroom rules cannot contradict the already established standards of the community and school. Next, think about what is really important to you and what behaviors are completely unacceptable to you? What behaviors are an absolute must for you? Write them on a piece of paper, review them, and select the three or four that are most important to you. These will become the inviolate standards of behavior for your classroom.

These standards must be clearly communicated to your students. Write them on poster-board or a large sheet of paper and present them to your students as the expected behaviors.

Standards should be phrased in positive terms...."Raise hand before speaking," rather than "Don't speak out."

Use positive terms

Although you will present the standards as a whole to your students on the first day of school, each standard actually becomes a social skill objective in and of itself and should be taught, modeled, and practiced, as necessary, by your students. Review the standards every day during the first week of school, then periodically throughout the school year. It is really helpful if you make a point of reviewing them after vacation times, such as winter and spring breaks.

Review the standards periodically.

Also, when a new student enters your classroom, an explanation of the standards is critical for the new student's success.

Be sure you explain the standards to new students.

The Nurturing Classroom

SAMPLE STANDARDS

The following list of suggested standards is offered only to help you in your own thinking. The standards you adopt must be suited to your school and your own teaching style. Students will understand your standards and will be more accepting of them if you also provide a brief explanation of why each is important.

> This is a **sample** list only -- you must decide what standards are best for you and your students.

1. *BE ON TIME:* This means that each student is responsible for being in his seat or work area at the appointed time. For lower elementary students, pictures of clocks depicting the expected times can be used; for older students, a chart listing the scheduled times can be posted. Being on time includes moving from one area in the classroom to another area without dawdling. Being late disrupts the group work already in progress.

2. *BE RESPONSIBLE FOR YOUR OWN LEARNING:* This is really a different approach than we typically use in our nation's classrooms. It means that the teacher will provide a stimulating and exciting learning environment including as much information, data, and materials, and as many experiences as possible. It is then the students' responsibility to avail themselves of these resources.

   If students have questions, are confused, or miss something, they should first ask another group member for the answer. If no one in the group knows the answer, the student may then ask the teacher. Students' questions should always be answered but the student must take the initiative to clear up any confusion.

   Learn how to learn

   This standard helps students learn how to learn; develop initiative and become responsible.

3. *BE RESPONSIBLE FOR YOUR OWN MATERIALS AND ASSIGNMENTS:* Each student has a responsibility to himself and the class as well as to his cooperative group members to carry his own share of the work load. He cannot wait for someone else to remember for him. A clear procedure outlining how to gain access to materials and books should be posted for students. This will help them actualize this responsibility.

Chapter 2: Creating A Cohesive Classroom Group

4. *ONLY ONE PERSON SPEAKS AT A TIME:* This is one of the beginning steps in teaching communication and meeting management skills. It cannot be assumed that your students have internalized this basic socialization skill. This standard gives a strong message that students are to respect each other's contribution to the group effort.

5. *KEEP YOUR WORK AND DESK AREA CLEAN:* Each person is responsible for his own personal space and the areas used by everyone. It is important to demonstrate what "clean" means in your classroom because a clean work space to one person may seem quite messy to another. A clean work area reduces distraction and teaches students self-responsibility.

To avoid misunderstandings, demonstrate what you mean.

GETTING ACQUAINTED

When students enter a classroom for the first time in a small school they may already know all or most of the other students. In larger schools, however, they may recognize only one or two other students. That first day in a new class may be a frightening experience for many. Helping students become acquainted with you and with each other will set a positive tone for your classroom.

Step 2: *Getting to know one another.*

Your students will begin to know you when you present your standards and describe the basic "housekeeping" procedures of the class. This needs to be done clearly and students should be encouraged to ask questions if they don't understand something.

Taking the time to help students become acquainted with each other will develop group cohesiveness more quickly. This, in turn, promotes a more accelerated degree of learning both social skills and academic content.

Getting Acquainted activities are carefully structured to ensure student/student and student/teacher interaction. Besides helping students get to know each other as people, these activities promote acceptance and understanding of classmates from different backgrounds and with different values. This, in turn, provides the foundation needed for developing

Getting Acquainted activities promote acceptance of others

The Nurturing Classroom

cohesive and cooperative groups.

Use Opening Activities to begin the day

Two other types of activities closely related to Getting Acquainted Activities are *Openings* and *Transitions*. Opening Activities are used at the beginning of the school day; they help students develop a "mind-set" for the day. Certain "Getting Acquainted" activities may also be used as "Openers," such as: *"What We Have in Common," "Similarities and Differences," "Focus Worksheet,"* and others identified in the Sample Activities section at the end of this chapter.

Transition activities help students refocus on the group activity.

Transitions are used after lunch, weekends and holiday breaks to bring the group back together.

When your students have been away from the group, their thoughts are diverted from the group goal. It's important to help them refocus their minds and energies on that group goal.

Transitions at the secondary level

At the secondary level, as students move from class to class, say from a math class to an English class, the English teacher tends to expect students to be thinking about English as soon as they enter the room. This is difficult, to say the least, especially if the student was involved in some fascinating problem solving discussion in the last class. A Transition activity will help the student "leave" math and begin thinking about English. At the secondary level, either an Opening or Transition activity should be used at the beginning of each period.

Transitons at the elementary level

Transition activities are a "must" at the elementary level after recesses, lunch, and between the end of one subject and the beginning of another, e.g., moving from spelling to math.

Energizers help everyone "wake up."

Energizers are another type of activity used frequently in cooperative classrooms. As the name implies, they are used when students seem to be "fading" — when energy is low, when it's too warm, when many students seem especially tired or are having trouble concentrating. The Energizer is a quick activity designed to "wake students up."

You will find sample *Getting Acquainted, Opening, Transition and Energizer* activities at the end of the chapter. These activities help ease student anxiety, reserve and shyness. They also help students become accustomed to working in groups.

Sample activities are at the end of the chapter

STUDENTS SETTING STANDARDS

This stage of group development provides an opportunity for your students to have "a say" in the class rules. It empowers them; it tells them their thoughts and opinions are important. Providing your students the opportunity, in fact, the responsibility to set standards of behavior for their class is collaborative management. Consider yourself and your feelings. Don't you prefer to be involved in establishing the rules in your school? And don't you feel like a real part of "the team" when you participate in making other decisions affecting your class, your school, and your life as a teacher?

Step 3: Students set standards

This step gives students the chance to become self-regulated which leads to a sense of social responsibility. It teaches them that by following a specific procedure, they *can* make a difference. This is a good time to mention to your students that there are also ways (such as voting, contacting legislators and local government officials) in which they can change laws and other aspects of our society.

*Empowering students leads them to a sense of social responsibility. Students learn they **can** make a difference.*

Another benefit of involving students in setting class standards is that they will be much more willing to abide by the class "rules" and will actually monitor their own adherance to those rules.

It's easier to "follow the rules" when you're involved in establishing them.

Conduct this session as soon as you believe students have mastered the skills involved in the initial standards you established. This could be any time within the first few months of the school term. (The sooner, the better, though.)

To lead the Student Setting Standards session:

1. *Discuss* the general purpose of a classroom: to maximize the potential of each student; to provide

an environment and experiences that allow each student to learn the social and academic skills necessary to lead a happy and productive life.

2. *Review* the present standards of behavior and identify those from your list that you absolutely require; point out that these may not be altered in any way.

3. *Ask* your students if there are other standards they believe would help reach the goals of the class.

4. *If you're willing to adjust* any of your initial standards, ask if they think an adjustment or deletion of these would better serve the class purpose.

This session could also be conducted in smaller cooperative groups. Each group would discuss possible changes, deletions and additions and report their results to the class. Group lists would then be combined and discussed and the class would make a consensus decision on which standards will be added, changed, or deleted.

Consensus decision making, which will be discussed in greater detail in a later chapter, is essential for this process to work. In other words, the entire class must agree to any additional standards, deletions or adjustments as well as the consequences, if any, of violating the class rules.

As mentioned above, this process gives your students a sense of ownership, a feeling of pride and responsibility, a sense of leadership and a basis for establishing standards within their cooperative study groups. Students learn that standards of behavior and attitude help accomplish tasks and goals more efficiently and effectively. They also learn that you, in fact, want to hear their opinions. This all leads to greater group cohesion and productivity.

"Consensus means everyone will support and abide by the decision."

Chapter 2: Creating A Cohesive Classroom Group

Group cohesion and enhanced productivity (i.e., increased achievement), in turn, raises self-esteem. These effects become circular in nature because greater self-esteem increases cohesion and achievement.

COMPLETING THE TASK

"Completing the task," the next step in the group development process, refers to students working, individually and in cooperative groups, towards academic and/or social skills objectives. As you give instruction and your students begin working on their assignments, you and your students will clearly see the results of the energy and time spent in Setting Standards and Getting Acquainted Activities — more learning will occur.

> **Step 4:** *Completing the Task*
>
> *or*
>
> *Working towards the social and academic goals*

"Completing the Task" is identified as the <u>fourth</u> step because some teachers will be able to involve their students in setting standards before any serious academic activity occurs. Other teachers will not introduce the Student Setting Standards procedure until weeks into the term. For those, "Completing the Task" will be the <u>third</u> stage in the development of their group.

In workshops, teachers frequently ask us if our sequence means that they should not conduct any academic lessons until their students are fully acquainted with each other. No, that is not what we're suggesting. We do believe, however, that if all teachers just forgot about academic content and spent the first week or two of school conducting *Getting Acquainted* activities, teaching effective communication techniques, diagnosing the initial skill and knowledge levels of students and providing an overview of the course work, including how the content relates to the world, academic learning would be greatly enhanced.

This approach gives you more real learning time. Think about it. How much learning time is lost in your classroom each year because students don't pay attention to your lesson; because they don't complete assignments; because they become distracted, or worse, disruptive; because some are bored?

How much learning time is lost in your classroom?

25

The Nurturing Classroom

> Now, imagine your classroom as one:
>
> √ where time on task and real learning time is maximized;
> √ where students want to complete assignments;
> √ where students don't want to be late or absent;
> √ where students cooperate and help each other.

Would you feel like you were in fantasyland? This is exactly what happens in cooperative classrooms.

Try it. Even if you're inititating cooperative techniques in the middle of the year, take some days and spend them mostly on assessing or re-evaluating student academic achievement levels, reviewing and establishing standards, getting acquainted, teaching social skills and see what happens.

A sample lesson plan format and sample lessons are included in the chapter entitled "Putting It All Together." Using the sample format will help you remember to include all the parts needed in a cooperative learning lesson.

BREAKING UP

Step 5: Breaking Up -- the group disbands.

There comes a time for each group to end, to *"Break Up."* This can be a difficult time for students in a Simple Cooperation classroom. Students will experience sadness and anxiety when it comes time for the group to disband. They can, and often do, go through a grieving period.

The end of the school year may be a very difficult time for your students

This is a time when conflict is likely to erupt in your classroom. Ironically, the very success of the Simple Cooperation classroom in building a close, effective, supportive group contributes to the possibility of conflict.

Remember, these students first entered your classroom not knowing exactly what to expect or how they would be accepted. Since that first day, they have become members of a cohesive group built on mutual trust, respect, and caring. Now they must leave the safety and support of this group.

You can help your students work through their feelings of loss and anxiety by carefully planning activities for the end of the year. These activities must help you and your students immortalize the group, provide a "living" memory **and** redirect their energy to the next phase in their lives. Activities such as exchanging photographs, planting trees, writing a letter to the next class, visiting the next grade level all help with this difficult transition.

A number of *Breaking Up* activities are offered in the sample activity section at the end of this chapter.

CONFLICT

The sixth and last stage in the group development process is conflict. In actuality, conflict is not a "stage" in the normal sense of the word. It doesn't occur at a specific time in the sequence; it can occur at anytime in the group development process.

Conflict is a normal part of any relationship development process. Consider the development of a friendship or other close personal relationship. As you become more familiar with a person you begin to feel safe; you begin to feel comfortable enough to express what you're really thinking and feeling. Your defenses are lessened and you show your vulnerability. When you and your friend or mate reach this level of emotional intimacy, it's very possible to say or do things that the other disagrees with. When there is strong disagreement, conflict may erupt.

This same phenomenon occurs in a group. Your students will feel safe enough to express their opinions, thoughts and feelings and you may find yourself faced with a conflict.

> *Stage 6:* Conflict.
>
> *Conflict is not really a "stage" of group development. It is a natural part of the process that can occur at any time, very often, when you least expect it.*

Conflict is likely to erupt during the last few weeks of school

Strangely enough, conflict is most likely to occur during the last weeks of school. The reason for this is simple - students are faced with losing the group they have come to trust. Anxiety and frustration accompanies this feeling of loss which is similar to the grief cycle. Disagreements and conflict occur as a way of dealing with these feelings.

Consider your own feelings and reactions when you had to move away from people you really cared about or when you attended a class or multi-day workshop where a very cohesive, caring group developed. How did you handle your own feelings of sadness and loss? This is difficult for people of all ages.

Planning and implementing *Breaking Up* activities will diffuse much of the conflict that can occur at the end of the year.

Teaching your students the problem solving procedures discussed later on in this book will diffuse conflicts that occur at other times. By handling conflict in a positive manner, you will provide an invaluable learning experience for your students.

GROUP GROWTH AND MATURITY

Dont rush -- taking one step at a time will result in greater progress.

Groups, like people, progress through phases of development. Within each stage, a certain level of maturity must be reached before the group can successfully move on to the next stage. While perfection isn't required, moving too fast through the stages may be counterproductive.

When a group tries to jump to a new phase before it has internalized the earlier stage, it won't be as effective in accomplishing its task. As an example, think of a committee that never seems to be able to reach a decision or take definitive action. The committee members just meet and meet and meet, endlessly circling the same questions and problems, never accomplishing anything.

If the committee members had taken the time to get acquainted, to set standards and norms, to define its goals, it might have been successful; it may have accomplished something. This same thing is true for classrooms.

If your students aren't achieving or meeting goals, review the earlier stages. Was sufficient time spent on establishing and learning the standards of behavior and attitude? Did students have sufficient opportunity to become acquainted with you, your expectations and fellow-students? Have you spent time providing instruction and experiences to develop communication and problem solving skills?

It's important to identify the weak spots and go back and repeat earlier activities to help students gain the skills necessary to reach goals. As the fundamentals are mastered, students will become a cohesive, cooperative group and learning both social and academic skills will take a giant leap forward.

SUMMARY

- *Cohesive groups do not occur by accident.*

- *Stages of group development include:*

    - *Teacher Setting Standards*
    - *Getting Acquainted*
    - *Students Setting Standards*
    - *Completing the Task*
    - *Breaking Up*
    - *Conflict*

- *Conflict is inherent in the group development process.*

- *You can help reduce conflict at the end of the school year by planning and implementing Breaking Up activities.*

- *Conflict is best handled using a problem solving process (a sample problem solving process is offered in a later chapter.)*

- *Getting Acquainted Activities are the foundation for developing a cohesive, cooperative group. These activities promote acceptance and understanding of classmates with diverse backgrounds, attitudes and values.*

- *Opening Activities are used at the beginning of the day.*

- *Transition Activities are used to bring the group back together after lunch, weekends, and at the beginning of departmentalized class periods.*

- *Energizers help give the group an energy boost.*

Superteaching Workbook:
Chapter 2 - DEVELOPING A COHESIVE CLASSROOM GROUP

Self-Evaluation Quiz

1. Name and describe the six stages of group development.

2. Why is it important to establish and explain initial standards?

3. What are the benefits of having students participate in setting standards?

4. When will you have your students set standards?

5. Why are Getting Acquainted activities important?

6. Describe how and when to use Transition Activities.

7. When do you use Energizers?

8. What is the purpose of "breaking up" activities?

9. Why does conflict frequently occur during the last weeks of school?

SUPPLEMENTAL INFORMATION AND ACTIVITIES

I. **Establishing Classroom Standards.....**

   A. **The first critical element in creating a cohesive, cooperative group is to establish Class Standards.** For maximum effectiveness, keep rules to a minimum and include only those that you can enforce. (It doesn't make much sense to have a rule that is impossible to enforce, or in having so many rules that it would take all your time to enforce them.)

   Phrasing class standards in positive terms eliminates confusion and is usually more effective. Example........

<u>Positive</u>	<u>Negative</u>
a. Raise your hand before speaking.	a. Don't speak out in class.
b. Be on time.	b. Don't be late.

   B. **A Process for establishing class standards:**

   1. Write all the behaviors you would like your students to demonstrate in your classroom. Remember to phrase them in positive terms.

   2. Prioritize your list in order of importance to you.

   3. Take the top two, three or four. These will become your beginning standards of behavior for your classroom.

   It's helpful to post these standards in your room in a place that is clearly visible to your students. For younger students, a visual representation of each standard could be used.

   Since the same words mean different things to different people, it is important to demonstrate and/or model each of your class standards. Example...Say "Keep your area clean" is one of your standards; it is highly unlikely that "clean" means the same thing to you as it does to each of your students.

   One final thought: What are the consequences of breaking the standards: How much leeway or flexibility will you allow and are there any exceptions to the rules? All of this should also be shared with your students.

II. Getting Acquainted vs Opening vs Transition Activities

A. Some activities may be used as Getting Acquainted, Opening and/or Transition activities; however it is important to remember the purpose of each:

1. *GETTING ACQUAINTED ACTIVITIES* are for the purpose of getting to know each other better. Knowing one another is a prerequisite to establishing a cohesive group and an environment that is perceived as safe and secure; one in which it's okay to risk attempting new things. This type of environment is most conducive to learning.

   Getting Acquainted activities are more important than most educators believe. The need for these activities in large districts is obvious — people just don't have the opportunity to meet each other. However, many people tend to think that because a district is located in a small town where students are almost raised with each other and have attended school together since preschool days, the children know each other and do not need to participate in Getting Acquainted activities. This is usually not true. There is a difference between "knowing" each other and "knowing about" each other.

   Whether your school is small or large, Getting Acquainted activities will help students "know" each other better. It is important to set a relaxed atmosphere and broaden awareness of how others think and feel.

   We always begin workshops with a Getting Acquainted activity. Here's one we use with school staffs who believe they know all about one another. It's called, *"Guess That Person."*

   a. On an index card or piece of paper, write one thing about yourself you think nobody knows.

   b.. Hang the cards or papers on a wall.

   c.. During the day, everyone reads the descriptions and writes below them who they think the person is.

   d. At the end of the day, read each card and the guessed identities.

   e. The real person identifies him or herself.

> POINT: There are many levels and degrees of "knowing" each other and most often we really don't know each other as well as we think we do.

2. *Transition Activities* bring each individual's thoughts and energies back to the group focus. They provide a mind set which focuses on the group task and goal rather than on what each individual was doing or thinking prior to joining the group. They are used when moving from one subject area to another, after lunch, and at the beginning of departmentalized class periods.

3. *Opening Activities* are used after your students have become acquainted. They are similar to Transitions in that they are used to put everybody in the right "mind set" for the rest of the day. The difference is that a Transition is used during the day while an Opener is used at the beginning of the day.

IMPLEMENTATION ACTIVITIES

1. *Establish initial standards.*

   Regardless of when in the school year you are initiating cooperation in your classroom, follow the procedure for establishing standards. If you initially listed a number of class rules:

   a. Review them and decide which *two, three* or *four* are most important to you;
   b. Take the time to discuss these with your students; and
   c. Hold a class meeting to review the others.
   d. Give your students the option of keeping, eliminating or modifying the rest of your list.
   e. Also, give students the opportunity to establish new standards to add to the list.

   ** Note: The decisions related to any changes, deletions, or additions must be made by class consensus.

2. Conduct *Getting Acquainted* and *Transition* activities every day. Also, use *Energizer* activities as appropriate.

LESSON/ACTIVITY ANALYSIS

DATE:_____

ACTIVITY/LESSON:

WHAT WENT RIGHT:

WHAT WENT WRONG:

ANALYSIS:

HOW TO MAKE ACTIVITIES/LESSONS MORE SUCCESSFUL:

NOTES:

SAMPLE ACTIVITIES

Getting Acquainted Activities

Title: **Introductions**
Grade Level: Kindergarten - Adult
Roles: None
Time: 20 - 35 minutes
Materials: Directions written on chart paper or on the chalk board

Activity: Students will each interview a partner, then each will introduce the other to the class using the information obtained during the interview.

1. Decide what questions students will use in the interview. The number and complexity of questions will depend upon your grade level, the attention span of your students and the time available for the activity. Questions might include things like: name, hobby, favorite TV show, number of brothers and sisters, place of birth, etc.

2. Write the questions on large chart paper or chalk board.

3. Students choose a partner — a person they don't know or, at least, a person they don't know well.

4. Students "interview" each other for three to five minutes each, obtaining the specified information.

5. At the end of the time period, each student introduces his partner to the class.

Title: **Similarities and Differences**
Grade Level: Kindergarten - Adult
Roles: None
Time: 10 minutes
Materials: Paper, Pencils, Measuring Instruments

Activity:
1. Place students in groups of two to five, depending on grade level (e.g. K = 2; grades 1 - 6 = 3; secondary - adult = 4 or 5.

2. Give students a list of characteristics or facts to compare, such as: longest/shortest foot; longest hair; tallest/shortest; longest/shortest fingers; how many have blue/brown/hazel eyes; longest time attending this school; lives furthest from school; and so on.

3. Groups gather information within the alloted time and share their results with the rest of the class.

* This activity can be used to reinforce various academic lessons, e.g., use both metric and linear measurements, reinforce vocabulary words, etc.

TITLE: **Self-Description**
GRADE LEVEL: 2 - Adult
ROLES: None
TIME: 15 - 20 minutes
MATERIALS: Paper and pencil

ACTIVITY: Students write a description of themselves. Teacher collects the descriptions and reads them aloud one at a time; class guesses who is being described.

VARIATION: Conduct in small group setting with a group "Reader" sharing the information for everyone in the group. The entire class would still guess who in each group is being described.

TITLE: **The Memory Game**
GRADE LEVEL: 3 - Adult
ROLES: None
TIME: 20 - 30 minutes
MATERIALS: None

ACTIVITY:
1. The class, including the teacher, sits in a circle.
2. Students, beginning to the right of the teacher, recite the alphabet in sequence, each student saying only one letter of the alphabet.
3. The sound of the letter each student says becomes the beginning sound of an adjective the student chooses to describe herself, example, Affable Jane, Bouncy Mary, etc.
4. Give students one to two minutes to think of an adjective.
5. Then, students take turns, again beginning with the student to the immediate right of the teacher, introducing themselves by adjective and first name.

VARIATION #1: After going around the circle, repeat the process with the added task of stating the names of students who have already introduced themselves. Example.........Jane, the first student on the teacher's right, will say only her adjective and name, "Affable Jane."
Mary, the next student, would say, "Affable Jane, Bouncy Mary."
The third student would say, "Affable Jane, Bouncy Mary, Cute Jamie."
And so on around the circle.

VARIATION #2: Allow students to the immediate right and left of the speaker help by whispering answers when the speaker forgets.

VARIATION #3: Students select adjectives that have the same initial sound or letter as the intitial letter/sound in their first name.

** Note: You may wish to seat students you know have short term memory deficits to your immediate right. This will avoid placing these students "on the spot" by requiring them to remember more names than they may be capable of.

TITLE: **Guess That Person**
GRADE LEVEL: 3 - Adult
ROLES: None
TIME: 10 minutes, additional time during day, and 10 minutes at end of day
MATERIALS: One Index Card or piece of paper per student, pen or pencil

ACTIVITY:
1. On an index card or piece of paper, write one thing about yourself you think nobody knows.
2. Hang the cards or papers on a wall.
3. During the day, everyone reads the descriptions and writes below them who they think the person is.
4. At the end of the day, read each card and the guessed identities.
5. The real person identifies himself or herself.

TITLE: **What We Have in Common**
GRADE LEVEL: 4 - Adult
ROLES: Recorder and Time-Keeper
TIME: 10 - 20 minutes
MATERIALS: Paper and Pencils

ACTIVITY:
1. Place students in groups of 4 or 5.
2. Teacher suggests categories of possible commonalities and gives examples.
3. Within groups, students discuss possibilities.
4. Group members then determine three things they have in common.
5. Each group's recorder shares with the rest of the class the commonalities found within his group.

A discussion about what students learned through this activity is a nice wrap up.

The following may be used as
GETTING ACQUAINTED OR TRANSITION ACTIVITIES.

TITLE: **Getting Acquainted Cards**
GRADE LEVEL: 2 - Adult
ROLES: None
TIME: 20 - 25 minutes
MATERIALS: Name tags or 3 x 5 index cards (pins or tape are needed if index cards are used), directions and sample Getting Acquainted card written on chart paper or chalk board.

ACTIVITY: Each student is given a name tag or index card and is instructed to write her first name in the center. Students then complete their name tag by following the instructions written on the sample.

You can help students by verbally "walking" them through the activity. Example....

"- In the upper right hand corner, write the location of your last vacation.
- In the lower right hand corner, write the number of your brothers and sisters.
- In the lower left hand corner, write the name of your favorite TV program.
- In the upper left hand corner, write the name of the city where you were born."

The completed Getting Acquainted card is attached to the writer's shirt or blouse. The class is then divided into groups of three or four. Group members share the information on their Getting Acquainted card.

VARIATION: This can be done in pairs, larger groups or with the entire class.

Figure 3: Sample Getting Acquainted Card

City where born	Last vacation place
Name	
Favorite TV program	Number brothers/sisters

Completed Getting Acquainted Card

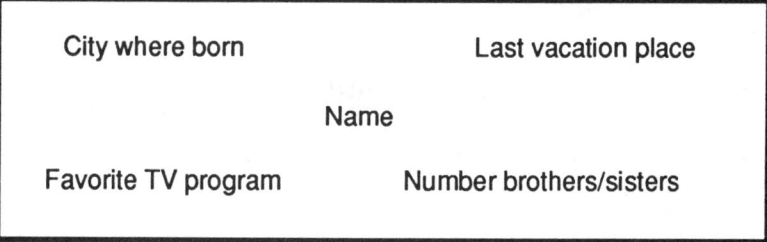

San Jose	Disneyland
Elaine	
Star Trek	1 brother/2 sisters

TITLE: **One Fact**
GRADE LEVEL: Preschool - Adult
ROLES: None
TIME: 20 - 25 minutes
MATERIALS: None

ACTIVITY: Students are seated randomly in a circle and instructed to tell one fact they have learned this year about the person on their right. The only restriction is that it must be a *positive* statement about the person.

You will lead the activity by stating one new fact you have learned about the person on your right then the process is continued around the circle until the student on your left tells one new fact he or she has learned about you.

The following may be used as OPENING, TRANSITION OR ENERGIZER ACTIVITIES.

TITLE: **The WHIP**
GRADE LEVEL: Preschool - Adult
ROLES: None
TIME: 10 minutes
MATERIALS: None

ACTIVITY: Students are asked to formulate a one word response to an open-ended question, e.g. "A one word description of how I am feeling this moment is...." Students are given a minute or two to think of their response.

Beginning with one student, "whip" around the room rapidly giving each student the opportunity to respond or "pass." Regardless of student response, simply say "thank you" and go on to the next student.

Students must be given the option to pass, i.e., not respond directly to the question, because some may not be able to think of an answer and others may feel threatened by the question. Students may also want to test you to see if you really mean it's okay to say "I pass" rather than offer how they are feeling, thinking, etc.

It's important that neither you nor other students react or respond to any student's answer. All answers are accepted without further comment.

VARIATION: Instead of a one word response, a short phrase or a sentence may be requested.

** Be sure to clarify exactly what type of response is required before beginning the activity, i.e., one word, fewer than five words, short sentence, etc.

Sample WHIP questions:
    a. One new idea I got during this activity was...
    b. One new fact I learned during class today (or yesterday) was...
    c. My favorite vacation spot is...
    d. My favorite subject in school is...
    e. The best thing about school is...

TITLE: **Aardvarks and Antelopes**
GRADE LEVEL: 5 - Adult
ROLES: None
TIME: 15 - 30 minutes
MATERIALS: One object to symbolize the Aardvark and one object to represent the Antelope

ACTIVITY:
1. The class, including teacher, is seated in a circle.
2. Teacher, turn to your right and say to Student #1, "This is an aardvark."
3. Student #1 asks, "A what?"
4. Teacher reply, "An aardvark" and hand the object to the student.
5. Student #1 then turns to Student #2 on his right and says, "This is an aardvark."
6. Student #2 asks, "A what?"
7. Student #1 turns to teacher and asks, "A what?"
8. Teacher reply, "An aardvark."
9. Student #1 then turns to Student #2 and says, "An aardvark" and hands Student #2 the object.

In other words, each time the aardvark is given to the next student in the circle, the question "A what?" must be passed back around the circle to the teacher. The teacher answers, "An aardvark" and the answer "An aardvark" is passed back around the circle until it reaches the person in possession of the object representing the aardvark. When the student holding that object receives the answer, he may then turn to the next student, say, "This is an aardvark." and pass the object to her.

The process is repeated until the "aardvark" is passed from one student to another, full circle, back around to the teacher.

As soon as you're certain the "aardvark" is moving smoothly counter-clockwise around the circle and students are following the correct procedure, you hand the object representing the "antelope" to the student on your left, saying, "This is an antelope."

The "antelope" then begins its "trek" in a clockwise direction around the circle in the same manner.

In other words, while the "aardvark" is moving counter-clockwise around the circle, the "antelope" is moving simultaneously around the circle in a clockwise direction.

The activity is completed when both the "aardvark" and the "antelope" have gone full circle and are both in your possession.

Variations: a. Begin with just one object.
        b. Use objects to represent new vocabulary words.

The Nurturing Classroom

The following may be used as:
OPENING, GETTING ACQUAINTED, TRANSITION
OR ENERGIZER ACTIVITIES.

TITLE: **Focus Worksheet**
GRADE LEVEL: 2 - Adult
ROLES: None
TIME: 10 - 20 minutes
MATERIALS: A prepared worksheet on which five to ten questions have been listed. The questions may be academic, social, trivia or a combination thereof. See Figure 4 for sample.

ACTIVITY:
1. A worksheet is distributed to each student with instructions to complete the worksheet by interviewing fellow students.
2. Students may not obtain more than one answer per student.
3. A specific amount of time is given to complete the activity, such as five or ten minutes, depending upon the complexity and number of questions.

Be prepared for a lot of movement and a relatively high noise level.

At the end of the activity, you may wish to have students turn in the worksheets, share the information they have gained in a small group, or discuss each question with the entire class.

This activity is excellent for reviewing material, preparing students for a test, reinforcing specific data or information you consider important, and getting better acquainted with each other.

Figure 4: SAMPLE FOCUS WORKSHEET

INSTRUCTIONS:
a. Find someone who can correctly answer the following questions or who fits the description.
b. have that person sign in the appropriate place.
c. Each question/description should be signed by a different person.

---

1. Explain paraphrasing _____

2. Describe the major stages of group development _____

3. Someone wearing blue _____

4. What is the purpose of Getting Acquainted activities? _____

5. Someone born in this city _____

6. When would you use a Transition Activity? _____

NOTE: Dana Lovitt reports that she has successfully used the Focus Worksheet with her first graders substituting pictures for words.

Chapter 2: Group Development Sample Activities

The following may be used as Transition or Energizer Activities

TITLE: **Exercises**
GRADE LEVEL: Preschool - Adult
ROLES: None
TIME: 5 Minutes

ACTIVITY: Lead your students in various physical exercises such as stretching, bending, jumping jacks, walking in place, etc., as appropriate for your grade level. (This is one of our favorites when people start getting tired and/or to begin the day.

VARIATION: Lead the class in a game of "Simon Says." This works especially well if you are teaching in tight quarters. Examples include: "Simon says touch your nose." "Simon says touch your left shoulder with your right thumb."

TITLE: **Guess That Number**
GRADE LEVEL: 2 - Adult
ROLES: None
TIME: 10 - 20 minutes
MATERIALS: Name Tags on which random numbers between 1 and 1,000 are written. Adjust the range of numbers according to your students' ability level. For grade 2, for instance, you might only include numbers between 1 and 50. Instructions are written on the chalkboard or on large chart paper hung on the wall.

ACTIVITY: The object is for each student to discover his number.
1. Numbered name tags are placed on students' backs.
2. Students may not see their own number.
3. Students discover their number by asking other students any of the following questions:
   a. Is my number lower than....?
   b. Is my number higher than....?
   c. Is my number ....?
   d. Responses may be "yes" or "no."

4. As students walk around the room they ask each other any of the three questions. They may not ask two consecutive questions of the same person. Example..Jamie may ask Maria, "Is my number higher than 50?" Maria may answer with a "yes" or a "no." Jamie must then ask another student one of the three questions. Jamie could then ask a third student another question or he could return to Maria to ask another question.

5. When a student discovers his number, he returns to his seat.

6. At the end of the allotted time period, all students return to their seats. Students who have not yet discovered their numbers may elect to continue the game during recess or break

time, or they may be told their numbers.

VARIATIONS: Use the alphabet, vocabulary words, mathematical equations, science facts, or any other facts you want to reinforce.

The following activities are ENERGIZERS

TITLE: **Bees**
GRADE LEVEL: Kindergarten - Adult
ROLES: None
TIME: 1 - 2 minutes
MATERIALS: None

ACTIVITY: All group members mimic the sound of bees (zzzzzzz) beginning very softly and gradually increasing in loudness.

TITLE: **Applause**
GRADE LEVEL: Preschool - Adult
ROLES: None
TIME: 15 - 30 seconds
MATERIALS: None

ACTIVITY: Students simply applaud for about 15 seconds.

The following are Breaking Up Activities ....

........to help students bring closure to the school year; to immortalize the group; to refocus and redirect student energy.

• **Sharing Individual Pictures** — Students may bring photos to class or use an instant picture camera to take candid shots at school. The pictures can be placed on a bulletin board before students take them home.

• **Cooperative Group Pictures** — Pictures of each cooperative group working together can be taken throughout the year with prints made for each group member. A copy of each picture can be put on a bulletin board until the end of the year. This reminds students of how many groups they participated in successfully.

• **Sharing Class Pictures** — Take a picture of the entire class involved in an activity, duplicate and distribute to each student. (Of course, the class picture taken by the school photographer can be used but it isn't quite as much fun.)

• **Copies of Special Small Group Projects** — Cooperative groups can reproduce a project that was special to the group. Each group member then keeps a copy of the project as a momento. (Examples: term papers; research papers; essays; literature critiques; an especially difficult test; any type of report; etc.)

• **Autograph Books** — These can be made by students so that each page has a statement or picture that is meaningful to students. They can be bound into a "book" in many ways: stitching; velobind; spindles; stapled; glued.

- **Journals or Scrapbooks** — As a final project, students could write a journal or make a scrapbook, noting special events and other memories. A journal or scrapbook could also be kept during the year with entries made periodically. This really helps students remember how they felt about the various activities.

- **Class Story** — At the end of the year students write a story about their class. This is a great creative writing assignment. The story would be duplicated for each student to take home. If the story were completed early enough, excerpts of it could be printed in the school newspaper or bulletin.

- **Sharing Feelings about what the year has meant and how much was achieved** — This can be done in small groups with each group writing their thoughts and feelings, then sharing their comments with the rest of the class. Another alternative is to have individuals share their feelings and thoughts with the entire class by conducting a WHIP. OR the entire class can brainstorm their feelings and achievements.

- **Visiting "next year's" classrooms or school.** — Elementary students often visit the junior high school and graduating junior high students visit the high school. But elementary students do not usually have the opportunity to visit the next grade level classroom. Even if a school has five classes of the next grade level, a brief visit (5 minutes) to each one would help alleviate some anxiety about their forthcoming move.

- **Orientation sessions with the next higher grade level teachers.** — If visiting the next grade level is impossible, the next best thing is to have those teachers visit the present classroom and briefly explain what can be expected in that grade level.

- **Sharing Future Goals or Planned Summer Activities**

- **Plant trees or bushes** on campus grounds with a sign "From the class of...."

- **An Art Project** such as painting a mural for the classroom or for the school, making a sculpture, stained glass designs that can be hung by the window, macrame plant holders, drawings, picture collage, etc. — The mural can be painted on canvas, plywood or cardboard and attached to a wall or it can be painted directly on a wall.

- **Giving Imaginary Gifts.** — Students' names are placed in a container. Each student draws a name and decides what he or she would most like to give to his recipient. Students then sit in a circle and each student "gives" his gift by describing what it is, walking to the student and placing the imaginary gift in his or her hands. Gifts can be intangibles such as happiness or fun for the summer or they can be tangible items such as a new bike or whatever.

- **Leaving a gift to the world.** — This is similar to the individual imaginary gift. The class (or small groups) decide, if it were possible, what they would most like to give the world. Responses usually include such things as peace, food for everyone, clear communication, happiness.

- **Artifacts.** — Students place different artifacts in a container with a note and bury it someplace on campus with the idea it will be found by later generations.

- **Letters.** — Students, in small groups or in one large group, write a letter to: the students who will follow them in this class; the principal; their parents; the teacher; each other.

- **Class Yearbook.** — Each page is devoted to one or two students. A picture of the student is placed at the top with information about the student, such as: birthday; where born; how long in school; brothers and sisters; the funniest/most interesting thing that happened to the student that year; accomplishments and achievements; and whatever else the students might want to immortalize. These books can be made easily with a computer and "desk-top" publishing or word processing programs. They can be stapled or bound in some other way.

SOURCES

THE WHIP: Developed by Dr. Stan Schainker, Associate Superintendent, San Francisco Unified School District, San Francisco, Calif.

SIMILARITIES AND DIFFERENCES AND SELF-DESCRIPTION: Peggy

WHAT DO WE HAVE IN COMMON: This activity was conducted by students in one of Peggy's classes a few years ago but we don't know if they created it?

GUESS WHO and GUESS THAT NUMBER: Jacquie

APPLAUSE and BEES: Adapted by Peggy to use as an energizer.

ONE NEW FACT: Adapted by Peggy and Jacquie from various activities they have experienced and conducted in workshops.

Breaking Up Activities: Developed, devised, remembered or modified for bringing closure to a group and redirecting group members' energies by Jacquie and Peggy.

ALL OTHERS: Original Source Unknown.

CHAPTER 3

SUCCESSFUL COMMUNICATION

OVERVIEW: This chapter discusses the four major areas of communication and points out that the two most used in everyday life, listening and speaking, are the least taught in public schools.

Effective speaking and listening techniques and nonverbal messages are explained in depth. A suggested teaching sequence is also provided.

TOPICS INCLUDE:

1. What is successful communication?
2. The communication process.
3. The steps involved in getting your message across.
4. Conflict language.
5. Becoming a better listener.
6. Nonverbal communication.
7. Congruence.
8. Feedback.
9. Supplemental information and activities.
10. Sample Activities.

WHY STUDY COMMUNICATION?

The student's success in the classroom, at play, in interpersonal relationships, and later, in the working world, all depend on the ability to communicate well.

Your effectiveness as a teacher is also dependent upon your skills as a communicator; if you can't get your message across, students will be unable to gain the knowledge and information you have; if you have poor listening skills, students will not get their specific questions answered. Before we can teach successful communication strategies, we need to have an understanding of the different techniques that have proven themselves effective.

Effective teachers are effective communicators.

There are four basic communication skills: reading, writing, listening and speaking. Schools normally teach these skills in reverse order of their importance in a person's life. The most taught are reading and writing, the least taught are listening and speaking. Reading and writing are certainly important, but in our normal daily lives we spend far more time listening and speaking than we do reading and writing. Simple Cooperation brings the critical skills of listening and speaking into their proper place in the curriculum.

The four communication skills are taught in reverse order of use in daily life.

Nonverbal communication, another element of communication largely ignored in the classroom yet vitally important in life, is also studied and taught in the Simple Cooperation model.

Verbal and nonverbal communication skills are taught directly and through many specific activities. In fact, developing effective communication skills and techniques becomes part of the daily classroom activity.

Because communication skills have been so widely ignored as

The Nurturing Classroom

Before you teach successful communication techniques you need to evaluate your own skills.

actual subjects of study in our school system, we'll first discuss some of the concepts and elements of sending and receiving messages; what these skills are, how they work and what sometimes stops them from working. Once you have this background, we'll show you how Simple Cooperation helps you teach communication through specific activities.

As teacher and model for your students, it is necessary to first evaluate your own communication skills. You will analyze, perhaps for the first time in your life, how well you send and receive messages.

A caution: for many people, self-examination is very threatening. We're not certain exactly why, but we frequently observe this phenomenon in workshops. It may be that in looking closely at our own communication techniques, we find that we're not as effective as we've always thought we were. It can be upsetting to discover that our own communication skills can be dramatically improved. There is a consolation — no matter how effective our communication patterns may currently be, no matter how much training we've had each and every one of us can always improve.

WHAT IS SUCCESSFUL COMMUNICATION?

Definition

Successful, i.e., effective, communication is defined as the transference of ideas, thoughts, attitudes, and opinions from a sender (the speaker) to a receiver (the listener) with the receiver understanding the content of the message in the same manner as the sender intended. In other words effective communication is transferring meaning from one person to another. That sounds easy enough until we look at everything involved in that process.

As Figure 5 reflects, there are two principal parties in a communication transaction — the sender and the receiver, commonly regarded as active and passive roles, respectively. But that is definitely not true; both are very active roles.

A communication begins when one person sends a message to another. That message is sent in some sort of code, words or behaviors, typically referred to as verbal and nonverbal language. This is where the first "trouble spot" may occur.

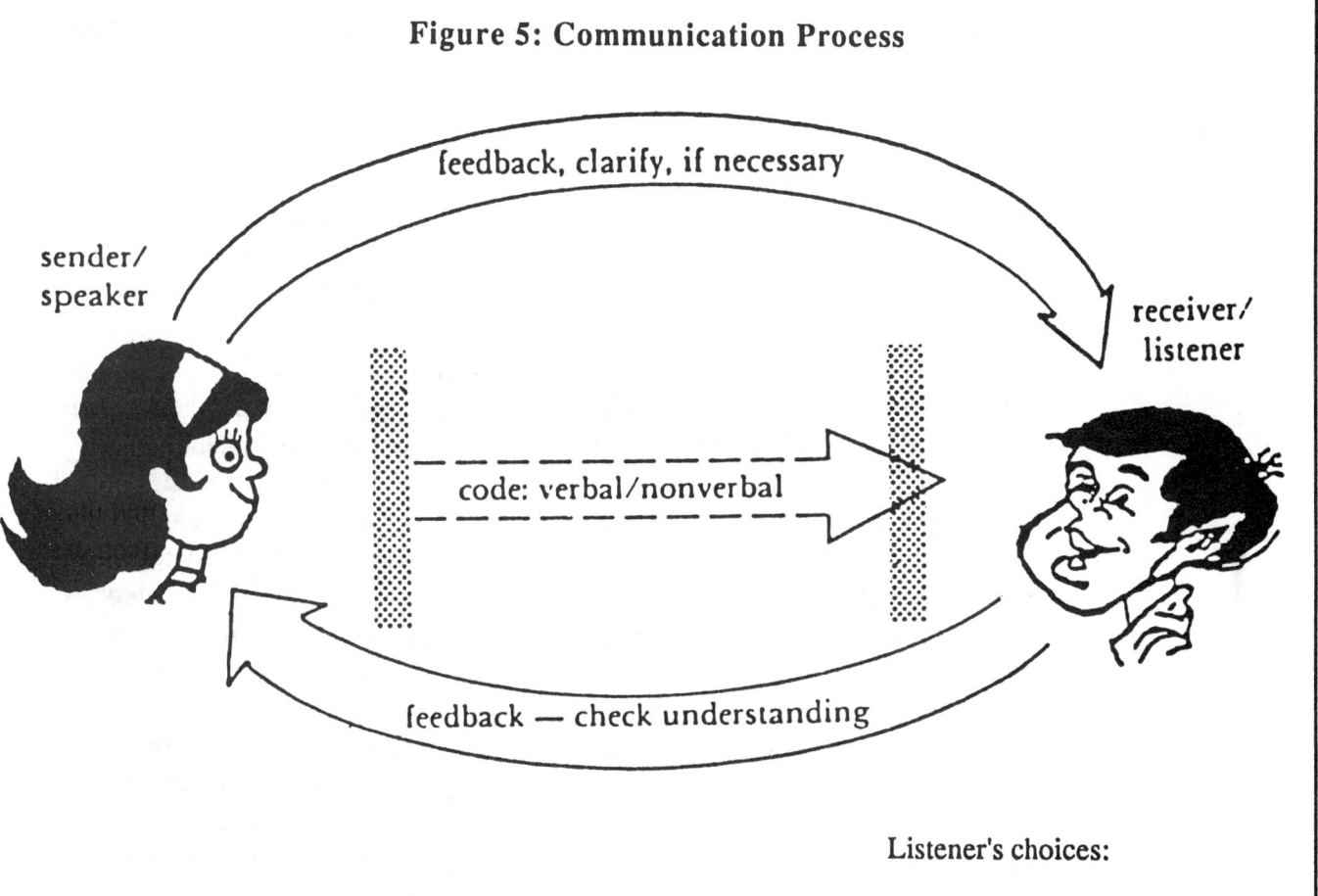

Figure 5: Communication Process

Note: The shaded areas reflect perceptual zones; each message, verbal or nonverbal, must travel through each individual's perceptual zone which is comprised of attitudes, opinions, knowledge, thoughts, values, feelings and previous experiences. Each person's perception and interpretation of any given behavior or verbal message is based on these and other variables.

It's easy to see how a message may be misinterpreted. The listener must, in fact, decode what the speaker intends to say; checking the accuracy of the interpretation becomes critical in many situations. It is equally important for the speaker to verify the listener's perceptions and interpretations and to clarify by restating the message if the receiver isn't "getting is."

Same word or action = different meanings

Each of us interprets words and behaviors differently. The meaning any word, action or other nonverbal signal has is dependent upon our own thoughts, attitudes, feelings, knowledge, and experience. So, I say something to you, using words and gestures that have specific meaning to me. But those words and gestures may mean something entirely different to you. For example, in certain parts of our country, a "soda" is a drink made with seltzer water and ice cream and a "pop" is a carbonated drink that you buy in a can or bottle. Here's another example from Peggy's experience when she first moved from New York to California.

Peggy and her brother, Bill, were shopping and purchased a small item in a variety store. (In 1956 variety stores had a clerk behind each small counter.) As Peggy paid for the item, the clerk asked if she wanted a sack. Puzzled, Peggy looked at Bill, turned back to the clerk and said "No, thank you." Naturally, the clerk then handed the item to Peggy. When they left the store, they discussed the clerk's "strange" behavior: first, asking if they wanted a sack, then not putting the item in a paper bag. (The only "sack" they had ever heard of was a burlap sack.)

In these two examples, there is immediate feedback about the success, or lack thereof, of the communication. Many of our communication interactions are much more subtle and it's possible for our conversation to go on for many minutes before we realize we're not thinking or talking about the same thing. We could even find ourselves in a disagreement because we did not fully understand what we each meant ten minutes ago.

Frame of reference is important

The communication process becomes more complex because we each communicate within our own "frame of reference." Your frame of reference is the sum total of your experiences and knowledge. If we get into a long discussion about a topic in which I have no knowledge or experience, I won't understand what you're trying to tell me. It's possible that I'll think I'd look or sound dumb if I stop you to ask questions so your message just gets lost while I pretend I understand. This happens frequently in the classroom and our students don't ask questions because they don't want to appear "dumb" to their teacher or peers.

Need to complete the communication loop.

Another thing that can go wrong in communication interactions is failure to complete the communication loop. The listener needs to send some sort of message (called "feedback") to the speaker to indicate how he is interpreting the speaker's message and the speaker must then let the listener know if the interpretation is correct or not.

An effective, or successful, communication has not occurred until all parts of the process have been completed.

As mentioned before, messages are traditionally divided into two types: verbal and nonverbal. For lack of any better classifications, we will use these same terms here. While it is possible to send a completely nonverbal message, a verbal message always includes nonverbal cues, such as tone of voice, inflection, tempo, volume, facial expression, body posture, breathing rhythm, pupil size, etc. These nonverbal cues are more powerful messages than your words.

For instance: a person might silently confront you with a flushed face and compressed lips, breathing rapidly with eyebrows drawn together over glaring eyes and fists clenched at sides OR he might say, in a loud trembling voice with clipped words, "You miserable so and so, I am absolutely furious with you." Both are very effective communications.

Verbal vs Nonverbal

For our purposes, the term "verbal message" will mean the spoken words, and "nonverbal message" will mean everything except the words. (Though perhaps we should coin a new communication term and call these messages "without words" rather than "nonverbal.")

SENDING MESSAGES — THE "SPEAKER"

To teach your students how to get their message across successfully, explain and model each of the following techniques:

1. GET YOUR LISTENER'S ATTENTION

• SAY THE PERSON'S NAME

Step 1: Get intended listener's attention.

The very first step in sending an effective message is to get the receiver's attention. The simplest way to get someone's attention is to say the person's name. If the response doesn't clearly indicate that the receiver is ready to be attentive (for example, if he just grunts or nods without looking up), it may help to say something else such as: "Do you have a minute?"

Getting the listener's attention may seem almost too obvious to mention, yet many people launch into their main message without doing so. Before the listener understands he is being addressed, much of the message has already been said. Taking a moment to establish the listener's attention also gives him time to stop thinking about whatever else was going on and refocus on the message about to be received.

2. ESTABLISH EYE CONTACT

Step 2: Eye contact but be aware of cultural differences

It is also important to establish eye contact with the receiver if at all possible. Eye contact allows the nonverbal part of the message to be sent: gestures, facial expressions, etc. that emphasize and illuminate the verbal part of the message. (More on this later.) A caution here, though: in some cultures it is considered disrespectful for a youngster to have direct eye contact with an adult. It is **imperative** that you are aware of and sensitive to the cultural differences of the students in your classroom.

3. CLAIM YOUR OWN THOUGHTS, IDEAS AND FEELINGS

Step 3: Claim your thoughts, ideas and feelings.

The next step in sending effective messages is to claim your own thoughts, ideas and feelings. We have a tendency in our society to talk about *"they"* and *"them"* a lot: *"they"* say", "it's up to *"them"*. Have you ever wondered who *"they"* and *"them"* are? It almost seems as if we're afraid to say, "*I* think..." or "*I* feel....". Students need a great deal of practice and reinforcement to learn to claim their thoughts as their own.

4. THE "3-C'S" — BE CLEAR, CONCISE, COMPLETE

Step 4: The 3 C's

Effective sending, or speaking, requires learning how to state a message clearly, concisely and completely.

• BE CLEAR

The speaker needs to stick to one topic at a time,

without jumping from one subject to another. The listener won't know what information belongs to which topic if the speaker plays a game of leap-frog.

One topic at a time

As the message proceeds, the speaker can and should check with the listener from time to time to determine if the message is being understood. This is particularly true when relating long or complex issues, instructions, reports or similar messages. A simple question such as: "Am I making sense?" or "Are you understanding (or following) all of this?" is all that's really needed.

Check to see if you're getting your message across

If the listener indicates that she is having difficulty understanding, the speaker can elaborate on the message or rephrase it. Watching your listener's nonverbal messages will also alert you to any confusion the listener may be feeling.

The speaker can also use visual aids such as graphs, charts or other types of visual cues to assist the listener in understanding unusually complex messages.

Draw a picture

Pronouns are another source of confusion in verbal communication: remember the rule that a pronoun refers to the noun that immediately precedes it. Better still, decrease your use of pronouns.

Watch out for pronouns

• **BE CONCISE**

Too much detail can confuse the message.

Remember, effective sending requires you to state your message CLEARLY and CONCISELY. You must say enough to let the listener know what's being talked about but not so much that the main point of the message gets lost in excess detail, and the listener gets tired of waiting for you to get to the point.

Being clear and concise not only enhances the listener's level of understanding but retains interest in what is being said. A rule of thumb is to use only as many words as are required to get the message across. Extra words do nothing but confuse the issue.

A general rule abut how many words to use

• BE COMPLETE

On the other hand, you must give the receiver the necessary background information to understand what you're saying.

Before launching into the main message, the sender should provide a context for the information which follows. Children often omit this step. How often have you had to stop a student in the middle of an excited rush of details about some incident and get them to say what they're talking about so you can understand their message?

Children are not alone in sometimes failing to give proper background for their message. For example....have you ever had someone tell you a fairly lengthy story which included several references to a particular person, let's say someone named Rick. Try as you might, you can't remember who Rick is. From the way the speaker is talking, she seems to be taking it for granted that you know this Rick person. You keep listening for clues and you search your brain but you just can't identify the man.

Finally, you give up and ask, only to learn that Rick is another friend of the speaker's whom you've never met. Had the speaker identified Rick immediately as "a friend of mine" you would have been able to relax and concentrate on the story. As it was, your attention was distracted as you tried to supply background information for yourself that *should* have been given to you by the speaker.

5. EXPRESSING AND NAMING FEELINGS

Another tendency we have in our society is to discount and/or deny our feelings through statements like: "It doesn't matter," and "No, I'm not hurt/angry/etc".

Clearly expressing feelings is neither expected nor encouraged in our society. Consider how many times a day

Give your listener enough background information to understand what you're trying to say

Step 5: *Identify your feelings*

you say or hear: "How are you?" or "How are you feeling?" Most often, this is nothing more than a social amenity. The expected response is "okay" or "fine."

Yet, expressing feelings clearly contributes to effective communication because the listener doesn't have to guess at what you're feeling.

It takes a lot of practice and conscious effort to state your own feelings and to teach your students to recognize and express theirs. (It also takes courage but it's worth it.)

6. FRAME OF REFERENCE

It's important to remember frame of reference discussed earlier. Be sure your listener has some knowledge or experience in whatever topic you want to discuss. If he doesn't, you need to use examples and analogies relating the new information to what the listener already knows. This is what we do when we teach students new academic information, isn't it? We explain how this information is like and/or relates to something we know they already know.

> **Step 6:** Stay within your listener's "frame of reference"

CONFLICT OR POTENTIAL CONFLICT SITUATIONS

Many people don't know how to express themselves in a diplomatic and tactful manner; they just blurt out their feelings and thoughts without thinking about how their comments will affect others.

Anger is often expressed in a verbally aggressive manner (intentionally or not). The listener could easily believe he or she is being criticized or attacked and may become defensive. The result is usually a heated argument with subsequent bad feelings between the individuals involved in the interaction.

We can avoid many arguments and conflicts by stating our feelings in ways that will be less offensive to the listener.

"I-MESSAGES"

"I-Messages," as developed and taught by Dr. Thomas Gordon of the Effectiveness Training Institute, are comprised of three specific and distinct parts:

1. your feeling,
2. the other person's behavior which preceded the feeling; and
3. the consequence, or tangible effect, the behavior has on us.

Conflict language

An "I-Message" tells the listener exactly how the speaker feels, why she feels that way, and what effect the listener's behavior has had on the speaker. This type of statement is clear and focuses on behavior rather than becoming an evaluation of the person's character; thus, it is less likely to result in an argument.

Teach students how to express anger in a constructive manner

Students are rarely taught how to express their anger in a way that can prevent, or at least, diffuse, conflict. For example...... a group member has failed to complete his part of the assignment. Typical reactions from other students include name-calling or some other form of verbal assault. An alternative communication strategy is an "I-Message" which could be phrased like this: "I'm really angry that you did not complete your part of the assignment because our group paper is now incomplete and we won't get as many bonus points."

(*Note:* "I-Messages" may also be used in a positive manner, "I'm really pleased that we've all completed our parts so well because we will surely receive a high grade for our paper.")

RECEIVING A MESSAGE — THE "LISTENER"

> *"Hurry up and finish talking, it's my turn now."*

A good listener does more than passively receive the message being transmitted by the speaker. Remember the definition of an effective communication is that the message is understood in the same way that the sender intended.

The listener has a responsibility to help achieve this goal. Learning to be an active, skilled listener is as important as learning to be a good speaker.

The listener is equally responsible for the communication being successful

All of us listen more than we speak, read or write; yet listening techniques are rarely, if ever, taught. Children and students are scolded and told to listen. So, how are youngsters supposed to learn effective listening techniques?

As with most things, learning to become a skilled listener takes training, lots of practice and appropriate feedback from others. Specific listening-skill activities that will provide the practice and feedback can be found in the "Sample Activities" section at the end of this chapter.

To teach your students how to become better listeners, discuss and model the following techniques:

How to teach listening

1. FOCUS ON THE SPEAKER

The first step in effective listening is to focus on the speaker and make a genuine effort to hear and understand the message. Listening, too often, takes the form of a game called, ***"Hurry up and finish talking, it's my turn now."*** In this game, very little listening really occurs. The listener is not receiving the message at all, he's just marking time until the speaker pauses or stops speaking.

Step 1: Focus

2. CLARIFY

As the message proceeds, the listener must try to judge whether or not she really understands what's being said. If not, the listener has basically two choices: to guess or to clarify. Sometimes guesses are accurate; more often they aren't. Clarifying, which is a form of

Step 2: Clarify

Three ways to clarify

feedback, makes a lot more sense than guessing. *Asking questions, paraphrasing* and *checking your perceptions* are three ways of clarifying a speaker's messages.

• ASKING QUESTIONS

One method of clarifying is to simply ask questions. In the example given earlier, when the listener couldn't identify "Rick," a simple question early in the story would have clarified everything. "I'm sorry, I can't figure out which Rick you mean. Is he someone I know?"

*Is it **really** okay for students to ask questions in your classroom?*

Students frequently do not ask questions because they're afraid to appear "dumb." It's up to you as the teacher to establish a safe environment for questioning, and encourage students to ask for clarification. This means that the teacher must be careful not to demonstrate any behavior, verbal or nonverbal, that can be interpreted as nonaccepting of questions.

When students ask questions about the assignment, statements such as, "Finish your workbook, of course! What did you think?" or "You have to learn to listen the first time!" tell students questions are not appreciated. Signals of impatience such as raised eyebrows, smirks and looks of irritation or exasperation all give students a very clear message that a "dumb" question has been asked.

Students model the teacher

> Students model teacher behavior. If the teacher demonstrates nonaccepting behavior when questions are asked, two things will happen: students will feel free to ridicule the questioner and students will stop asking questions.

Give direct and positively-phrased answers to students' questions.

- **PARAPHRASING**

    Another clarifying technique is paraphrasing. To paraphrase, the listener states in his own words how he has interpreted or understood the message. Note that paraphrasing is not simply restating the message in different words; this would not guarantee understanding. For example, consider the following exchange:

    Teacher 1: *"Suzanne shouldn't be in this classroom."*

    Teacher 2: *"You're right, she really shouldn't be in this classroom."*

    Are they both thinking the same thing? Do they have the same idea about Suzanne? They may certainly think they're talking about the same thing but it's more likely they aren't which would have been revealed if Teacher 2 had paraphrased instead of restated:

    Teacher 1: *"Suzanne shouldn't be in this classroom."*

    Teacher 2: *"She does seem a bit disruptive!"*

    Teacher 1: *"Oh no, that's not what I mean. It's that Suzanne is so advanced I'm having trouble challenging her mind."*

    Teacher 2: *"Oh, I see what you mean."*

    In the second dialogue paraphrasing was used to clarify the message and a clear communication occurred.

    To better understand the difference between restating and paraphrasing, it might be helpful to remember that *restating is a tool for the sender of the message*. The sender restates his own message using different words to make certain he's getting his meaning across to the listener.

    Paraphrasing is a tool used by the receiver, to make sure that her understanding of the message is what the sender intended.

> *The listener paraphrases; the speaker restates*

- ### CHECK OUT YOUR PERCEPTIONS

A third clarifying technique is to "check out" your perceptions. Checking your perceptions means that the listener looks beyond the words and attempts to understand how the speaker is really feeling. This is important when the listener is unsure of the speaker's feelings.

Checking your perceptions is also important when the listener thinks she is getting a double message. That is, when the words say one thing and the nonverbal message says something else. Perception-checking helps the listener understand the "true" message the speaker is trying to convey.

Since perception-checking concerns primarily nonverbal communication, it is discussed in the following pages.

NONVERBAL COMMUNICATION

We have referred to nonverbal messages already, and defined them as *all parts of a message except the spoken words*. Depending on which researcher you read, somewhere between 70 and 85% of our communication is nonverbal. Yet, schools do not teach students what nonverbal communication is or how it relates to the spoken word.

Some of the many aspects of nonverbal communication

Earlier we listed some of the many aspects of nonverbal communication: tone of voice, inflection, tempo, volume, facial expression, body posture, breathing rhythm, flushed face, pupil size and perspiration rate. To this list may be added gestures, eye movement, non-word vocalizations, i.e. guttural sounds, any and all behavior during a communication other than the spoken words.

Note that much of what we refer to as "nonverbal" involves the spoken message: the way in which words are delivered. Tempo, volume, inflection, etc. are nonverbal components of the verbal message. (Also, note that nonverbal communication is not synonymous with the "body language" that many of us studied in the '60s, although body language is certainly one aspect of nonverbal communication.)

Nonverbal communication ≠ "body language."

Most of the time, we're not aware of the messages we're giving nonverbally. Worse, our nonverbal messages can be easily misunderstood.

Many people believe that nonverbal messages are really simple to interpret; a flushed face obviously means embarrassment, right? And a person who closes his eyes during a conversation is simply not interested in what's being said, true? Not necessarily.

Consider this before you jump to conclusions about another person's nonverbal messages: Blushing certainly can mean that a person is embarrassed but some individuals blush when they're irritated, excited, hurt, or just overly warm. And, the person who closes his eyes during a conversation *may* be inattentive or perhaps he can concentrate better with closed eyes.

Becoming aware of some of the aspects of nonverbal messages and knowing how easily nonverbal cues can be misinterpreted will increase your communication success. Explaining the many different messages we give each other nonverbally to your students will enhance their ability to interact with others. Role playing can be especially valuable in practicing nonverbal communication.

Role playing is valuable when teaching students

WATCHING YOURSELF

If nonverbal signals can be so easily misinterpreted (or used to manipulate others) is there any way to avoid misunderstanding? Yes. Perhaps not perfectly, but there are several ways to greatly improve clarity and understanding for both the receiver and speaker.

Begin with yourself. Become aware of your own nonverbal messages. What signals do you give when you're anxious? Happy? Sad? Depressed? Insecure? Annoyed? Do you cover your embarrassment with a steady string of words? Do you avert your eyes and blush when you're embarrassed? When do you speak loudly or softly, faster or slower? Do you sometimes isolate yourself from a group with subtle body movements?

Become aware of your own nonverbal cues

As a receiver, how do you signal your interest or lack of interest? Do you look intently at the speaker and use nonverbal sounds and nods to indicate your attention and understanding? When you doodle as you listen, does that mean you're bored or that you listen better when your hands are busy?

The listener gives nonverbal cues, too

After you've observed your own nonverbal messages for a week or so, ask a friend to tell you how she knows when you're happy, sad, annoyed, embarrassed, hurt, etc. You may have to reassure your friend that you really do want honest feedback and that you will not be insulted or offended by her report. In all probability, your friend will tell you some things you didn't know.

Ask a friend to help

Once you've checked your own nonverbal messages, you can begin to change those mannerisms that are causing you to be misunderstood or that you are personally dissatisfied with. You'll also gain more awareness of how you may be misinterpreting the nonverbal cues of others and you'll be on the way to becoming a more effective communicator.

Being aware of yourself can help you understand others

- **PROXIMITY**

An aspect of nonverbal communication seldom considered is where you are physically in relation to the person with whom you're speaking, i.e., how close you are, if you're sitting or standing.

*How close is **too** close?*

Each individual has a "comfort zone." Some people are very comfortable when they are four inches away from your face; others prefer to be no closer than twelve or more inches. No matter how far or close someone stands, don't jump to conclusions here, either. The distance selected may be related to visual acuity.

Where you position yourself in relation to the person with whom you're speaking also sends some very clear messages. For example, standing over a person could be interpreted as an attempt to control. Or, giving the parent of a primary student a small chair while you sit at your desk could be interpreted as an attempt to intimidate.

Where are you?

Determining where another person's comfort zone is and staying within it will enhance communication; it communicates respect and concern. It's fairly easy to determine at what distance other people are comfortable; they will usually back away if you're too close or, conversely, move in if you're too far away.

As with all aspects of communication, it's important to be aware of where your own comfort zone is. Pay attention to how close you get to someone when you're conversing. This is the first step in recognizing the "comfort zone" message you are sending to others.

Where's your own comfort zone?

Be aware, also, of your physical size as compared to others. How much taller are you? If you're several inches taller and you stand right next to a person, to maintain eye contact, the shorter person may feel intimidated or, at best, will get a stiff neck This is especially important with young students. Always try to get down to eye level: stoop, sit on a chair, or whatever so that the child is not in the position of looking up two or three feet.

Even though your can't change it, be aware of your physical size

• <u>CHECKING PERCEPTIONS</u>

Checking your perceptions is a part of what Dr. Thomas Gordon calls "active listening" -- listening to and for the speaker's feelings as well as the words.

"Active Listening"

Observe your students and think about what they're telling you with their nonverbal language. What is the "obnoxious" child really feeling? Or the student who goes off by himself at recess? How about that child who swaggers and brags, or the one who rarely speaks up in

What are your students really saying to you?

class or in groups? Is the braggart really so sure of himself, or does that nonverbal behavior mask an inner insecurity? Is the quiet child really timid, or is she simply absorbed in what's being said?

Adults too seldom check their perceptions about a child to determine what the child is really feeling. We don't know if it's because adults think they <u>know</u> what the child is feeling better than the child does, or if adults consider it "beneath" them to check with the youngster. We DO know that very few teachers take the time to discern the student's real feelings.

You can also help your students, even young ones, learn about nonverbal language. One way to do this is to check out your perceptions with them, "It sounds like you're really hurt?" Or, "I get the impression that you're confused. Are you?" Or, "Your face is flushed. Does that mean you're embarrassed or angry or....?" "It looks like you may not be very happy, right now. Is that true?"

Don't jump to conclusions

You have to determine how best to approach your students to check out your perceptions of what their nonverbal messages are really saying. With some students, you can simply ask them. With others, you'll need to take a much more indirect approach. *Remember to always leave room for the student to correct you, or even not respond.* Feelings are a very personal thing and once again, in some cultures and families, it is not acceptable to discuss one's feelings. Whatever you do, remember not to jump to conclusions about what their nonverbal cues mean.

This technique of checking your perception of nonverbal messages accomplishes a great deal. By doing so, you avoid making assumptions about the student which could be wrong, you bring nonverbal behavior to the student's attention in a nonthreatening way, you help students clarify and express their feelings and you've modeled the "checking it out" process for them.

CONGRUENCE AND INCONGRUENCE

Congruence means that your verbal and nonverbal messages are both expressing the same thing. Incongruence is the opposite: the words are saying one thing while the nonverbal cues are saying something quite different.

When your verbal and nonverbal messages are incongruent, the listener is forced to make a choice - which message shall I, the listener, believe, or should I believe either of them? Most often, it is the nonverbal message that is believed.

Nonverbal messages are more powerful

FOR EXAMPLE...your new site administrator has assured the faculty that she is there to help and support you; that if you have a problem you can't seem to resolve you have only to make an appointment and she will be happy to explore alternative solutions with you. Well, one day you *do* have a problem with a student and you seek the guidance of your new principal. She welcomes you into the office and five minutes later, as you're relating the specifics surrounding the problem, she begins shuffling papers on the desk and glancing at the clock. You ask if she's too busy now and should you make another appointment. She curtly assures you that she is not too busy and really wants to help you.

Are you going to believe her words or actions. Most likely, you will begin to feel uncomfortable, start talking faster, and wish you hadn't made the appointment in the first place. It'll probably be a long time before you make another appointment to discuss a problem with this administrator.

Why do people give incongruent messages? There are many reasons: sometimes we're simply not sure about how we feel; other times we deliberately try to hide our feelings because allowing others to know what we're feeling makes us vulnerable. We fear being ridiculed, rejected, or looking stupid; these fears are powerful motives for trying to conceal our feelings.

We also try to hide feelings that we know are "wrong." We are *supposed* to be patient and calm in most situations but instead, we feel frustration and sometimes, intense irritation. For example, the response we give to the second or third student who interrupts our concentration might be genuinely patient and calm. The response to the tenth student who interrupts, however, might be given using the same words, but may

The Nurturing Classroom

be accompanied with exasperated sighs which gives a very different message to that student. You can be certain that no matter what your words are, this tenth student will not believe it was okay to interrupt you.

Because a major source of incongruence is fear, it is imperative for the teacher to create and foster a safe and secure environment in which students may learn and practice congruence.

Another reason to create a safe environment

In the cooperative classroom, standards of behavior are established very early. These standards must include the fact that each and every individual in the class is to be accepted and respected.

Respect and acceptance are inherrent in cooperative classrooms

No one should ever be allowed to ridicule or demean another. You, the teacher, must model this behavior and help enforce these rules. Should ridiculing occur, it's important to take the offender aside and firmly tell him or her that this type of behavior is simply not allowed in your classroom.

If this problem is pervasive with the group, it would be appropriate to review the group standards, emphasizing "respect." Teach this skill by explaining what "respect" means. Provide examples and perhaps, have your students role play what respect looks like compared to what disrespect looks like, in other words, use examples and nonexamples to teach the concept of respect. (Mary Rose, who teaches in a high school dropout prevention program, has implemented what she calls, "Give 'em three!" Any student who puts down anyone else must give three "build-ups" or three compliments to that person. — Great idea!)

"Put-downs" = "Give'em three"

POWERFUL LISTENING

Earlier, we stated that listening is an active role in a successful communication, not a passive role. Nonverbal language may be the listener's single most powerful tool for achieving effective communication.

A "good listener" is highly prized and what makes a good listener is often the way in which she signals interest and attention through non-verbal language. Eye contact, nodding, subvocalizations and other signals assure the speaker that he is being understood and that the listener values what he is saying. A frown or quizzical look may let the speaker know that something isn't being understood and could be an implied request for clarification.

When working with younger children, getting to the same eye level as the child is a good nonverbal assurance of attention. It's often an excellent technique to crouch, sit in chairs side by side or even sit the child on a desk or table so that the two of you talk at the same eye level.

We've said it before but it's worth repeating

You can help encourage good nonverbal listening habits by remarking on them and praising them, in addition to modeling these techniques. Example: "Suzanne, I like it when you nod and smile like that. It lets me know that I really got my message across to you."

Praise good listening techniques

TEACHING EFFECTIVE COMMUNICATION

Each of the major components of effective communication (Figure 6) must be taught, and no matter what age group you are working with, begin at the beginning. Don't automatically think that high school or adult students remember to get the attention of their intended listener before they start speaking. Since effective communication skills are seldom taught in schools, it is counterproductive to assume that your students know even this first step.

Also, whatever your students' age level, it is important to teach one technique at a time and to be sure this is mastered before moving to the next. You'll find a communication skills continuum at the end of this chapter (Figure 7) — but note: it should be used as a *guideline* only. Your own perceptions of your students' skill levels is the best guide for you to follow when introducing new skills.

Always begin at the beginning

and

Teach one thing at a time

FEEDBACK

In interpersonal communication, feedback helps the receiver become more aware of how he or she is coming across to the rest of the world. Feedback is a very important tool in teaching communication skills, but it can be dangerous unless you are careful and firm about its use.

Figure 6: Major Components of Effective Communication

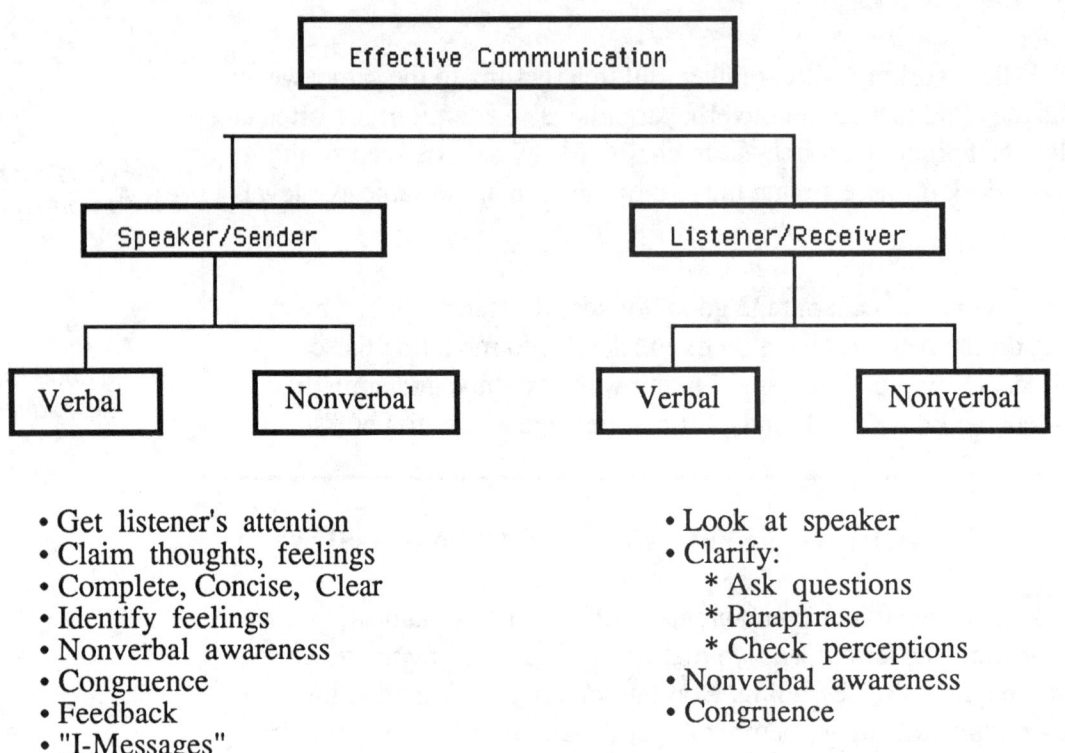

- Get listener's attention
- Claim thoughts, feelings
- Complete, Concise, Clear
- Identify feelings
- Nonverbal awareness
- Congruence
- Feedback
- "I-Messages"

- Look at speaker
- Clarify:
  * Ask questions
  * Paraphrase
  * Check perceptions
- Nonverbal awareness
- Congruence

Feedback Rules

There are a number of rules for giving feedback, the most important to remember and to teach are:

1. Feedback *should never be forced on an individual.* Sometimes a person simply cannot cope with feedback and will perceive it as negative criticism or an attack.

2. Feedback should *always focus on a specific behavior* rather than a vague generalization. e.g., "You did not turn in your math homework today" rather than, "You never do your homework."

3. Feedback *should be timely and be given as immediately as possible*, e.g., "You fell asleep in class last period." rather than, "You

fell asleep in class twice last semester."

4. *The person giving feedback should not be allowed to use it as a means to make him or her feel like a better person or more important than the receiver of the feedback.*

Figure 7: Communication Continuum

<u>SENDING</u>:

1. Get Listener's Attention
2. Claim Own Thoughts, Ideas, Feelings
3. 3 C's — Be Clear, Concise, Complete
4. Identify Feelings
5. Nonverbal Awareness
6. Congruence
7. Feedback
8. "I-Messages"

<u>RECEIVING</u>:

1. Look at Speaker
2. Clarify by Asking Questions
3. Clarify by Paraphrasing
4. Nonverbal Awareness
5. Perception Checking
6. Congruence

SUMMARY

- *Communication skills are usually ignored as specific subjects of study in the public schools.*

- *Verbal messages always include nonverbal messages.*

- *Techniques for sending effective messages include:*

    - *Getting the attention of your intended listener.*
    - *The 3 C's — Be clear, concise, complete.*
    - *Identifying feelings.*
    - *Using "I-Messages".*
    - *Using visual aids for complex messages.*
    - *Demonstrating congruence between verbal and nonverbal messages.*
    - *Staying within the listener's frame of reference.*

- *Listening can be enhanced by:*
    - *Attending to the speaker.*
    - *Clarifying the message by asking questions, paraphrasing and checking perceptions.*

- *More than 70% of all communication is nonverbal.*

- *Nonverbal messages are more powerful than verbal.*

Superteaching Workbook Chapter 3 - SUCCESSFUL COMMUNICATION

Self-Evaluation Quiz

1. Define "successful/effective communication"

2. What is:
    a. Verbal communication

    b. Nonverbal communication

3. What does "congruence" mean

4. What is an "I-Message"

5. When would you use an "I-Message"

6. Paraphrase the following:

    John: "I'm giving a test today and I don't have enough pencils for my students. Do you have 15 pencils I can borrow?"

    Your paraphrase:

7. What does it mean "to check your perceptions"

8. Identify at least three actions you're going to take to become a more successful communicator:

SUPPLEMENTAL INFORMATION AND ACTIVITIES

SENDING EFFECTIVE MESSAGES

A. SUGGESTIONS FOR GETTING YOUR INTENDED LISTENER'S ATTENTION:

1. Say his or her name.
2. Give a light pat or tap on shoulder or arm.
3. Walk over and stand next to or in front of the person. This is frequently necessary with very young children who are engrossed in something else.

To get the attention of your whole class:

Teachers use a lot of different methods for getting their students' attentions: switching off lights; blowing whistles; raising the voice; shouting; etc. Two techniques we have found very effective are:

1. Stand quietly, saying nothing, in front of the group scanning the faces of your "audience" until everyone is attending.

2. Establish a signal with your students, e.g., when you raise your hand, that means you need everyone to be quiet and paying attention to you. (Another idea from Mary Rose is *to shake a raisin box - this is instead of "rais'n your voice."*)

These two techniques will work consistently <u>ONLY if you wait until everyone is quiet and ready to listen before you begin speaking.</u>

B. PRACTICE WITH THE 3-C'S

Rewrite the following paragraph to be clear, concise and complete:

Background: Your friend is telling you about an unexpected meeting she had with some mutual friends, two teachers, Guy and Rosemary, who moved three years ago. Your friend refers to a third person, Ruth, whom you've never heard of. (Ruth is Rosemary's sister and Earl is Ruth's husband.)

YOUR FRIEND: "Guess who I saw yesterday...no, you'll never guess! I'll tell you. There I was in the mall looking for some shoes for my son and I had just left Sears. I was looking around trying to decide where I'd have lunch; it was so crowded over there yesterday, anyway, I was deciding between that little coffee shop and the deli when there they were......Guy and Rosemary! Remember them?

They were just passing through town and decided to see if the sandwiches were still as good as they used to be at the deli. Ruth was with them. They sure looked good. They're very happy. Hard to believe two people determined to remain single being married to each other. Ruth left teaching two years ago, just before Earl retired, and opened up a very successful little dress shop. She's really trying to get Rosemary to go into the business with her. She is certainly making more money than she was teaching. Rosemary is seriously considering it but she hasn't decided yet. She really loves teaching high school business. Ruth has persuaded Rosemary to do the books for her and to spend some time in the shop "just to get an idea of how it would be," she said. And Guy is such a whiz with computers and stuff — some big company has been trying to entice him to leave the school system and work for them at triple his salary.

He's decided to talk with them seriously about it. He enjoys teaching but he thinks he'll just teach some night classes or do some guest lectures, if he misses it too much. In fact, they were on their way to talk with the big bosses at the head office.

They said they were really sorry they didn't have time to call or stop to see everybody. Sure was great seeing them; we all had lunch at the deli.

Your Rewrite:

C. RESTATING AND USING OTHER MODALITIES TO GET YOUR MESSAGE ACROSS

When your listener does not seem to understand what you've said -- there may be a quizzical or confused look on her face -- or when you have to give complicated information to your class or some other group, restating and using illustrations are great ways to help clarify your message.

There are many ways to clarify your message:

   a. Say it again using different words, i.e., restate your message.
   b. Use illustrations, charts, drawings, etc., i.e., add other modalities.
   c. Say it differently and use illustrations, i.e., restate and add other modalities.

Note that restating and paraphrasing are **not** synonymous; restating is done by the speaker. If the listener restated the speaker's message using different words, that would be called, "word swapping."

> Paraphrasing is done by the listener. It is saying in your own words what you **think** the speaker meant by whatever he said.

C. PRACTICE "I-MESSAGES" AS DEVELOPED BY DR. THOMAS GORDON

SITUATION: You have a very good friend who borrows your reference books "for a week" which always turns into months. This has been very inconvenient for you and you always have to ask your friend to return your books.

Your "I-Message:"

SITUATION: Your school has a full time clerk whose sole responsibility is to duplicate material for you. The requirement for having material duplicated is to turn in whatever you want with a request form at least three days before you want the copies. You always submit your request at least four days before you need the material, yet, more than half the time your material isn't ready and you have to alter your lesson or ask the clerk to copy it immediately.

Your "I-Message:"

SITUATION: You carpool with another teacher who lives only a few blocks from you. When it's his turn to drive, you make sure you're ready, in fact, you're usually standing on your front step waiting as he drives up. BUT....when you drive, you frequently have to wait for him. Typically, you have to wait any where from two to five minutes. A couple of times you waited 10 minutes, then got caught in the worst traffic which made you late for school.

Your "I-Message:"

Now, construct an "I-Message" related to some actual situation in your life.

BECOMING AN EFFECTIVE LISTENER

Being a good listener brings many rewards. A good listener learns more, has fewer arguments, has more friends, and is a valued colleague.

Practice by paraphrasing the following statements:

1. Effective communication strategies are usually not a part of the regular school curriculum. As a result, we have a society filled with people who are unable to express themselves and very few people seem interested in listening to others anymore.

Your Paraphrase:

2. I'm giving a test today and I have 15 pencils and 30 students. Do you have any pencils I could borrow?

Your Paraphrase:

3. It's no wonder we have such a high rate of illiteracy in our country - nobody wants to read books anymore. Everyone just watches the idiot box.

Your Paraphrase:

HOW TO CHECK OUT YOUR PERCEPTIONS

Perception checking, or checking the accuracy of what you believe another person is feeling, is truly valuable. The person who checks things out does not jump to conclusions, thus, has far fewer misunderstandings with others.

It's really easy to check your perceptions: You just simply ask the other person if what you perceive is what they are really feeling. What a surprise to ask a child who is so "obnoxious" and find that she is scared stiff and doesn't know how else to deal or cope with her fears and anxieties.

Dr. Thomas Gordon of Effectiveness Training Institute calls this "Active Listening" which means listening to the feelings as well as the words. He suggests that you "active listen" by beginning your sentence with something like, "It sounds like you're feeling............" or "You seem to be..........."

Whatever words you use, it is critical to give the other person the clear option of saying, "No, that's not what I'm feeling." or "No, that's not what I mean."

Practice Perception Checking, every day.

SAMPLE COMMUNICATION ACTIVITIES

LISTENING: CLARIFY BY ASKING QUESTIONS

TITLE: **Learning to Ask Questions**
GRADE LEVEL: Kindergarten - Adult
ROLES: None
TIME: 30 minutes
MATERIALS: Short story or newspaper item

ACTIVITY:
1. Read a short story or news item to your class, leaving out at least half the critical facts of the story.

2. Students then ask questions to gain the necessary facts.

3. You respond to each specific question without volunteering additional information.

4. Following the question and answer period, students review the questions that were asked and discuss which questions resulted in gaining the most information.

5. Students then examine how those questions were phrased to gain the necessary information.

6. The last step is to determine what kinds of questions would have gained necessary information faster.

LISTENING: CLARIFY BY PARAPHRASING

TITLE: **Paraphrasing Verbal Messages**
GRADE LEVEL: Grade 2 - Adult
ROLES: None
TIME: 10 - 15 minutes
MATERIALS: None

ACTIVITY:
1. In pairs, one student tells the other what she did during the weekend and how she felt about it.
2. The second student, the listener, paraphrases the message.

3. The speaker responds by validating the listener's interpretation of the message or clarifies her message.

TITLE: **Paraphrasing Written Messages**
GRADE LEVEL: 4 - Adult
ROLES: Recorder for Single Assignment
TIME: 5 - 10 minutes
MATERIALS: Any printed material

GROUPING PATTERN: Assign students to groups of three or four. and specify a recorder for each group.

ACTIVITY:

1. Distribute a short paragraph of two to four sentences. (This can be from a newspaper, magazine, or even part of a textbook.)

2. Students work together to paraphrase the content.

3. Discuss each group's paraphrase, helping to improve student ability to use this skill.

TITLE: **Paraphrasing Student Writing**
GRADE LEVEL: 4 - Adult
ROLES: None
TIME: 10 - 15 minutes
MATERIALS: Short Stories written by students

GROUPING PATTERN: Pair students

ACTIVITY: .

1. Each student takes a turn and paraphrases the partner's short story.

2. The original author validates the correctness of the reader's interpretation, or if the interpretation is incorrect, clarifies.

COMBINED LISTENING AND SPEAKING ACTIVITIES

TITLE: **News Reporter**
GRADE LEVEL: 3 - Adult
ROLES: None
TIME: 20 - 40 minutes
MATERIALS: Short Newspaper Article

ACTIVITY: Select a space within or near the classroom where students can talk softly, yet not be heard by other members of the class. This space is called the "safe" area, out of earshot of other students.

1. Take one student to the "safe" area and read a short news article to him.

2. You then leave the "safe" area taking the news article with you, and direct another student to go to the "safe" area.

3. The first student repeats the news story to the second student, then leaves the area.

4. A third student is then selected by you to go to the "safe" area where student #2 repeats the story to her.

5. This process is continued until each student in class has the opportunity to hear the news story and tell it to another student.

6. The last student hearing the story returns to the room and tells the story to the entire class.

7. You then read the "real" article to the class. In most instances, the story told by the last news reporter will vary greatly from the original text.

8. The last step is to lead a class discussion on the importance of effective speaking and listening skills.

VARIATION: Any reading material, including academic content, may be used in this activity. It is important, however, that the material is no longer than one page in length and is complete in and of itself.

TITLE: **The Verbal Map**
GRADE LEVEL: Kindergarten - Adult
ROLES: None
TIME: 10 - 20 minutes
MATERIALS: None

ACTIVITY: Pair students.

1. One student, the speaker, gives verbal directions from the classroom to the office, restroom, playground or some other campus location.

2. The second student, the listener, may use clarifying techniques, then follows the directions exactly as given.

3. Upon returning, the listener reports whether or not he actually arrived at the desired location.

Follow this activity with a discussion about what went right and wrong, pointing out the necessity for clarity when speaking and clarifying when listening.

Variations: a. Allow the listener to take notes when directions are being given.
b. Listener may not use clarifying techniques. The activity then focuses primarily on clear message sending.

The following activity focuses on:
CLEAR SENDING, CAREFUL LISTENING, and FOLLOWING DIRECTIONS

TITLE: **The Unknown Design**
GRADE LEVEL: Kindergarten - Adult
ROLES: None
TIME: 10 - 15 minutes
MATERIALS: A geometric design drawn by the teacher; paper and pencils for students.

ACTIVITY: The design is drawn and placed outside the visual range of students, such as the back side of a portable chalkboard or behind a room divider.

1. One student is selected to be the "director." She verbally instructs the class to individually reproduce the given design on the paper provided to them.

2. The students, "artists," may not ask the "director" any questions.

3. After the "director" has completed giving directions, she shows the design to the "artists." They, in turn, compare their drawings with the original design.
4. The last step is for you to lead a discussion related to the experience asking such questions as: "What did the 'director' say that helped you reproduce the design?" "Why were some "artists" successful in reproducing the design and others not successful?"

VARIATION: Conduct activity in pairs, one person being the "director," the other, the "artist."

Figure 8: Geometric Design Samples

Activities to practice: EXPRESSING and NAMING FEELINGS

TITLE: **Find the Feeling**
GRADE LEVEL: Kindergarten - Adult
ROLES: None
TIME: 10 - 15 minutes
MATERIALS: Anything displaying pictures of people, e.g., magazines, newspapers.

ACTIVITY: In small groups of two or three, students are instructed to find all the pictures reflecting a specific feeling such as: happy; worried; confused; sad; excited, etc.

TITLE: **Identify the Feeling**
GRADE LEVEL: Kindergarten - Adult
ROLES: None
TIME: 5 - 10 minutes
MATERIALS: Pictures of People

ACTIVITY: In groups of two or three, students are given two pictures of people exhibiting different emotions/feelings and are asked to identify what they think the people are feeling.

IDEA: Use cartoon or "smiley" faces for primary age children.

TITLE: **Music is my Business**
GRADE LEVEL: Preschool - Adult
ROLES: None
TIME: 5 - 10 minutes
MATERIALS: Prerecorded tape or phonograph record with appropriate playing machine.

ACTIVITY:

1. Play music to class.

2. Discuss with students the "way the music makes me feel."

3. Play the same selection again; students may dance around classroom reflecting the way the music makes them feel.

TITLE: **Literature and Feelings**
GRADE LEVEL: Kindergarten - Adult
ROLES: None
TIME: 30 - 60 minutes
MATERIALS: *The Rotten Chicken*; Drawing Paper; Crayons

ACTIVITY: Read *The Rotten Chicken* aloud to class. A specific discussion question is then presented to students.

> Students are divided into dyads (two students per group) and instructed to do the following:
>
> 1. Decide how to depict the group's feeling response to the question.
>
> 2. Draw a group picture representing the feeling response to the question; all students must participate in the drawing.
>
> 3. If group members disagree about how to depict the feeling in the drawing, this should be reflected in the drawing.

Sample Questions to ask class:

> - *How do you act when you feel rotten?*
> - *How does it feel when you believe in yourself?*
> - *How did the willow tree feel after it helped the hen?*
> - *How did the young rooster's feelings change about himself and his mother?*

After the pictures are completed, they may be posted on the bulletin board or used as a kick-off for further discussion.

Note: *The Rotten Chicken* is a modern allegory and may be interpreted on many levels. While written in a format appropriate for children, the story line inherently includes themes of adult complexity, among which is psychological abuse.

This title is offered as an example of the use of literature in listening skills activities. Select titles that will be most appropriate for your class. Some criteria to consider when selecting stories for this activity:

> a. Story should be brief, taking no longer than 10 minutes to read.
> b. Story should contain a message that elicits a feeling response.
> c. It is extremely beneficial when the author has provided discussion questions - this will decrease preparation time.

The following activities may be used to:
GAIN AWARENESS OF NONVERBAL MESSAGES

TITLE: **Mirroring**
GRADE LEVELS: Kindergarten - Adult
ROLES: None
TIME: 6 - 8 minutes
MATERIALS: None

ACTIVITY: This is a fun activity that enhances nonverbal anticipation. It also dramatically demonstrates the difference between leaders and followers.

1. Students choose partners and stand facing each other.

2. One partner is designated the leader, the other is the "mirror."

3. The leader makes a series of movements, which are followed as closely as possible by the "mirror."

4. After two to three minutes, switch roles.

5. Discuss how students felt in each role.

Note: Initially, students will need to be directed to begin with slow movements to give the "mirrors" a fair chance to imitate with ease.

VARIATION: When first beginning this activity, it may be helpful for primary grades to have the teacher be the leader, with all students mirroring the teacher.

TITLE: **Music Interpretation**
GRADE LEVEL: 3 - Adult
ROLES: None
TIME: 15 - 30 minutes
MATERIALS: Prerecorded tape or phonograph record

ACTIVITY:

1. Students select groups of three or four.

2. Students are instructed to listen to the musical selection (suggested length: 2 - 3 min-

utes) and, as a group, develop a nonverbal interpretation of the music.

3. The group product is limited to two to three minutes and may be performed with the music as a direct interpretation or without the music as an indirect interpretation.

4. Groups perform for the class at the end of their planning time. Planning time can be 5 - 15 minutes during which time, it will be helpful to have the music playing softly in the background. The interpretation could take the form of a dance, pantomimed skit or any variation thereof.

TITLE: **Expression!**
GRADE LEVEL: 3 - Adult
ROLES: None
TIME: 20 - 40 minutes
MATERIALS: 4 x 6 index cards. A specific feeling/emotion is written on each card, such as happy, disgusted, worried, confused, excited, etc. At least 20 different feelings are needed.

ACTIVITY: Place cards face down on a desk or table.

1. Students take turns drawing a card (don't let anyone else see the card) and acting out the feeling that is written on their card. *It will be helpful to place a time limit of two or three minutes on each demonstration.*

2. The rest of the class guesses what feeling is being demonstrated.

3. At the end of each student's turn, he or she shows the class what feeling is written on the card.

4. The card is then placed at the bottom of the stack.

VARIATION: Conduct activity in small groups of four or five students each.

TITLE: **Giving Directions**
GRADE LEVEL: 3 - Adult
ROLES: None
TIME: 10 - 15 Minutes
MATERIALS: Direction cards showing cubes in different patterns; Patterned cubes or blocks

ACTIVITY: Students are grouped in dyads. Object is for one student to give the other nonverbal directions to assemble a pattern with the cubes or blocks.

1. First student has activity card (be sure partner does not see card), second student has

cubes/blocks.

2. Student #1 gives nonverbal directions to student #2.

3. Allow 3 - 5 minutes for the activity, then have student #2 look at direction card and compare to his design.

4. Reverse roles.

5. Discuss the degree of success students experienced; what contributed to this success; and how directions can be given nonverbally to allow others to follow them.

TITLE: Becoming Aware
GRADE LEVEL: Adults
ROLES: None
TIME: 5 - 10 minutes
MATERIALS: Chairs

This exercise will help adults remember what it's like to be a child.

ACTIVITY:

1. Place chairs in a semi-circle.

2. Half of the group members are directed to stand on a chairs.

3. The other half "pretend to be children" and travel from one "adult" to another saying either, "I've had a good day today." or "I've had a really bad day."

4. The "adults" are to respond to the statement before the "child" moves on to another "adult."

5. Continue for about three minutes, then switch roles.

6. Group discussion: as "children" what verbal and nonverbal messages were received and how did they feel during the exercise.

TITLE: **Tangrams**
GRADE LEVEL: 2 - Adult
ROLES: Facilitator as Monitor; Optional - Observer
TIME: 15 - 20 minutes
MATERIALS: Tangram packets for each group of students. Packets contain the pieces for five separate tangrams of three pieces each. See Figure 9 for sample tangrams.

ACTIVITY:

1. Establish groups of two to five students each, depending on grade level.

2. Appoint a Facilitator as Monitor for each group.

3. Distribute packet of materials to the Facilitator of each group.

4. Facilitator distributes the 15 pieces one at a time to group members in same manner as dealing out a deck of cards. Some group members may have more pieces than others.

5. The group then begins the task of solving the puzzle, i.e., putting the four squares together from the pieces.

Rules: a. No speaking or sounds of any sort.

b. Students communicate with each other by trading and moving tangram pieces until the four squares are made.

c. Students should be told that their tangram pieces will make four squares of identical size.

VARIATION: *For Grades 5 - Adult, the role of Observer may be included in this activity.* An observer would be appointed for each group. Behaviors to be observed could include: following directions; cooperation/sharing of pieces; nonverbal messages being used and/or what process the group used to complete the task

Figure 9: SAMPLE TANGRAMS

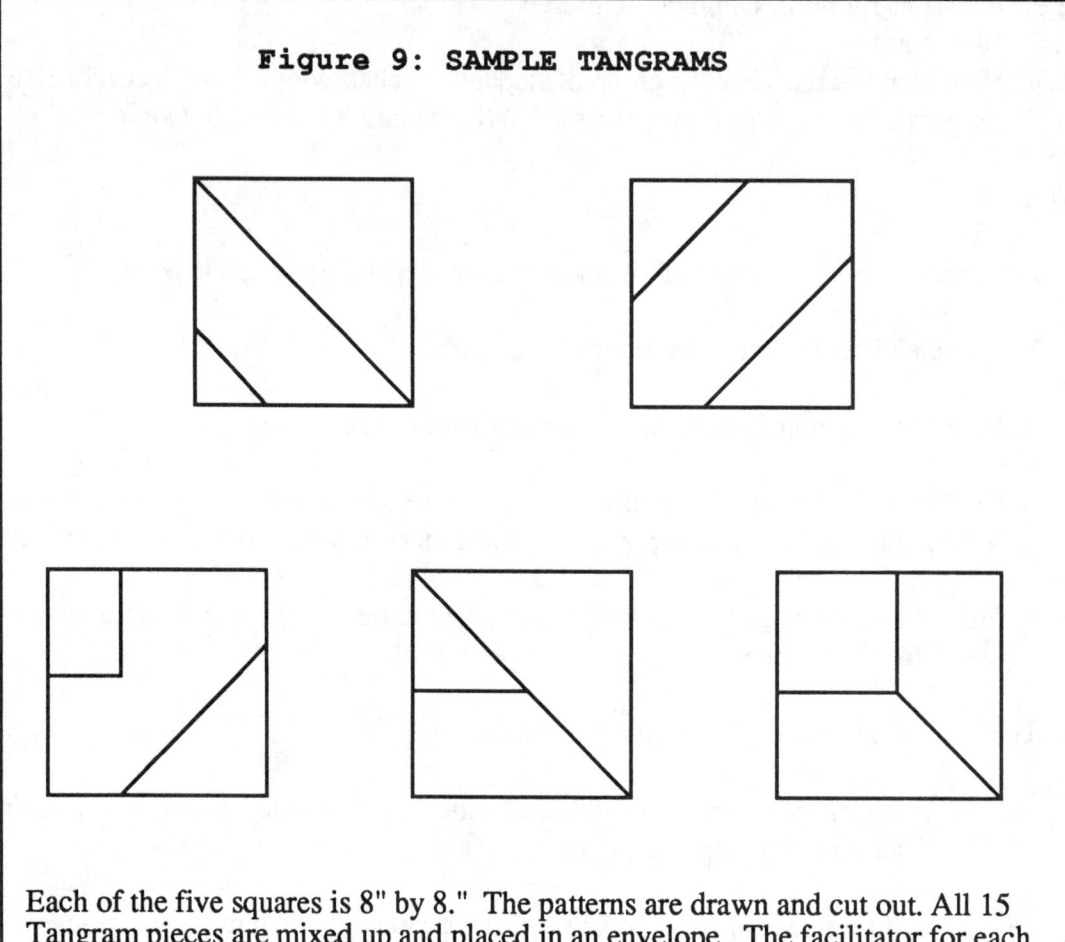

Each of the five squares is 8" by 8." The patterns are drawn and cut out. All 15 Tangram pieces are mixed up and placed in an envelope. The facilitator for each group opens the envelope (packet) and distributes the 15 pieces, one at a time, to group members.

You will need a set of five tangrams for each group.

Activities to practice PERCEPTION-CHECKING

TITLE: **Becoming Aware of Your Nonverbal Messages**
GRADE LEVEL: 6 - Adult
ROLES: None
TIME: 10 - 15 minutes
MATERIALS: None

ACTIVITY:

1. In pairs, students tell each other how they "know" the other one is happy, sad, excited, embarrassed, angry or whatever feelings you specify.

2. The receiver/listener affirms or denies that is what she is actually feeling when she demonstrates that nonverbal action.

3. When both students have had the opportunity to share their perceptions with feedback, have a class discussion about how easy it is to misinterpret another person's nonverbal messages, and the importance of checking out our perceptions.

Activities to practice CONGRUENCE: SPEAKING

TITLE: **On Becoming a Poet**
GRADE LEVEL: 2 - Adult
ROLES: None
TIME: 15 - 25 minutes
MATERIALS: One piece of paper and pencil for each student.

ACTIVITY: Pair students.

1. Each pair decides who will be "A" and who will be "B."

2. Without looking at each other's paper, the "A" students write their greatest wish or fantasy; while the "B" students write the most perfect place, activity, or circumstance they can think of.

3. Pairs read their "poem" aloud to the class, hearing it for the first time themselves: "A"s read their part first, followed immediately by "B."

Sample Poem: "A" - "I would like to be floating on clouds in the sky."
"B" - "Eating chocolate ice cream."

TITLE: **On Becoming an Actor**
GRADE LEVEL: 2 - Adult
ROLES: None
TIME: 15 - 20 minutes
MATERIALS: Charted poem or tongue twister at an appropriate reading level for your students; 15 - 3 x 5 index cards with one emotion or feeling written on each one, e.g., happy, sad, angry, excited, dull, brave, surprised, etc.

ACTIVITY: The poem or tongue twister written on a chart pad or chalkboard must be placed within easy view for all students. <u>Sample tongue twister:</u>
Sister Susie sits by the Sea Shore Sewing Skirts (or sifting sand).

1. The deck of emotion/feeling cards is placed on a table or desk.

2. Students take turns going to the front of the room, drawing a card (no one else should see the card),

3. Student demonstrates the emotion or feeling while reading the poem or tongue twister. Demonstration of the feeling can be done with intonation, volume, facial expression, and body language.

4. Other students attempt to identify the emotion/feeling being demonstrated.

VARIATION: Students may be divided into smaller groups of 3 - 6; each group is given a stack of index cards with a feeling written on each one.

Activities to practice CONGRUENCE: LISTENING

TITLE: **How to be a Good Listener**
GRADE LEVEL: Kindergarten - Adult
ROLES: Speaker and Listener
TIME: 20 - 30 minutes
MATERIALS: None

ACTIVITY: This activity has four distinct parts. Begin by grouping students into triads. Each triad decides who will be "A," "B" and "C."

Part 1: *Experiencing "Plops"* - a "plop" happens when someone says something and the listener(s) do not acknowledge the comment.

  a.) "B's" and "C's" leave the room or congregate at the far end of the room. They will be the "listeners" and are instructed to pay no attention to the speaker. Instead, they are to look around the room, doodle, and/or pick up and scan through a book. It's important that the "A's" do not hear these instruction.

  b.) Instruct "A's" to discuss their favorite activity, what they did over the weekend, or any other topic appropriate to the age group.

  c.) Reestablish the triads and direct them to begin the activity. You can only allow one or two minutes for the "A's" to try to get their message across.

Part 2: *Experiencing Disinterest* — Change roles. "B's" become the speakers.

  a.) "A's" and "C's" are instructed to demonstrate lack of interest by checking their watch or clock, yawning, looking at speaker, then looking away.

  b.) Instruct "B's" to discuss a topic appropriate to their age level, anything will do such as: "how to be a friend."

Again, stop the activity after one to two minutes.

Part 3: *Experiencing Attentiveness* — Switch roles. "C's" become the speakers.

  a.) Instruct "A's" and "B's" to demonstrate effective listening behaviors.
  b.) Instruct "C's" to discuss what animal they like best and why, or any other topic appropriate to age level.

Part 4: *Class Discussion*
   a. Following the activities, ask how students felt in each situation.
   b. Discuss how important listening techniques are in any discussion or conversation.

SOURCES:

LITERATURE AND FEELINGS: Adapted from *The Rotten Chicken* by Letitia Solomen.

BECOMING AWARE: Mary Rose, Teacher, Ukiah, Calif.

ON BECOMING AN ACTOR and EXPRESSION!: Marvin Roupe, Teacher, Point Arena, Calif.

ON BECOMING A POET: Ann Marie Samson, Teacher and Poet, Willits, Calif.

VERBAL MAP; CONGRUENCE: LISTENING; CLARIFY BY ASKING QUESTIONS; CLARIFY BY PARAPHRASING; FIND THE FEELING; IDENTIFY THE FEELING; BECOMING AWARE OF NONVERBAL MESSAGES: Peggy

NEWS REPORTER: Adapted by Jacquie and Peggy from the "old" telephone gossip game. Original source unknown.

TANGRAMS; THE UNKNOWN DESIGN; MIRRORING; MUSIC IS MY BUSINESS: Original source unknown.

GIVING DIRECTIONS (NONVERBALLY): Jacquie and Peggy

Chapter 4

PROBLEM SOLVING
AND
CONFLICT MANAGEMENT

OVERVIEW: Conflict, while frequently viewed as a negative, is a natural event in any social environment. This chapter suggests using a problem solving process to manage conflict.

TOPICS INCLUDE:

1. How we approach conflict is a learned behavior.
2. How the teacher can approach conflict to enhance student learning.
3. One Problem Solving process.
4. Brainstorming.
5. Decision Making models.
6. Supplemental Information.
7. Sample activities.

Chapter 4: Problem Solving and Conflict Management

What are your first thoughts and feelings when you believe you're in a conflict situation? Many people think "trouble" and feel a certain degree of anxiety. And, teachers often think conflict in the classroom means a loss of classroom control. All in all, conflict is most often viewed as a "negative" -- something to be avoided.

It's easy to understand why so many people prefer to avoid conflict. Emotions usually run high which often causes people to behave in irrational ways — some individuals become verbally or physically aggressive while others withdraw from the situation altogether. Conflict certainly can be unpleasant and uncomfortable but conflict in itself is not the negative, it's how we approach and resolve the conflict that is positive or negative.

The situations or occurrences we interpret as "conflict" as well as how we approach these situations are, for the most part, learned behaviors. For example, in some families, a raised voice is interpreted as a conflict, while in other families, arguments or heated discussions are normal ways in which to communicate and/or ways to "clear the air." It's easy to see how family and cultural styles can confuse the issue of what we perceive as conflict — a perfectly normal, lively discussion to some people will seem like a verbally violent and threatening conflict to others.

What we perceive as conflict and our reactions in a conflict situation are learned attitudes and behaviors.

The manner in which we approach what we perceive as a conflict situation is also learned. In some families, the appropriate thing to do is to withdraw until everyone "cools off," then to sit down and discuss the issue. Other families exchange words without really resolving the disagreement, then simply forget about it; i.e., they behave as though nothing happened. Others sit and talk it out calmly, or relatively so, until a resolution is reached. And still others "fight it out" until the issue is resolved. And, these are only four of many approaches we and our students may be accustomed to.

The point is that "conflict" means different things to different people. For our purposes, we'll define conflict as *any situation that involves a strong difference of opinion, where the persons involved are emotionally*

Definition

involved, and where each individual or group is attempting to win while the other loses.

Whether on the school grounds, in the classroom as a whole, or in small cooperative groups, as a teacher you will be faced with conflict situations and you will have to deal with them. How you approach these situations will determine if they will be learning, growing experiences for your students or just another time when the "adult took over."

It's tempting to use direct intervention strategies at these times but consider what this approach tells students. As an example, let's say you have a particularly argumentative or nonparticipating student in your classroom and conflicts consistently erupt in her group during cooperative assignments. Moving that student to a different group might seem like a reasonable solution but switching a student from one group to another usually will *not* solve the problem. In fact, this action could be a disservice to all students inhibiting their learning.

Direct teacher intervention gives four very clear messages to students:

> *1. You believe student group members are not capable of solving problems and finding satisfactory solutions themselves.*
>
> *2. You know best and will solve all problems in the classroom.*
>
> *3. Students can depend on you to make certain that the group completes its assignment.*
>
> *4. Students don't have to be responsible for their own behavior or learning.*

We're not saying that direct intervention should never occur; there are crisis situations when you must intercede. We *are* saying that whenever possible, it will help students more if you act as a facilitator and guide students through problem solving strategies when they encounter problems in their cooperative groups or elsewhere.

Sidebar: The four messages direct intervention gives students.

You can turn this potential negative experience into one that is a positive force for learning and growth by using and teaching your students the following problem solving technique. As your students become more adept using this problem solving process, the frequency of conflicts will decrease — students will begin taking preventive actions, thus, disagreements will seldom become conflicts.

PROBLEM SOLVING

The techniques that follow are not used only, or even primarily, to resolve conflict. In fact, they might be better termed "Solution Finding" techniques. They are as valuable in academic lessons as they are in social situations. In other words, these techniques can be used when Cindy and Mike are quarreling about whose turn it is to be group Praiser or they can be used by a social studies group to plan ways of completing a major research project.

There are nine steps in this problem solving model. It is **not** necessary to include each step with each and every problem. However, we suggest you use each of the steps when first using this process. Once you and your students become fully acquainted with each of the steps, eliminate those that are not applicable to the problem at hand.

The Steps:

1. STATE THE PROBLEM - Write it down, just as you perceive it. Example: two students fighting.

    Nine Steps

2. IDENTIFY THE COMPONENTS OF THE PROBLEM - Before you can resolve a problem, you need to identify and analyze its component parts, such as: who and what is affected by the "problem," when does it occur; who's involved. This step provides greater clarity about the problem situation and often results in valuable clues for resolving it.

    For example, when two students are arguing have each write down how they perceive the problem and how it might be resolved.

    This step helps diffuse emotionality and starts to give you the information necessary for an effective solution.

3. **DETERMINE WHAT YOU WANT TO HAPPEN INSTEAD OF WHAT'S HAPPENING.** - Example: "Students settle disagreements through discussion rather than physical or verbal assault." Most of the time, your students will be able to identify behaviors that would be more effective in settling disputes. Once in a while, you may need to offer suggestions or help them generate a list of alternative actions.

4. **REDEFINE THE PROBLEM AND STATE IT AS A QUESTION.** - This step requires you to analyze the information gathered in the previous three steps. After you have identified and reviewed the components and how you want the situation to change, you will have a clearer idea of what the issues really are. At this time, you will probably find it helpful to redefine the problem and to state it as a question. Example.... How can Jack and Marie settle their disagreement without fighting? While two students involved in fisticuffs is a problem, the real issue may be that they lack the skills to resolve their differences in any other way.

5. **IDENTIFY THE CONSTRAINTS.** - Constraints are factors outside the problem itself that have an impact on the solution to the problem. Among the constraints to be considered are: time - by when must the problem be resolved? resources - what resources, e.g., money, trainers, materials, are available for resolving the problem? politics or social norms - what community or school rules. must be considered when determining a solution? For example....there is a school rule prohibiting fighting, therefore, students must resolve their differences without hitting each other.

6. **SPECIFY THE FINAL DECISION MAKER AND WHAT DECISION MAKING MODEL WILL BE USED.** - Will the decision be made by consensus? By democratic vote? By the teacher? By the principal? By the board? Example... students and teacher must arrive at a consensus decision on how to resolve these two students' differences. (Decision making models are discussed later in this chapter.)

7. **BRAINSTORM POSSIBLE SOLUTIONS.** Once the real problem has been defined, the constraints clearly identified, the final decision maker and decision making mode specified, possible solutions

are brainstormed. Everyone involved in the problem should be included in the brainstorming process. This is a time to share all ideas, without judgment. (How to conduct an effective brainstorming session is discussed at length later in this chapter.)

As an example, our fighting students might brainstorm this list:

* not play together
* sit in office during recess
* kick the other kid out of school
* learn a different way to settle disagreement

8. **EVALUATE THE POSSIBLE SOLUTIONS IN LIGHT OF THE CONSTRAINTS AND IN TERMS OF THEIR FEASIBILITY AND PROBABILITY FOR SUCCESS.** - Following the brainstorming session, compare each idea against the list of constraints. Using a matrix like the one shown is an easy and effective way to determine which ideas fall within the constraints.

The next step is to examine each idea that meets the constraints in terms of feasibility and probability for success. With our fighting students, "not playing with each other" may meet the constraints but it has a low probability of success because it doesn't change anything. Eventually, these two students will interact on the playground, in the hall, etc.

9. **SELECT AND IMPLEMENT A SOLUTION.** - Since it was previously determined that teacher and students must reach a consensus decision, it would be up to them to decide which of the possible solutions will be implemented.

Once the solution has been selected, it is critical to clearly outline who will do what, when it will be done, and when and how the solution will be evaluated to determine its degree of success.

This becomes the implementation plan and should be written and signed by everyone involved. For example, if our fighting students agreed they would prefer to learn different ways in which to handle their differences, the agreement might look like this:

AGREEMENT BETWEEN JACK AND MARIE

1. "Jack and Marie agree they will not hit, push or shove each other.

2. Jack and Marie agree to learn how to handle their differences by sitting down and talking about it with Ms. Johnson.

3. Ms. Johnson agrees to help Marie and Jack learn how to solve their differences by discussing exactly what each one thinks and feels until they reach a mutual understanding.

4. Jack, Marie and Ms. Johnson will meet again in one week on (month and date) to reevaluate this agreement.

Signed:_____ _____ _____

Date: _____

BRAINSTORMING

Brainstorming is a free-wheeling, but not chaotic, session in which individuals offer ideas. Brainstorming is one of the most powerful techniques to use when looking for solutions to problems, innovations, or any other time you want to generate a lot of ideas.

The rules for brainstorming are:

Brainstorming rules

1. Set and adhere to a specific amount of time, usually between 3 and 5 minutes;

2. Write all ideas on the chalkboard or on a large piece of paper taped to the wall. Every idea is written, no matter how "way out" it seems.

3. Absolutely no evaluation or judgment of ideas is permitted during the idea-generating period, not even smiles, smirks, nods, "good," "ugh," or any other form of approval or rejection.

4. Remember: the objective of brainstorming is quantity. You want to generate as many ideas as possible.

When the time is up and all ideas are listed, they are read aloud with any necessary clarification being given by the originator of the idea.

Clarify, as necessary

The second part of the brainstorming process is to evaluate the ideas. One effective evaluation tool is a graph/chart where the constraints are listed across the top and the ideas are written down the left side of the page. Make a checkmark (√) under each of the constraints that the idea meets. For example, if time is one of the constraints such as having two weeks to resolve an issue, then any idea that would result in a solution within two weeks would have a checkmark in the "time" column.

Use chart to evaluate ideas vs constraints.

The ideas with the greatest number of checkmarks become alternative solutions. Each alternative is then analyzed in terms of feasibility and probability of success.

DECISION MAKING MODELS

Teaching students different decision making models will give them flexibility when faced with a problem. Although there are numerous ways in which decisions are made, understanding the following four models will give your students a good foundation:

Four basic models

AUTOCRATIC: One person, unilaterally, makes the decision for all without taking input, ideas, or suggestions. This model is based on the premise that one person knows what is best for the group regardless of what group members think or feel. This is obviously the easiest and quickest way for anyone to make a decision. It is also the mode most students are accustomed to: teachers generally make most, if not

One person arbitrarily

The Nurturing Classroom

**Figure 10.1: Sample Brainstormed Ideas vs Constraints Chart
Part 1**

Brainstormed ideas; i.e. possible solutions	Constraints				Comments

EXAMPLE: *Comparing brainstormed ideas to constraints using chart.*

> **PROBLEM:** *What to do for year-end party?*
> **DECISION MAKING MODEL:** *Consensus*
> **DECISION MAKER:** *Entire class, including teacher*

The next step is to identify the **constraints(School rules, teacher judgement** and **cost** must all considered.)

1. For this example, we will assume that school transportation is not available, therefore, one constraint is: ***"The activity location must be within walking distance of the school."***

2. Based on familiarity with students and their families, the teacher has specified: ***"A maximum cost of $3.00 per student."***

These two constraints will be written on the chart.

Figure 10.2: Sample Brainstromed Ideas vs Constraints Chart

Part 2

Brainstormed ideas; i.e. possible solutions	Constraints		Comments
	Within walking distance	Maximum cost: $3.00 each	
1. Go to zoo			
2. Go to beach			
3. Have potluck in classroom and play games			
4. Have picnic at park			
5. Go to Mary's house for Bar-B-Que			
6. Have film festival in classroom; eat in cafeteria			
7. Go to MacDonald's			

The teacher has written the constraints on the chart.

Students were given four minutes to brainstorm ideas.

All ideas have been listed on the chart.

The next step is to determine which ideas fit within the constraints.

Figure 10.3: Sample Brainstormed Ideas vs Constraints Chart

Part 3

Brainstormed ideas; i.e. possible solutions	Constraints Within walking distance	Maximum Cost: $3.00 each	Comments
1. Go to zoo		√	Need bus & 4 chaperones
2. Go to beach		√	Need bus & 6 chaperones
3. Have potluck in classroom and play games	√	√	
4. Have picnic at park	√	√	Need 4 chaperones
5. Go to Mary's house for Bar-B-Que	√	√	Need to talk with Mary's parents
6. Have film festival in classroom; eat in cafeteria	√	√	Need to check on availability of films
7. Go to MacDonald's	?	?	May be too far to walk if hot; cost could be more

This comparison chart reveals *five possibilities* (alternatives # 3, 4, 5, 6, 7) three of which are dependent upon the availability of specific resources: <u>films</u>; <u>chaperones</u>; and <u>Mary's parents</u>. The teacher does not want to impose on Mary's parents so *alternative #5 is eliminated.*

The cost per student at McDonald's is questionable as is the distance (it's just over a mile and it is frequently very hot in June) so *alternative #7 is also eliminated..*

Films will probably be available; the teacher will have to inquire at the media center and since this class has never had a problem getting enough chaperones, there are now **three possibilities left: Alternatives # 3, 4 and 6.**

The next step is to have the class prioritize the three remaining alternatives by first discussing the advantages and disadvantages of each; then asking if there is an option someone "definitely does not want to do." If there is, eliminate it from the list.

Following these steps, the class will typically reach a final decision easily and quickly.

all, their decisions in the classroom and parents make most of them at home.

The result of this type of decision making, however, is that many individuals feel others are trying to control them and they have no voice in what is happening or what they are required to do. Feelings of resentment occur and some people may simply ignore the decision or try to sabotage it.

DEMOCRATIC: This model uses some type of voting, usually with a majority rule aspect. A potential draw-back of this model is that voting creates visible winners and losers.

Voting: Majority rules

"Losing" can be embarrassing to some individuals and they may attempt to prove the decision was the wrong one by doing or not doing things that will cause its failure.

PARTICIPATORY: Everyone involved has an opportunity to state their opinions and offer suggestions. The decision maker considers the input when making the decision.

Giving input

Too often, this is simply autocratic decision making wearing a false face. Be sure if you're the decision maker that you genuinely consider the opinions and suggestions of others.

CONSENSUS: In this model, all group members participate on an equal basis, thus no one really loses. Consensus does not mean that each and every individual thinks that the final decision is the best possible alternative. It does mean, however, that each person believes the decision has a chance for success and each will sincerely support it.

Everyone wins

Consensus has many advantages over the other models whenever time constraints permit its use. For one thing, people affected by the decision are much more likely to "buy-in" to the decision when they've been involved in the process. Consensus is a concept which permeates all levels of the Simple Cooperation model. It reflects the fundamental premise that each member of the group is respected and encouraged to

The Nurturing Classroom

participate in all activities.

Although consensus is clearly preferred, here are some examples of times when the other models are appropriate:

All models appropriate at different times.

- A teacher uses the *autocratic* model when establishing initial classroom standards as well as when designing lessons.

- The *democratic* model is useful when deciding between two equally appealing activities or when time is short and no one in the group is going to feel they will lose no matter what the decision.

- The *participatory* model is valuable in any classroom situation when the teacher must be the ultimate decision maker but where suggestions from the group would be helpful, e.g. selecting among possible destinations for a field trip.

Figure 11: Problem Solving Examples

Example #1 -- Issue: Two students fighting

STEPS

1. State Problem

    1. Two students fighting

2. Identify Components

    2. Seems to be sporadic, no particular time. Each believes "it's the other guy's fault." They seem to disagree about something, shout, then start shoving, pushing, and/or hitting.

3. State Preferred Solution

    3. Settle disputes without use of verbal or physical aggression.

4. Redefine problem; State as question

    4. How can students gain skills needed to settle disputes without fighting?

5. Constraints

    5. Time: Immediately

6. Decision Making Mode
   Decision Maker

    6. Consensus
       Teacher and two students

7. Brainstorm Possible Solutions

    7. Either the entire class could be involved in this process or just the two students.

8. Evaluate Ideas

    8. Compare the brainstormed ideas with the constraints.

9. Select & Implement

    9. Evaluation is easy for this: no fights means success. Even so, it would be a good idea to have a discussion with the students in two weeks and again a month later to get their opinions of how well the plan is working.

Example #2 -- Issue: Reading Scores

Steps

1. State Problem	1. Spring reading scores down.
2. Components of Problem	2. All grade levels? All classrooms? What materials are being used? What methods? Daily time spent on reading? What are perceptions of each teacher?
3. State Preferred Situation	3. All students reading at or above grade level.
4. Redefine problem; State as question	4. Analysis shows new reading program introduced but teachers did not receive any training for it.-- How can teachers gain training for new program?
5. Constraints	5. Time: By Sept. Money: $2500 available
6. Decision Making Mode Decision Maker	6. Consensus at school Ultimately, Superintendent
7. Brainstorm Possible Solutions	7. Send teachers to training sessions; bring in trainer; revert to program teachers already know; get new program; etc.
8. Evaluate Ideas vs Constraints	8. Use chart to compare each idea against each constraint, then look at probability of success.
9. Select & Implement	9. Decide and Write it down, include when and how to review progress.

SUMMARY

- *Conflict, in itself, is neither negative nor positive.*

- *Conflict situations can be used to teach students valuable skills.*

- *Use problem solving techniques to manage conflicts.*

- *Problem Solving is most effective when a sequential process is used.*

- *All steps in the Problem Solving process are not required for all situations.*

- *Each model of decision making is appropriate at specific times.*

- *Consensus decision making means that each member of the group agrees to support the decision.*

- *Consensus decision making creates a win-win setting for group members.*

SUPERTEACHING WORKBOOK: Chapter 4 - PROBLEM SOLVING

Self-Evaluation Quiz

1. List and explain the steps in problem solving:

2. Should you use all steps with all problems?

3. Explain each of the following decision making models:

   a. Autocratic -

   b. Participatory -

   c. Democratic -

   d. Consensus -

4. Which model do the authors prefer?

   Why?

5. How would you explain "Brainstorming" to your students?

SUPPLEMENTAL INFORMATION AND ACTIVITIES

BRAINSTORMING

At first glance, the concept of brainstorming seems simple: generate as many ideas as possible within a given amount of time and do not evaluate the ideas while you are brainstorming. In reality, implementing the most important rule, no evaluation, is very difficult to do. Why? Because it means that **you cannot say things like**, "*great idea!*" "*yea*" "*oh, that's good*" **or** give any nonverbal judgments such as nodding, grunting or other gutteral sounds.

People, in general, and teachers, in particular, like to reinforce or, at least, acknowledge another person's comments and contributions. It's very hard to *not* do this.

The second issue in brainstorming is the temptation to immediately begin discussing the pro's and cons of an idea or to make comments such as: *"We've tried that already"* or *"There's not enough money for that,"* etc.

One technique to use when first learning brainstorming is to have a nonparticipating member designated as a "flagger." The "flagger" sits or stands outside the group and literally throws a flag (a nerf ball, handkerchief or some other piece of material) into the group when members wander off into discussion or evaluation.

The last major difficulty with brainstorming is that people are still hesitant to offer ideas they consider "farfetched." In fact, some individuals are just shy about offering any idea, believing their ideas are not as good as some others. It takes time and lots of encouragement to eliminate these fears. It also takes time and practice to dust off some of the creative cobwebs. With persistance and the actualization of a safe and secure classroom, brainstorming sessions will become lively and enthusiastic.

ACTIVITIES TO PRACTICE BEFORE TEACHING PROBLEM SOLVING

Problem solving is one skill that must be well established in the teacher's mind before being taught to students.

Using a real issue at your school or in your classroom which requires a decision, follow the problem solving model and develop a possible solution. (A real issue will generate a higher level of interest.)

After practicing this process several times, you will be ready to teach problem solving techniques to your students.

SAMPLE ACTIVITIES

Activities to practice BRAINSTORMING

TITLE: **The Future**
GRADE LEVEL: 2 - Adult
ROLES: (Grades 4 - Adult, use Advance Facilitator and Recorder;
in primary grades, teacher acts as Facilitator)
MATERIALS: Chalkboard or Large Chart Paper and Marking Pens

ACTIVITY: The idea is to brainstorm what something will be like in the year 2000, or any year in the future.

The purpose of this activity is to simply gain experience brainstorming and to allow oneself to be creative.

Ideas:
- Transportation
- Games & Sports
- Television and Movies
- Homes
- Heating and Cooling Systems
- Anything you can think of!
- Schools
- Stores
- Work
- Government
- Computers

TITLE: **Creative Uses**
GRADE LEVEL: 3 - Adult
ROLES: Advanced Facilitator and Recorder
TIME: 10 - 15 minutes
MATERIALS: Large Chart Paper and Marking Pens, OR Use Chalkboard

ACTIVITY: Using almost anything found in a classroom, generate ideas about how it can be used aside from its general use.

Examples:
- Chalk board eraser
- Pencil eraser
- Chalk
- Pencils
- Ruler
- Paper Clips
- Computer Disk
- Stapler

After the brainstorming session, the facilitators share their respective groups' ideas with the rest of the class.

TITLE: **The Inkless Pen**
GRADE LEVEL: 4 - Adult
ROLES: Advanced Facilitator and Recorder
TIME: 10 - 15 minutes
MATERIALS: Felt tip water color marking pens and large chart paper hung on the wall OR use chalkboard

ACTIVITY: Groups of 3 - 6 students are formed, depending upon grade level. An **Advanced Facilitator** and **Recorder** are selected for each group .(*Note:* if using groups of 3, the Facilitator and Recorder will participate in the brainstorming. If using groups of 5 or 6, they will not participate.)

Tell the following story:

"A company has one million felt tip marking pens and they don't know what to do with them — they forgot to put the ink in them. They don't want to throw them away because they will lose thousands and thousands of dollars. We have to think of how we can use these no-ink pens."

Each group brainstorms as many ideas for using the pens as they can within four minutes. Teacher acts as time-keeper. Remember to give students a minute or two thinking time before the actual brainstorming begins.

At the end of the brainstorming session, each Facilitator shares the group's ideas with the class.

Note: Ideas generated from various groups have included such things as: baby's toy, sell as invisible ink pens, mobiles, new kind of toy boat or missile, take the felt out and use as tooth pick holders.

SOURCES

THE INKLESS PEN: Experienced by Peggy in Leadership Workshops.

CREATIVE USES and THE FUTURE: Peggy

Chapter 5

THE CLASSROOM AS A MEETING

Helping students develop responsibility and dependability

OVERVIEW: This chapter will introduce you to the use of group roles as a means of teaching students responsibility. The use of group roles also allows students to realize how important they and their activities are to the group's success.

TOPICS INCLUDE:
1. How a classroom is like a meeting.
2. Each of nine group roles is discussed.
3. How to teach each of the group roles.
4. Sample appreciation and observation forms are provided.
5. Supplemental information includes creating new roles and combining roles.
6. Implementation Activities are offered.

Chapter 5: The Classroom As A Meeting

A meeting occurs any time two or more people come together or assemble for a specific purpose. Since the classroom has a single broad purpose - learning - it can, and should, be considered a meeting.

Definition

This is also true when your class is divided into cooperative groups; students in each group can be considered to be in a meeting. Their goal is to complete whatever assignment you have given them.

Obviously, there are differences in both the content and the structure of different types of meetings **but** each meeting has a purpose (a goal) and an agenda. The purpose in your classroom is to learn and the agenda is your lesson plan. The same is true for the small cooperative groups. The purpose is to learn and the agenda is to plan how to approach and then, to successfully complete the assignment.

Meetings of any kind will be more effective and successful when they operate within a structure designed to accomplish the goal while assuring each member an equal chance to participate and succeed. The use of group roles is one such structure.

Group roles increase rate of success.

The group roles most often used in a Simple Cooperation classroom are reflected in Figure 12. Each is important for the successful functioning of the group while teaching valuable skills to each student.

Teaching and using group roles will encourage shy students, students with a low self-image, and low performing students to participate. Roles will also build their self-confidence which will be reflected in greater academic achievement. At the same time, group roles will encourage verbose students to share some of the "limelight" with quieter students.

Roles help the shy as well as the gregarious student.

Group roles also help students learn to be responsible for their own

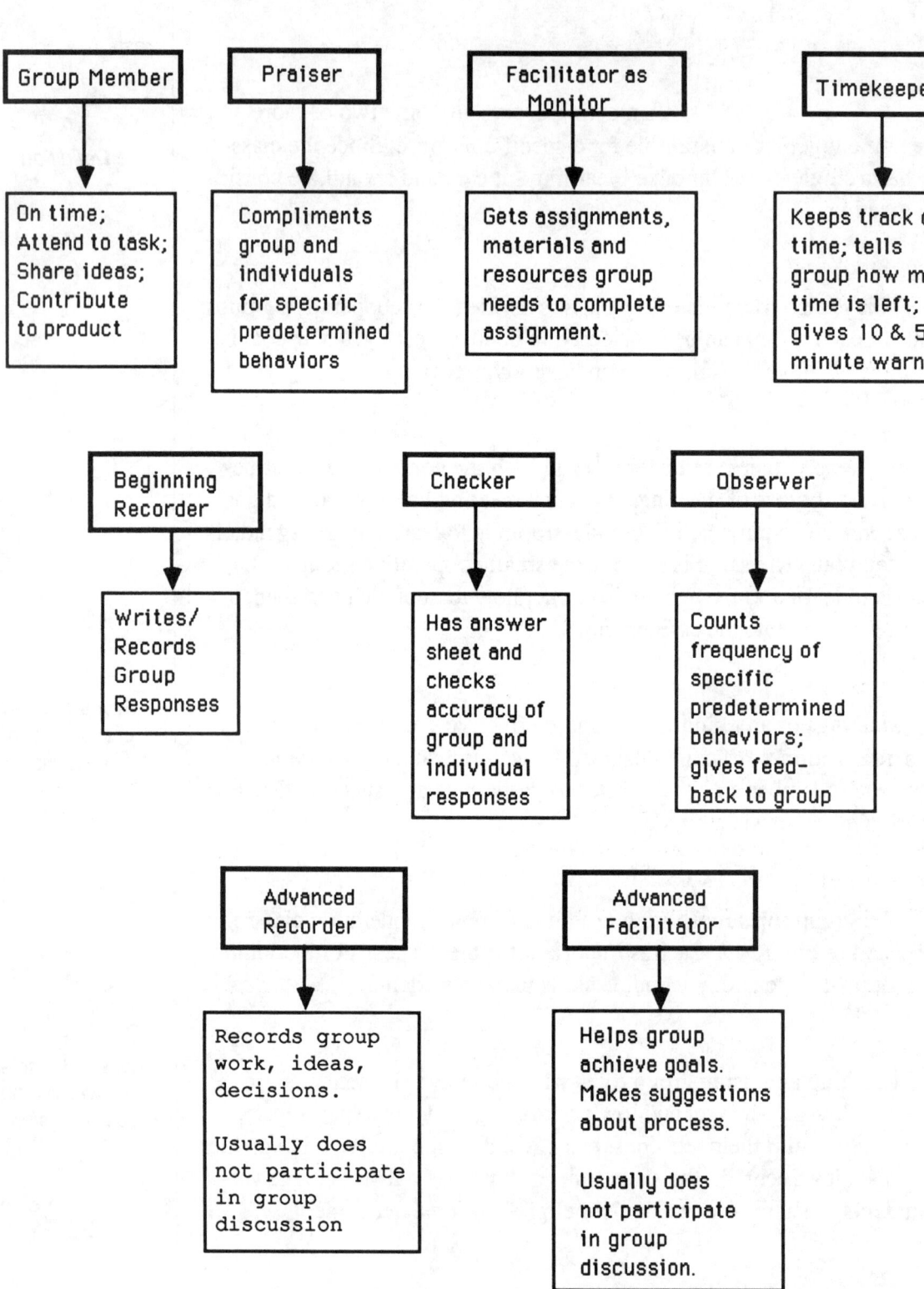

Figure 12. Cooperative Group Roles

actions. Students become aware of how their actions affect the group's productivity and that each student is an important part of the group. This awareness, in turn, leads to greater levels of dependability.

Group roles help students develop responsibility and dependability

Group roles do not occur spontaneously. Each must be introduced, explained to the class, modeled and practiced. Introduce one role at a time and give students sufficient time to practice and master each role before moving on to the next one. Be sure to rotate the roles within groups; each student needs the opportunity to develop the skills inherent in each role. Each student also needs to know he or she is important to the group.

Rotate the roles to give each student the opportunity to learn the skills

Two roles, facilitator and recorder, are taught first at a simple level and are reintroduced later at a more advanced level.

A suggested sequence for teaching the discussed roles is provided in Figure 13. This should be used as a guide and modified to fit the skills and abilities of your students.

As you implement cooperative groups in your classroom, you and your students will no doubt create additional roles to fit specific assignments. To assure your students' success, your new roles, whatever they may be, need to be taught, modeled and practiced.

All activities and lessons do not require the use of all roles. The specific group roles selected for any activity or lesson are dependent upon the lesson content and objectives. For example, the role of recorder would not be used when there is nothing to be written. Except when performing the responsibilities of advanced facilitator, advanced recorder, and observer, each individual involved in a group activity is always a "Group Member."

All roles are not needed for all lessons

THE GROUP MEMBER

Students, and even some teachers, may assume that they already know what a group member's role is — it's someone who attends a meeting, period. This is emphatically **not** true. Each member in any group has very definite responsibilities.

The most important role

The first thing to tell your students is that each member of the

Figure 13: GROUP ROLES CONTINUUM

```
SUGGESTED GROUP ROLES SEQUENCE

  1. Group Member
  2. Praiser
  3. Facilitator as Monitor
  4. Recorder: Single Assignment
  5. Time Keeper
  6. Checker
  7. Observer
  8. Advanced Recorder
  9. Advanced Facilitator
```

group is equally important and valuable. Unless each and every member does his part, the group will not successfully accomplish its task.

Group Member responsibilities

You will need to discuss the responsibilities of the Group Member's role as outlined below and why each is important:

- *Arrive at the meeting (classroom or area in the classroom) punctually.* Tardiness breaks the flow of work already started.

- *Actively participate; contribute ideas; give feedback.* It isn't fair to anyone, including oneself, if a group member doesn't contribute ideas and suggestions for the group task and product.

- *Attend to the task and refrain from distracting the group with off-task behavior.* Time is wasted and quality lowered unless every member gives undivided attention to the task at hand.

- *Help the group complete its assignment..* Members are collectively and individually responsible for the completion of the assignment. Also, group members' grades, bonus points or rewards are dependent upon everyone working together towards a common goal.

- *Follow through on assignments or agreements.* This is the same as keeping one's word. The group depends on each member doing what has been agreed upon. It hurts everyone (and the group grade or reward) when one person does not fulfill the agreement.

- *Listen to other members of the group.* Every member is important and has ideas to contribute. Group members must learn to respect others by really listening to each person.

- *Take turns speaking.* No one person should monopolize the discussion. Each individual must be given the opportunity to voice thoughts, ideas and reactions.

- *Encourage other members of the group.* Members should ask for each other's opinions and ideas, and compliment each other for good suggestions, for a job well done, or for active participation.

THE FACILITATOR AS MONITOR

The responsibilities of this role are the same as the traditional role of "monitor:"

- *Get and distribute* worksheets and/or written assignments to group members.

- *Quietly and quickly, get other materials necessary for the completion of the assignment or project.* These would include resource materials located somewhere in the classroom such as the dictionary, thesaurus, or other reference works.

- *Collect group work and turn in to the teacher.*

Using the term "Facilitator" will familiarize students with the terminology, concepts and responsibilities that will come with the more ad-

Like the traditional "monitor" role

vanced facilitative role.

THE BEGINNING RECORDER

"Recorder" role has two levels.

The role of Recorder also has two levels: beginning and advanced. The beginning role is used when the group is to produce a single response form to submit to the teacher.

RESPONSIBILITIES:

•*Keep a record* of the group's discussion and ideas as they relate to an assignment and

•*Write the group's responses* for a test or assignment.

Might also act as group spokesperson

During specific types of assignments the Recorder may also act as spokesperson for the group.

When the group is to submit a single response sheet to you, each student may be given individual worksheets; this is especially true for math and science practice. Students may work through the math, science, or other questions together or alone.

If they approach the task individually, they should share their answers and how they arrived at each answer. If working through the questions together, they should discuss each item separately and determine the correct response before going on to the next question.

Each student must sign the pages that are turned into the teacher

The Recorder uses a clean worksheet to write the group's responses. Each student is required to sign the page(s) that are to be submitted to you. Their signatures indicate their agreement with the recorded answers.

The Recorder role helps students practice effective listening skills as well as reinforcing the ability to take and write notes.

THE PRAISER

The praiser's job is to give compliments and praise to members of the group or to the whole group for specific preselected behaviors such as: staying on task; completing assignments; returning quietly after a break; etc.

Students typically don't know how to give and receive compliments or praise, yet this social skill is extremely important. (Consider your feelings about the supervisor who knows how to praise as opposed to the one who doesn't, who never seems to notice a good idea, extra effort, or a job well done.) *Giving and receiving praise gracefully and sincerely is a special skill.*

A very special skill

Because most students are so unfamiliar with praising, it's important to have an initial discussion about these skills. At elementary levels, you might begin by asking the class to define "praise" or "compliments." Ask students how they feel when giving a compliment or receiving one. Then ask for examples of praise and compliments and how the receiver might respond.

How to teach "praising"

Elementary students

With older students, you might begin this discussion by asking how people usually react when praised or complimented: by blushing or brushing the compliment aside? Brushing the compliment aside is a put-down because it rejects or contradicts the praiser's comment. Think about the last time you complimented someone on an article of clothing and she said something to the effect of "What, this old thing? It's been hanging in the closet for years." How did you feel? This type response (which is rather common) might even leave you feeling a little embarrassed. The response, in effect, invalidated your opinion.

Older students

The next step is to ask for volunteers to describe how they feel when they're complimented or praised: Embarrassed? On the spot? Singled out? Uncomfortable? Good? Grateful someone noticed their efforts?

The Nurturing Classroom

What to say when given a compliment

Then ask for suggestions about how to receive compliments and praise. If your students don't seem to know how to respond, explain that a simple "Thank you" is fine, including the praiser's name is even better: "Thank you, David." Longer responses are good, too, as long as they don't include a denial or put-down: "Thank you, Evelyn. I'm glad you like it."

Why we might feel embarrassed when someone compliments us

It might be helpful to have a brief discussion about the reasons some of us are embarrassed or uncomfortable when praised. These could include: being taught that nobody is better than anyone else; that humility is virtuous; that it isn't nice to be the center of attention; that we shouldn't get "swelled heads;" that a job well done is reward enough; and so on.

Role-playing and modeling are especially effective when teaching praising. Example..."Mellissa, I really liked the way you came into the room and got right to work today." "Jenna, I really appreciated your help with the door this morning." Whatever examples you use, be sure they are specific and sincere.

Next, students can practice giving and receiving praise and compliments in pairs.

Superficial praising at first

You might be surprised to find how difficult it is for students to learn how to give and receive praise gracefully. At first, they may be able to praise only at a superficial level: "I like your hair/I like your shoes/Your shirt is pretty." And, students may go overboard during the first few days. Most often, praising sounds really phony during the beginning stages of learning but eventually, students will become more sincere and perceptive and praising will become a normal part of their communication and interaction process.

Help students learn to praise by giving them cues in the beginning

One activity that helps students is to have the class brainstorm some praising statements and write them on the board. Those that come up frequently include: *"Good Job;" "Good Idea;" "You're really listening to others."* It also helps if you, the teacher, assign praising as a general social skill for students to use and practice in their groups while you monitor. At the end of the session, report to the class how much praising you heard.

As soon as your students seem to have a good grasp of what praising is, you can appoint a Praiser for a specific part of the class day, perhaps for the "next 15 minutes." Select one behavior for the student to praise, such as being on task or listening to other group members. If you assign this role during whole class activities you will be able to monitor and support praising behavior. Later, after several students have had the opportunity to practice during entire class activities, you can assign the role of Praiser in each cooperative group.

It's important to tell students what behaviors the assigned Praisers will be watching for during the activity. This will heighten students' awareness and place the target behavior at the forefront of everyone's attention. Throughout the time period, the Praiser should watch for students who deserve praise and give it to them quietly and simply. The Praiser might simply say: *"Good job of staying on task."* or *"You're really paying attention. That's great."* The student would accept the compliment/praise just as simply, perhaps with a *"thank you."*

Announce what behaviors will be praised

The role of praiser helps students learn to focus on the positive rather than criticizing or finding fault with others.

Students learn to focus on the positive

The Praiser remains an active member of the group and participates fully in task completion.

The list of behaviors on the next page is just a sample of what you might praise. The important thing to remember is to start with just one behavior, one that has been taught and practiced.

Sample List of Behaviors For Praising
(remember, begin with just one)

- arriving at work area promptly
- being on-task
- asking questions
- perception checking
- sharing ideas
- initiating discussion
- providing additional resources for group to complete task
- helping others
- listening to other group members
- taking turns speaking
- encouraging others

This is only a sample list

Praise can also be written; personal notes to each other or from you as well as more formal notes placed on the section bulletin board become very special for all ages (including adults).

Figure 14 provides samples of written praise forms.

Figure 14

Sample Written Praise, Compliment, Appreciation Forms

```
IDEA: Copy
these on 3" x
5" cards
```

An Apprecia-Gram

_____

Thank you for _____

_____

from _____

I like _____

Because _____

_____

signed _____

Chapter 5: The Classroom As A Meeting

```
I appreciate  _____

Because  _____
         _____


signed   _____
```

Recipient's name on first line, then be specific

TIME-KEEPER

The role of Time-Keeper is a simple but important role in the group. The Time-Keeper helps the group pace itself by keeping track of how much time has been used for a task and how much time is left to complete the task.

Teaching this role is simply a matter of explaining and modeling the responsibilities:

Responsibilities

- *To tell the group periodically how much of the allotted time has been spent on the task or assignment and how much time is left.* For example....if an hour has been allocated to writing a paper describing a recent news event, at the end of 30 minutes, the Time-Keeper would say something like: "We have used 30 minutes and we have 30 minutes left."

- *To give 15, 10 or five minute warnings before the expiration of the time, as appropriate.* The warning times depend upon the amount of time allocated. When an hour is provided, it's helpful for the group to know when half the time is used,

The Nurturing Classroom

then to have 15 and five minute warnings. If a half-hour is allocated, fifteen and five minute warnings are helpful and when only 15 minutes are provided, five and two minute warnings are appropriate.

• *To advise the group when time is up.*

Primary-age students can also act as Time-Keeper

The Time-Keeper role can be used with students who cannot yet tell time but who can recognize when a picture of the hands on a clock are in the same position as the hands on an actual clock. A stop watch or egg timer could also be used for young students.

CHECKER

The Checker has the answer key and tells group members whether their answers are right or wrong.

Immediate feedback enhances learning

Whether or not the Checker provides the correct answer when the group member is wrong is left to your own discretion. However, research reveals hearing or seeing the correct answer immediately following the response is a beneficial learning experience.

The role of Checker may be rotated around the group by passing the key to the next "Checker" after each question.

OBSERVER

Like the praiser, the role of Observer is to provide feedback, but of a very different kind:

Observer's feedback is quantitative only

- The Praiser's response is evaluative or judgemental while the *Observer's response is strictly quantitative*, with no evaluative or judgmental content;

Observer vs praiser

- The Praiser sits with the group and participates in the activity, while the *Observer usually sits just outside the group and does not participate in the group activity.*

Purpose

The Observer's role is *descriptive only*. Its purpose is to improve group interaction and increase the efficiency and effectiveness of the group by giving an objective report about how often a desired behavior is occurring.

The Observer is assigned a specific behavior to observe. He sits just outside the group in a position that allows him to see each member. Using a simple form, the Observer counts and records the frequency of the specified target behaviors. At the end of the time period, the Observer reports back to the group.

The Observer's report recognizes and reinforces behaviors that enhance group success without condemning the lack of those behaviors with judgements and evaluations.

What's a behavior?

A key to understanding the Observer role is knowing what a "behavior" is. *It is something that can be seen or heard; it is tangible and it can be counted, in other words, it is quantifiable.* A behavior is not an attitude, value, feeling, judgment or evaluation. "John is polite" is **not** a behavior, it is a judgment. It doesn't tell anything about John, it only tells how the speaker feels about him. "John raised his hand before speaking." is a behavior. It can be counted and it gives solid information.

How to teach behavior vs feeling, judgments and attitudes

To teach this difference, write two columns on the chalkboard. In one column, generate a list of behaviors from your students. In the other column, generate a list of feelings, values and judgments that might be confused with behaviors.

In the "behavior" column you might have words like: interrupt; make noise; come late to class; praise; offer ideas; ask questions; raise hand.

In the "feelings" column, you might have words like: rude; impolite; distracting; nice; mean; neat; pretty; nerd; argumentative; courteous.

If a student offers a judgment word for the behavior list, simply ask if it can be counted. If the student says "yes" ask for clarification — how

Can it be counted?

would others know what this "behavior" looks like? After one or two clarifying questions, the student will usually realize the word belongs in the "feeling" column. It's always important to gently lead students to learning the difference; under no circumstances should students be embarrassed or made to feel or look "dumb" for making a mistake.

You will have the opportunity to bring up another critical point during this activity: **the feelings associated with behaviors are subjective.** Behaviors perceived as "rude" to one person may not seem so to others. Remember, for example, the question of eye contact between children and adults: polite and expected in one culture; impolite and disrespectful in another.

Teaching "How to Observe"

The next step is to give instructions on how to observe. An Observation form is used which lists behavior(s) to be observed and group members' names in such a way as to create a grid. Figures 15.1 and 15.2 are examples of Observation forms. Let's use "Praising" as an example of a target behavior. You've taught the concept of praising, students have practiced it and you're confident they understand how to give and receive praise. Now the group is ready to be observed on this behavior.

Model

Initially, you may want to act as Observer yourself to model this role for your students. First, inform the group that you will be observing "praising" behavior during the next cooperative activity. Circulate among groups and record praising behavior for each student. At the end of the activity, total the number of praises each student gave and report that number back to the students without editorializing: *"Michael praised three times; Suzanne praised four times; David praised two times."* and so on. If a student hasn't praised at all, do not say his name.

Beware of subtle nonverbal cues

It's important that the report be given with neither emotion nor editorializing comments - this includes such subtle cues as: *"Suzanne praised four times, David only praised two times."* The interjection of the word "only" is a qualifier and denotes an evaluation. Tone of voice, raised eyebrows, smiles, frowns and other nonverbal cues also act as powerful evaluations and have no place in the Observer's role.

After you have modeled the Observer's role a few times, you can

Chapter 5: The Classroom As A Meeting

Figure 15. 1: Sample Observation Form (Primary)

```
                    Make a check mark (√) each time some-
                    one praises another person in the group


Jess  _____


Sylvia _____


Greg  _____


Maria _____


```

assign one student in each cooperative group to act as observer. Identify the behavior to be observed and provide the observers with a checklist similar to the one shown above. You can have students observe during the entire activity, but if it's a long one, the observers will become bored and restless. Five to ten minute observations are usually best to begin with. At the conclusion of the activity, Observers provide a frequency count to their groups.

Here are some other activities and points to remember about the Observer role:

- The Observer may record how many times the group collectively demonstrated the behavior without naming individuals or how many time individual members demonstrated the behavior.

133

Figure 15.2: Sample Observation Form

Behaviors to be observed:	Cavaliers	Co-op Kids	Genus		
Praising	✓✓✓	✓✓✓	✓✓✓✓✓		
Eye Contact with Listener	✓✓✓✓	✓✓✓✓	✓✓✓✓		
Eye Contact with Speaker	✓✓✓✓	✓✓✓	✓✓✓		
Clarifying by Asking Questions	✓✓	✓✓	✓		
Clarifying by Paraphrasing					
Summarizing What Has Been Said					
Claiming Own Thoughts, Feelings					
Encouraging Others					
Helping to Keep Group on Task					
Sharing Ideas					
Perception Checking, i.e. asking others how they feel about progress or process					
Initiating Discussion					
Identifying own Feelings					

Student or Group Names appear as column headings.

This is for demonstration purposes only. Begin by observing _one_ skill that you have taught and which students have practiced.

- Primary-age children can be taught to observe even if they can't read or write. Symbols or pictures can identify the behavior, e.g., a picture of children engrossed in reading or writing to represent "on-task" behavior or a picture of children listening quietly to someone else could represent "listening to others" or "only one person speaks at a time."

  Color codes can be used instead of names, with each student wearing a colored tag that matches a space on the observation form. The "observer" would make a mark next to the appropriate colored space.

- At any grade level, it's important to teach, practice and observe one behavior at a time and to be sure of mastery before adding another. At the secondary level, by the end of the school year, it may be possible to observe as many as five or more behaviors simultaneously, while primary students may be able to observe just one at a time.

- Have students observe only behaviors that have been taught, practiced and mastered and always inform the group of the behavior that is being observed.

- Observe only positive behaviors, for example, observe "taking turns speaking" rather than "did not interrupt others." Positive-based observations enhance the supportive atmosphere of the classroom and focus on what you are trying to have students learn.

Primary-age children (and nonreaders) can be Observers

Observe positive behaviors only

ADVANCED RECORDER FOR PROBLEM SOLVING AND BRAINSTORMING

Earlier, we introduced the Recorder role at a simple level. As your students become well-skilled in communication, and with older students, you can teach a more complex level of the Recorder role. This role's major responsibility is to capture an accurate record of the group's discussion and decisions.

The Nurturing Classroom

When to use this role

This role is used primarily in brainstorming and problem solving sessions but it can also be used any time it is important to have an accurate account of a group discussion.

The Recorder at this level usually does not participate in the group discussion. It will take all his concentration to perform his recording responsibilities.

When the Recorder makes a mistake

It's best if the Recorder uses large sheets of paper hung on the wall. This allows everyone to see what has been said and what decisions have already been made. Also, if the Recorder has made an error, the correction may be made immediately. If the Recorder **does** make a mistake, it is the group member's responsibility to request a correction. The Recorder should make the correction, without comment.

Record major points using speaker's words

The Recorder does not write every single word; rather, he writes the key words from a speaker's comments...verbatim. For example, if the group's task is to plan a study unit on local history and decides that one of their activities will be to take a walking tour of historical sites in the town or city, the Recorder would **not write** *"see old houses and buildings."* He **would write**: *"Walking tour of historical sites."* Paraphrasing and editorializing are not allowed. The importance of using the speaker's own words becomes clear during a long discussion when someone believes he or she said something different thirty minutes ago.

Helps students listen carefully and write clearly

The role of Advanced Recorder helps students learn to write neatly. Because the notes he takes are important to the group task, group members will tell the recorder if they can't read them. It also helps students learn to listen closely and selectively and to gain the ability to identify and pull out key words from long statements.

When group members talk too fast

If the group is talking too fast for the Recorder, he should ask them to slow down or wait a moment until the record can be brought up to date.

Review of the Advanced Recorder's responsibilities:

1. Using marking pens, write key words of group discussion on large pieces of paper which are in full view of group members. Writing should be about one inch high.

2. Write the speaker's words; don't paraphrase or interpret in any other way.

3. Abbreviate whenever possible.

4. Write as neatly as possible.

5. Listen carefully.

6. If Recorder cannot keep up with the group, ask group members to slow down or hold comments for a few moments so he can catch up.

7. Make corrections without argument (even if you believe you recorded accurately).

Responsibilities

Recording is a skill that must be modeled and practiced extensively before you can expect mastery. As students become more skilled in the role, and at secondary or adult levels, other techniques may be added:

When more experienced, Recorder can add variety to charts

- Different colors may be used for each major point of a discussion; yellow or orange can be used to highlight critical points or decisions.

- Abbreviations and symbols, such as +, =, >, <, and other geometric symbols can be used instead of words to identify or note certain concepts or actions. This helps the Recorder keep up in a fast-paced discussion.

ADVANCED FACILITATOR

This is the most difficult role to master.

Earlier we described the Facilitator as Monitor role, as a preparation for this more advanced level of facilitation. To perform this role successfully, students need to have mastered most of the effective communication skills.

The responsibilities of the Facilitator are to:

Responsibilities

1. Define the responsibilities of the group, making sure the group's purpose is clearly understood by all members.

2. Focus on the group PROCESS rather than the product. The Facilitator is concerned with HOW the group is working, not with the specific content of the discussion.

3. Encourage all members to participate, to contribute ideas, opinions, suggestions.

4. Make sure that all members have a chance to speak; that the discussion is not monopolized by one or two members.

5. Help the group reach its goal and objectives by suggesting processes to be used. For example: the Facilitator might suggest polling the group, breaking into smaller groups with subtasks, brainstorming, stopping general discussion to go around the circle sharing ideas individually, or whatever other process she thinks would help the group reach its goal.

6. Call time-out if the group seems to be stalled, perhaps suggesting a break and specifying a time at which to reconvene.

7. Help the group agree on a decision making model, if decisions are to be made, and to ensure that all members agree on the model to be used.

8. Keep the group within the time parameters of the task; help it pace itself along the various stages of the process in order to complete the task on time.

The Facilitator does not participate in the group discussion. Like the Recorder, it will take all her concentration to facilitate successfully and effectively.

Reviewing these responsibilities, it becomes clear that this role requires excellent communication skills as well as extensive practice. It takes intense training to become a skilled Facilitator; however, don't wait until you feel certain that your students will perform this role expertly before you introduce it. When your students have a good grasp of effective communication techniques and they are able to perform the other group roles successfully, introduce the role of Advanced Facilitator. You'll need to model it a few times, then give your students the opportunity to volunteer to try it. They may surprise you and do very well. Some people seem to be natural facilitators.

> *The Advanced Facilitator is like a "traffic cop" directing discussion, assuring everyone has a turn, that no gets "run over," and that the discussion stays on track*

When to introduce the role of Advanced Facilitator

Some people are natural facilitators

REMEMBER TO ROTATE ALL ROLES AMONG THE MEMBERS OF EACH GROUP. EACH AND EVERY STUDENT SHOULD HAVE THE OPPORTUNITY TO PRACTICE AND GAIN THESE SKILLS.

SUMMARY

- *The classroom as a whole, as well as smaller Simple Cooperation groups, can be viewed as meetings.*

- *Group Roles are a critical element in the Simple Cooperation Process.*

- *The most frequently used Group Roles are: Group Member, Praiser, Time-Keeper, Checker, Beginning Recorder, Facilitator as Monitor, Observer, Advanced Recorder, Advanced Facilitator. Other group roles may be needed for specific assignments.*

- *Except for the Observer, Advanced Recorder and Advanced Facilitator, students are always Group Members, no matter what other role they may be assigned.*

- *Group roles should be rotated among students to provide each an opportunity to gain skills.*

- *Group roles teach students to be responsible for their own actions.*

- *Group roles help students realize they are important members of the group and their actions contribute to the group's success.*

- *Group roles help students become dependable.*

- *The Group Roles Continuum should be used as a guide and modified, as appropriate for your students.*

Superteaching Workbook: Chapter 5 - THE CLASSROOM AS A MEETING

Self-Evaluation Quiz

1. In what way is the classroom like a meeting?

2. Why are group roles important in the classroom?

3. Briefly describe the responsibilities of each of the following group roles:

    - Group Member:

    - Facilitator as Monitor:

    - Beginning Recorder:

    - Praiser:

    - Time-Keeper:

    - Checker:

    - Observer:

    - Advanced Recorder:

    - Advanced Facilitator:

4. What are the major differences between the Praiser and Observer roles?

5. What is the purpose of "observation?"

6. What is a distinguishing characteristic of a behavior as opposed to a value judgment or feeling?

7. List some behaviors that might be praised or observed:

8. How will you begin teaching group roles to your students?

SUPPLEMENTAL INFORMATION

ADDITIONAL GROUP ROLES

The nine group roles discussed in the text are those that we believe you will use most often in your cooperative classroom. You may want to devise others for specific activities, such as:

The Reader

The Reader, as the name implies, reads the assigned material aloud to the group. Each group member may or may not have a copy of the material. Other group members might take notes, as appropriate while the material is being read. If other group members have a copy of the material, they may "follow along" as the assignment is read and/or take notes, as appropriate for the specific lesson.

The only caution is to be sure the student assigned as Reader is able to read the material fluently.

COMBINING ROLES

Participants in our trainings typically ask about combining roles. This is certainly an option but only with certain roles and only for specific lessons and activities. The roles that can be combined most easily and effectively, depending upon the content and assignment are:

Facilitator as Monitor and Time-Keeper;
Praiser and Time-Keeper;
Facilitator as Monitor and Reader.

> It's worth repeating here that **you will not use every role with every assignment or activity**. Group roles are assigned as appropriate for the lesson content or process.

The only constant role is that of Group Member and students should always be aware of their responsibilities. Each group's success depends upon each member fulfilling his responsibilities.

Do *not* appoint a "Group Leader" — the word "leader" immediately conveys a position of authority; all others are supposed to follow. This contradicts the foundation of cooperation which is that each and every student is equally responsible, important and valuable, and that all share as leaders.

One other point is that you will probably not introduce all of the roles in a year. Primary age students may never get beyond the Checker role.

The Advanced Facilitator and Recorder roles require exceptional communication skills. While it's possible for upper elementary to perform the Advanced roles, it isn't likely they will be able to do so unless they have experienced Cooperative groups for a couple of years and have gained mastery of the effective communication skills needed to perform these roles. This is also true of secondary students. How many roles you actually implement in your classroom in a year will depend upon the social skill levels of your students.

PRAISER vs OBSERVER

Of the roles described in the text, the two that sometimes cause some minor confusion are Praiser and Observer. They are similar in that each is concerned with watching for specific and identified behaviors; however, the Praiser is directly involved in the group activity, and makes a subjective judgement. The Observer, on the other hand, usually does not participate in the group activity, typically sits just outside the group and is involved with objective frequency counts of observed behaviors. The Observer is not allowed to make judgements or evaluations when reporting back to the group.

It is important to remember that behaviors and skills to be observed (or praised) must have been previously taught and mastered.

They must also be phrased in a positive manner:

Yes: Speaker gets attention of listener before sending a message.
No: Speaker doesn't make sure intended listener is listening before talking.

Yes: Group members take turns sharing their thoughts.
No: Group members interrupt each other to speak.

The reason for positive phrasing is because you want to monitor and encourage the occurrence of specific behaviors, not punish the nonoccurrence of them. This also sets a positive tone for the class.

It is imperative that you demonstrate the Observer role to show that voice inflection, insertion of the word "only" and other words denoting some type of comparison or judgement, raised eyebrows, etc. are **not** to be used in the observer's report.

The other issue is that only measurable and specific behaviors may be observed. If you can't count it, you can't observe it. Example.........you cannot count "polite" - it's not a behavior, it's a value judgement; waiting your turn to speak, however, is a behavior.

IMPLEMENTATION ACTIVITIES

1. *Begin by discussing the importance* of each student and the fact that the group's success is dependent upon each group member doing his or her share of the work, following through on agreements, and contributing ideas and opinions.

2. *Explain the responsibilities* of the Group Member. Writing the responsibilities on the chalkboard or on large chart paper on the wall will help remind students of what they are expected to do as a Group Member.

3. *A discussion with your students* about what each of the responsibilities means and how they would be demonstrated behaviorally will also help students internalize these expectations more quickly. (Note that some of the responsibilities may overlap your class standards.)

We've found that **elementary school teachers**, including primary grades, have great success introducing the roles of Group Member, then Praiser followed almost immediately by Facilitator as Monitor.

Upper elementary then introduce Beginning Recorder, Time-Keeper, and Checker.

Secondary teachers have reported better success introducing roles in this order: Group Member; Beginning Recorder for Single Assignment; Time-Keeper; Checker; Praiser and then Observer. We know a couple of secondary teachers who were able to teach and implement the Advanced roles towards the very end of the first year but this is rare.

Because the first group roles are simple, it's possible to introduce them quickly - you may have your students acting as Facilitator as Monitor and Beginning Recorder, within a week or two. Be sure, though, that each student has the opportunity to perform and master each role before introducing another role.

During the first several weeks, you will act as Time-Keeper and Observer. In fact, there will be times throughout the year when you will assume either or both of these roles. Some assignments are too intense for students to remember to keep time, they just get too involved in the content.

Before introducing the Observer role, students must have some degree of expertise in Feedback and Nonverbal Messages. Without a clear understanding and good ability in these skills, students will not be able to perform these roles successfully.

The Nurturing Classroom

> Remember: One role at a time; don't try to do too much too fast. Give yourself and your students an optimum chance for success.

IDEA: Use name tags, buttons, or badges to identify group roles. Make them up ahead of time and give the appropriate badges to students acting as Facilitator, Recorder, Praiser, etc. (This idea came from Elaine Skeete in Shasta County, California)

Bonus: Smiley-faces are something we all like to receive. Use for praise or anytime you want to give someone a "boost."

LESSON ANALYSIS

Lesson: _____ Date: _____

What went right? _____

_____

What went wrong? _____

_____

Analysis: _____

_____

_____

_____

Ideas to improve lesson: _____

_____

_____

_____

_____

Other notes: _____

_____

_____

_____

Chapter 6

GROUPING STUDENTS FOR SUCCESS

OVERVIEW: This chapter discusses the variables you need to consider when assigning students to cooperative groups. Careful planning will save time and increase the degree of success your students experience both academically and socially.

TOPICS INCLUDE:

1. Purpose of grouping.
2. Duration of groups.
3. Group size.
4. Academic Groups.
5. Methods of Teacher Group Selection
6. Methods of Random Group Selection
7. Supplemental Information
8. Implementation Activities

One of the first questions teachers ask is: *"How do I group students for success?"* While you have little or no choice in who will be assigned to your classroom for the year, you *do* have a choice in how you assign your students to cooperative groups. Following certain guidelines will assure successful grouping.

Grouping students must be done with conscious and careful thought. It's important that you choose a grouping pattern that is appropriate for your lesson objectives, that meets the needs of your students and that "fits" within the atmosphere of your classroom.

Group students carefully

Groups may be large or small, homogeneous or heterogeneous, short- or long-term, have academic and/or social skills objectives, be teacher or self-selected, and be formed by random or structured selection methods.

Regardless of the group's goal or method used to group students:

- *Know what you want to achieve* with your grouping as well as with your lesson. In other words, have an objective clearly in mind when you group students.

Things to remember

- *Tell your students what group selection method you are using,* just the process, not the rationale behind the process. For example: if you had student groups written on the chalkboard, you would show students the group to which they are assigned and where they should congregate. You would not tell them that you selected the groups according to ability level, behavior, personality factors, etc.

- If necessary, *model the grouping procedure.*

- *Be sure your students understand:* which group they are to join or by what criteria they will self-select their groups; where they will be working; and what they are to do as soon as they reach their assigned location. Check students' understanding before you begin forming groups.

- If your first few attempts at group selection aren't as successful as you would like, *don't despair!* Talk with your students about what worked and what didn't; then give it another try. Remember that you are all learning, teacher as well as students, and learning takes time and practice.

ABOUT GROUP ROLES

Use only roles that have been taught and only those needed for the lesson.

- Introduce just one new group role at a time, model it, and have students practice the role until they have mastered the responsibilities associated with that role.

- The number of group roles assigned in a group depends upon the number that have been taught and mastered and which roles are appropriate and necessary for the lesson.

DURATION OF GROUPS

The group stays together

A group may be together as briefly as three minutes for an opening or getting acquainted activity or as long as six weeks for a long-term academic assignment. Once a group is formed, however, it should stay together for the entire length of the project. (During the first week or two of implementing Simple Cooperation in your classroom, it's a good idea to limit the cooperative group assignments to one or two days. This will give you an opportunity to see how your students interact with each other; you'll learn their strengths and weaknesses. After you know how your students interact in small groups, you can give longer assignments with confidence.)

Students must get a clear message that they will be together until the task is completed. They will be working through their group development process, and this could well include conflict. If conflict does occur, resist the temptation to remove a student in order to resolve it. Remember, conflict should not be regarded as a negative condition. Students need to learn how to turn conflict into a problem solving situation and they can use their developing communication skills to resolve it themselves. If it seems that the conflict centers around one student and you remove him from the group, you will be telling your students you don't really expect them to be able to resolve their own problems.

When students learn how to resolve their own problems, they gain confidence and enhance their self-esteem.

GROUP SIZE

As a rule of thumb, *the less skilled the students are in group management and communication techniques, the smaller the group should be*. As these skills improve, group size can be increased. Larger groups require the members to have a greater degree of effective listening, speaking, problem solving and decision making skills. It takes a greater degree of sophistication, patience and skill to do well in larger groups; students need to work up to this gradually.

Rule of thumb

Recommended group size by grade level:

Grade Level	Group Size
Preschool	2
Kindergarten	2-3
Grade 1	2-3
Grades 2 & 3	2-4
Grades 4 & 5	2-5
Grades 6 - Adult	2-6

ESTABLISHING GROUP IDENTITY

Establishing group identity is an important element in conducting successful coopertive lessons. As the group establishes its own identity, each person in the group begins to feel as though they belong to the team and that their team is important. This can be accomplished in a number of ways:

* Have each team choose a team name. This must be done by

consensus so that each member has a genuine investment in the team.

* The team makes a group banner that best describes the team name and them members.

* Banners can be hung from the ceiling above the group's working area, folded in half and placed on desk, or hung on the bulletin board.

When referring to teams during lessons, using the team names enhances and solidifies team identity. Team names should be chosen for lessons lasting one week or longer.

ACADEMIC GROUPS

Academic groups are teacher-selected and are normally scheduled for one to six weeks. The academic group may have a single, specific objective such as practicing for a spelling test or completing a social studies report, or it may have a multi-objective assignment such as several members drawing a pictorial sequence of the War of 1812, while others are writing the captions. It may be made up of students with similar skills and aptitudes (homogeneous) or be a mix of skill levels (heterogeneous).

Homogeneous groups

Homogeneous groups may be assigned a single, specific objective which is appropriate for the group members' abilities. It is important to recognize here that there is really no such thing as homogeneity. No two students have exactly the same skill level; there are always differences. Each "homogeneous" group will be a combination of specific strengths and weaknesses. These differences become a definite asset to the group because sharing thinking processes will help group members individually as well as collectively.

"Homogeneous" grouping is most appropriate for such activities as study groups, completion of worksheets and, in fact, any other task you would normally assign to individual students.

Heterogeneous groups

Heterogeneous grouping is beneficial when the assignment includes two or more objectives within the lesson. For example...if the group is working on capitalization, two objectives might be: 1) capitalizing the first word in a sentence and 2) capitalizing proper nouns. Given ten sentences on a group worksheet, specific students are assigned to each of the objectives. Set a time limit for the lesson. Tell students they will work individually for a specified part of the time, then they will discuss each answer until they agree on a response for each sentence. If the role of Time-Keeper has been taught, one may be assigned; if not, you will act as Time-Keeper. Signal when the group should begin discussion and give ten and five minute warnings before the end of the allocated time.

Example of lesson objectives.

As we discussed in the first chapter, the heterogeneous group benefits students at all skill levels because it provides an opportunity to share thinking skills. As group members discuss how they arrived at their responses, each student gains new ideas and new ways to approach tasks.

Share thinking skills

METHODS OF TEACHER GROUP SELECTION

As we mentioned before, to assure successful group activities and to provide each student an opportunity to maximize her potential, academic group selection must be based on specific criteria. Group selection must also directly relate to your objectives.

A number of methods for grouping students are described in this section. These grouping processes add variety and fun to the school day.

Use different selection methods to add fun and variety

1. Name Tags

Name tags allow you to form either heterogeneous or homogeneous groups carefully, without calling unwanted attention to the reasons underlying your selection (academic levels, social skill development, etc.)

a. **Choose** an identifying number, letter, or name for each group and determine the work location for each group.

b. **Make** a sign to identify each group and place it at the appropriate workspace.

c. **Write** each student's name on a tag and lay the tags out in the groups you are forming. This will help you visualize the groups.

Just like a hostess working out a seating arrangement for a dinner party, you can shuffle the tags around until you have a grouping that seems that it will work best for your objectives.

d. When you've decided on the composition of each group, **write** that group's identifying symbol on the student members' name tags.

e. **Give** each student his name tag and tell the class that everyone should go to the workspace or table with the symbol (letter, name, etc.) that matches the one on his own name tag.

Idea for pre-school

For preschool and primary-age students, you might want to use color codes, pictures, or other symbols on the tags instead of names. You could also use paper hats made by you or your students.

2. Wall Charts

Write the names of students, by group, on a wall chart or chalkboard as in the sample, Figure 16, and point out the location in your room where each group should assemble. If time permits, you could have students choose a name for their group as their first task.

Figure 16: Sample Wall Chart

Group 1: Bright Idea
    Mellissa
    Jenna
    Joshua

Group 2: Willits' Wonders
    Suzanne
    Michael
    Jo

Group 3: Rancho Tops
    Cindy
    Michael
    Jamie

Group 4: Chino's Greats
    Cleo
    Clarence
    Tom

Group 5: Sunny Sides
    Marge
    Billie Jo
    Anthony

Group 6: Deltona Tigers
    Billy
    Kathy
    Robert

Wall Chart Sample, Continued

Group 7: Dolphins	Group 8: Surfers
Gregory	Ginny
Pat	Tommy
Jason	Dawn
Group 9: Lions	Group 10: Co-Ops
Heath	Kim
Jose	Roberto
Midge	Jan

3. Mystery Envelopes

You'll need an envelope for each student. You'll also need a selection of small objects.

    a. **Write** the name of each student on an envelope.

    b. As in the name tag method, **sort** the envelopes into groups.

    c. **Place** the same object or assortment of objects inside the envelopes of students belonging to the same group. For example, place a paper clip in the envelope of each student belonging to Group #1; a piece of chalk inside the envelope of each student belonging to Group #2; a piece of chalk and a paper clip inside the envelope of each student belonging to Group #3; etc.

    d. **Seal** the envelopes.

When you distribute the envelopes to your students:

    a. Tell them to <u>feel</u> the contents of their envelopes; they may not open the envelopes, they can only "feel" what's inside.

    b. Also tell them how many other students have envelopes with the same contents. If you've prepared for groups of three, for instance, you could say, "Two other students have envelopes exactly like yours. Your task is to find them. When all three of you are together, find a place in the room and sit down together."

c. Students should then open their envelopes to be sure they are really in the correct group.

4. Like-Sounds

a. Decide how many groups you will have and who will be in each group.

b. On 3 x 5 index cards, write the name of the same animal (examples.......horse, dog, cat, owl, sheep, cow) or the same title of a song (examples......"Twinkle, Twinkle Little Star;" "Baa, Baa Black Sheep;" "Happy Birthday to You") for students who are to be in the group.

c. Distribute the cards being sure that students you want grouped together receive the same animal or song title.

d. Students find their group members by walking around the room making the sound of the animal or humming the song. As one student finds another making the same sound, they become a pair and walk around together continuing making their animal sound or humming their song until they have found the rest of their group.

e. When all students have located their group members, direct them to a work location.

METHODS OF RANDOM GROUP SELECTION

Random selection of groups is most appropriate for nonacademic activities. Groups can also be randomly selected when ability levels are nonessential to the task.

Chapter 6: Grouping Students For Success

1. Mystery Envelopes

The process is the same as mystery envelopes described in the previous section with one difference — you do not write student names on the envelopes.

2. Counting Off

a. First, decide how many students you want in each group. Divide that number into your total population. The result is the "count off" number.

Example: You want to have groups of four students each and you have 28 students. Going around the class, you would count off from 1 - 7. (You could have the students count themselves or you could do the counting.)

You would then tell and show each number where to gather, e.g. all the 1's sit in the right back corner of the room, all the 2's by the pencil sharpener, etc. OR you can place numbered signs at selected workspaces in the room and tell students to gather at the number that matches theirs.

Since we aren't always lucky enough to have evenly divided groups, add the one, two, or three additional students to other groups; thus, you will have groups of four with one to three groups of five.

b. Another way to count off is to determine how many students you want in each group and simply count off that many students, i.e. count one, two, three, four - these four students are a group, and so on until all students are grouped.

3. Self Grouping by Category

Sometimes a bit of controlled chaos is a welcomed breather. This method is a good one for such times. It also gives students an element of choice in forming groups while insuring a good "mix-up."

This is just a sample list

Tell students to sort themselves into groups of four, or whatever size group you want to form. Each group must have at least one member who represents one of a list of categories; for example, each group must have someone:

1. wearing shoes with laces;
2. with brown hair;
3. wearing blue;
4. born out of the state.

It's okay to have a person who fits more than one criterion but all criteria must be represented in each group. If one person *does* fit more than one criterion, then there could be persons in the group who don't fit any of the categories.

Groups are then directed to their workplace.

4. Line Formation

This method is really a variation of the "count-off" method.

a. Students are instructed to form a line.

b. Then you simply count off to the group size you want. For example, for groups of three, beginning with the first student in line, you would say, "1, 2, 3, you're a group. I'd like you to sit at the table by the door." After these students are seated, continue the process until all students have been grouped and seated.

5. The Birthday Line

(This group selection method was developed by Dr. Stanley Schainker from San Francisco and is used with his permission.)

a. Have students arrange themselves according to the month and date of their birthdays. Begin by asking who was born in January and help the January group discover who has the earliest birth date.

Chapter 6: Grouping Students For Success

b. This student is first in line.

c. Direct her to stand in a specific spot in the room.

d. Then help students discover who has the last birthday in December and direct that student to stand at a spot that will be last in line.

e. Other students should then correctly arrange themselves in a line between the identified first and last students according to the month and date of their birthdays.

f. Once the line is formed, conduct a check by having each student, in turn, identify the month and date of their birthdays.

g. Count off to form groups.

6. Alphabet Line

Students are to arrange themselves in alphabetical order according to first name (or surname, if you prefer, or for diversity). Some groups may need visual cues. If this is true for your students, name tags can be used.

As in the Birthday Line, help students determine who will be first and last in line and tell these students where to stand.

Note: Other ideas for line arrangement include: height, shoe size, and distance between home and school.

Other ideas

7. The Color Spectrum

This is a good method to use when selecting groups for art projects.

Great for art projects

Begin by reviewing a color spectrum chart, if you have one. If not, you could write the names of colors on the chalkboard. Have students arrange themselves according to the color of socks, shirts, or some other article of clothing. (In schools where uniforms are worn, consider using colored name tags.)

8. Subject Area Selection

Best for projects in which you want a heterogeneous mix of students and where group size can vary somewhat, such as an art collage project in which each group will bring pictures related to specific subjects for inclusion in the collage.

In this example, you would designate areas in the room for each subject or element in the collage, and have students stand by the area in which they'd like to work.

It's very possible to have many students want to work with a specific subject area and no students wanting to work in another area. If this should happen, divide the large groups into smaller groups, and eliminate the subject area in which no one has an interest to work.

SUMMARY

- *Simple Cooperation groups must be formed with careful consideration to your lesson objective, subject area content, student ability level, and student personalities.*

- *Groups may be heterogeneous or homogeneous, teacher selected or student self-selected.*

- *Groups may be formed for academic and/or social skills objectives.*

- *For most activities and lessons, group size should not exceed six students.*

- *Groups may be selected in numerous ways, eleven examples were provided.*

SOURCES:

THE BIRTHDAY LINE: Dr. Stan Schainker, Associate Superintendent, San Francisco Unified School District.

THE COLOR SPECTRUM and SUBJECT AREA SELECTION: Jacquie

SOUNDS - HUMMING SONGS: Mary Rose, Ukiah High School

WALL CHARTS, COUNTING OFF, ALPHABET LINE, GROUPING BY CATEGORY, MYSTERY ENVELOPES, NAME TAGS, ANIMAL SOUNDS: These have been used by Peggy and Jacquie separately and together. We suspect that most have probably been used by many workshop leaders and teachers at various times. Obviously, someone had to be the first to use the methods but we don't know who.

Superteaching Workbook: Chapter 6 - SELECTING STUDENT GROUPS

Self-Evaluation Quiz

1. In general, how long should a group stay together?

2. What is the recommended group size for your grade level?

3. When are homogeneous groups appropriate?

4. When are heterogeneous groups most effective?

5. Identify at least three methods for:

   -teacher-selected grouping

   -randomly selected grouping

SUPPLEMENTAL INFORMATION

This chapter is straightforward; the only point to emphasize is that student grouping must be done with care. When you group students heterogeneously for an academic lesson, it is important to consider boy/girl ratio, proportionate minority grouping, ability level and personality.

You need to give a very clear message to your students that they will be together for the duration of the lesson or activity, whether that is for ten minutes, a day or six weeks. They must cooperate and help each other; **no one in the group is finished with the task until all group members know and understand the material and complete the assignment**.

If a problem or conflict occurs in a group and you intervene by either removing a student from the group or providing the solution, you have told your students: a) they can't solve their own problems; b) you don't believe they can solve their own problems even if they might think so; and c) only you have the *right* answers. Facilitation is the key. You need to help and guide, but not solve, the problem. (Of course, if students get into physical altercations or a shouting match, you will have to intervene directly.)

IMPLEMENTATION ACTIVITIES

Begin by grouping students randomly for short-term nonacademic activities. Any of the "counting-off" methods would be appropriate for this.

The next step is to select groups for a short-term, i.e., 20 - 30 minutes, academic activity. One idea is studying math facts or vocabulary words. Then extend the assignments to a two or three day time period.

Once students have demonstrated success with these short activities, select groups for an academic assignment that will last one week. This might be studying for Friday's spelling or vocabulary test, math worksheets, or any other assignment that will be completed in one week.

Gradually work up to assigning groups for long term projects, such as science, math, term papers, etc.

Chapter 7

MONITORING STUDENT PROGRESS

OVERVIEW: This chapter presents two methods of monitoring student progress in learning and applying effective social skills.

TOPICS INCLUDE:

1. Teacher Observation
2. Observation Forms
3. Wrap-Up
4. Supplemental Information
5. Sample Activities

Chapter 7: Monitoring Student Progress

Throughout your teaching career, you've had a lot of practice monitoring the academic progress of your students. You know if they're learning the content of the material you're teaching. But, if you're like many teachers, you may be asking yourself how you will know if your students are really learning the social skills you're teaching.

There are several ways to measure and monitor social skills acquisition. For example, if you want to measure your students' knowledge of the concepts involved in any of the social skills, you could administer a test just as you do in any academic area. Such a test might include questions like: *"What are two ways a listener can check her understanding of what the speaker has said?" "What are the responsibilities of a group member?" "When should a group use a recorder?"* etc.

Test knowledge of concepts.

While acquiring knowledge of social skills is important, **mastering** the application of social skills is really the key to successful living, therefore, the Simple Cooperation model provides two other methods that can be used to monitor and assess student ability to apply the social skills you have been teaching: *teacher observation* and *wrap-up activities.*

Two methods assess ability to apply social skills.

TEACHER OBSERVATION

Teacher observation provides a systematic method of monitoring student behavior relative to academic and social skill objectives. It's also an excellent vehicle for providing immediate feedback to your students.

We use a simple observation form, one that can be adjusted to meet different needs. A sample form is provided in Figure 17. We have found that this basic form adjusts easily to a variety of observation requirements. (The form can be duplicated and ready for use when needed.)

Begin by observing the whole class.

Observations may be conducted by targeting behaviors of individual

The Nurturing Classroom

Begin by observing the whole class

students, groups of students, or the class as a whole. While it is beneficial to vary the observation method, it helps students become accustomed to the process if you *first observe the class as a whole.* Tell students what behavior you will be observing. During the cooperative activity, using an observation form, make a checkmark each time you observe anyone in the class using this skill.

Observe only skills you've taught and students have practiced.

Following the lesson, total your checkmarks and tell the class the total number of times you observed this specific skill being used. Remember that you only observe a skill that you have taught and which your students have had time to practice.

You might consider doing this for a week and keeping a running tally on the board by day. At the end of the week you would total all five days for the week's grand total.

The second step would be to observe by group; following the cooperative lesson or activity, you report the number of times you observed group members, collectively, using the preidentified skill.

Finally, you would observe individuals within each group, reporting to the group the number of times you observed each individual using the preidentified social skill.

Example: Let's assume that "praising" is the social skill behavior to be observed. You could conduct three to five minute observations of each group; standing slightly outside the group, count the number of times members of the group praised during that time period.

How to report observations to students.

Examples of reporting your observations.......

1. If you conducted a *full class* observation you would say, "During this activity, I observed 32 praising behaviors and/or comments."

2. If you conducted a *group by group* observation, you might

Chapter 7: Monitoring Student Progress

Figure 17: Sample Teacher Observation Form

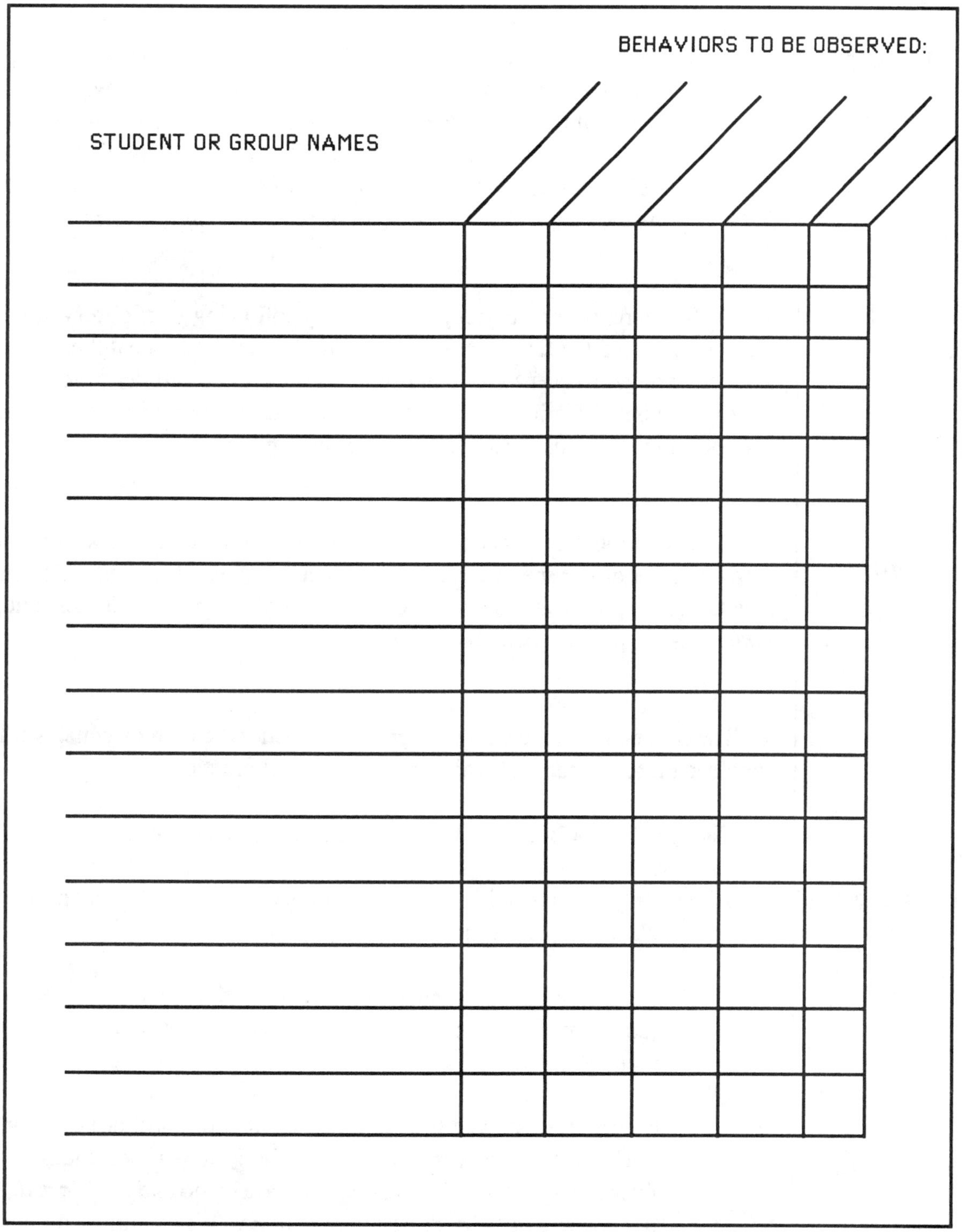

BEHAVIORS TO BE OBSERVED:

STUDENT OR GROUP NAMES

say, *"During this observation period, Group 1 praised 6 times; Group 2 praised 8 times; Group 3 praised 5 times; etc."*

Observing individuals within groups

3. When conducting individual group member observations, you can give your report to each group immediately following your observation or you can wait and return to each group at the end of the activity. Your report would sound something like this: *"During these last three minutes, I observed: Margie praised 4 times; Jan praised 2 times; Juan praised 6 times; etc."*

If you report to the group immediately following your observation: after you observe the first group, move on to the next and repeat the process. You may not get to every group during one cooperative activity or lesson. That's okay but it *is* important to observe all the groups periodically, even if your observations must be spread out over two or three cooperative lessons.

Purpose

The purpose of Teacher Observation is to help you and your students know whether or not specific skills have been mastered. The feedback you give the class, group, and individuals within each group will heighten student awareness of specific social behaviors.

The observation report gives everyone a good indication of which skills have been internalized and which need additional practice.

Certain "rules" apply to the observation and its report:

Rules for giving observation reports

a. Only observe skills and behaviors that have been taught, modeled, and practiced.

b. Observation reports must be delivered without evaluation or judgment, be aware of your words as well as your nonverbal messages.

c. If a group or student has not demonstrated the skill or behavior during the observation period, omit the group or individual from the report. In other words, you **would not say:** *"Mark did not praise"* or *"Mark praised zero ttimes."* You simply do not say Mark's name.

d. In addition to providing a gauge by which to measure areas where additional practice is needed, observation is intended "to catch kids doing something right."

Catch kids doing something right

WRAP-UP

The Wrap-Up is a very brief activity which occurs immediately after each Simple Cooperation lesson. Its primary purposes are to:

a. Give each student the opportunity to think about his own cognitive and/or social behavior in a structured manner.

b. Provide you, the teacher, with immediate feedback regarding the process each group or individual used to accomplish the task.

c. Help measure the learning that has occurred.

d. Reinforce a specific social skill, such as how each student helped his group complete the task.

e. Reinforce prior learning, new learning or the integration of prior and new learning.

Purposes of Wrap-Up

To conduct a Wrap-Up, you ask a question related to the academic lesson or the social skills involved in the group's process. Because Wrap-Up activities pose a question to students, they provide a natural integration of communication and thinking skills. Students must think about what has just occurred, what they have learned, how their group functioned, and how they, themselves, behaved within the group during the lesson or activity.

Integrates communication and thinking skills

Wrap-Up activities may be general or specific and related to either the lesson's social or academic objective.

Examples:

a. A **"general"** question related to the academic content could be, "Name one new thing you learned during the lesson."

General - Academic

Specific - Academic

b. A **"specific"** question related to the **academic** content could be, *"Identify the most critical element in...."whatever the lesson was about."*

General - Social Skills

c. A **"general"** question related to **social skills** might be, *"Identify how the group worked together to complete the task."*

Specific - Social Skills

d. A **"specific"** question related to **social skills** might be, *"Rate your group's use of paraphrasing during this lesson."*

There are numerous ways in which the Wrap-Up activity may be conducted. Some examples include:

- Verbally within each Cooperative group;

- Verbally with entire class;

- Written and submitted to you - you would then read the responses to the class with or without identifying the student;

- Written on index cards, shuffled, then distributed to group or class members who read them aloud.

- Written, signed, and submitted to you for your own review;

- Written as a diary/journal entry or as a letter to self, submitted to you for your review and return to students.

Do not underestimate the importance of the Wrap-Up activity. Besides reinforcing academic content and social skills, Wrap-Ups integrate thinking and communication skills, thus allowing each student to contribute something unique to the small group or class as a whole.

Wrap-Up activities also bring closure to a lesson. They act as a transition, allowing students to prepare themselves to move on to the next lesson or activity. They also provide valuable feedback to you which gives ideas on how to adjust your lesson in the future.

The most important factors to consider when planning Wrap-Up activities are:

1. The activity must relate directly to the academic or social skills objective of the lesson, or act as a reinforcement for previously learned skills.

2. A Wrap-Up activity should immediately follow each Simple Cooperation lesson.

3. The activity should take no more than ten minutes.

4. It should be on a level that allows each student to participate easily.

5. Wrap-Ups should not put anyone on the spot. In other words, students should not be placed in a position where they would look or feel less valuable than other students.

6. Wrap-Ups should vary in process, sometimes conducted in small groups, sometimes in pairs, and sometimes with the entire class.

7. Wrap-Ups should also vary in form, sometimes written, sometimes verbal.

Sample Wrap-Up activities may be found in Figure 18 in the Implementation Section at the end of this chapter.

Things to consider when planning Wrap-Ups

SUMMARY

- *Student knowledge of social skills concepts may be measured by administering a test.*

- *Teacher Observation and Wrap-Up activities provide systematic methods for monitoring student ability to apply social skills.*

- *Teacher Observations may be of the entire class, cooperative groups, or of individual group members.*

- *Students should always be told what specific skill will be observed.*

- *Observation reports are made in a nonevaluative, nonjudgmental manner.*

- *Observe only skills that have been taught, modeled and practiced.*

- *Wrap-Up activities should be conducted following each cooperative lesson or activity.*

- *Wrap-up activities provide a natural integration of thinking skills and communication. Wrap-Up activities also reinforce learning, bring closure and act as transitions to the next lesson.*

Superteaching Workbook: Chapter 7 – MONITORING STUDENT PROGRESS

Self-Evaluation Quiz

1. Briefly, how do you conduct Teacher Observations?

2. When and how do you report your observations back to students when you conduct:

    whole class observations:

    group observations:

    individual observations:

3. What is a Wrap-Up?

4. What is the purpose of a Wrap-Up?

5. What are some ways in which a Wrap-Up may be conducted?

6. What are some factors to consider when using:

    Teacher Observations:

    Wrap-Up Activities:

SUPPLEMENTAL INFORMATION

TEACHER OBSERVATION

Monitoring student progress in social skills is equally important as monitoring academic progress. Two effective ways to determine student social skill levels are "Teacher Observation" and "Wrap-Up" Activities.

Teacher preparation programs do not always include instruction or training in observation skills. It sounds easy enough, you just watch your students. But, if that is all you do, the observation will not be very helpful. Observations must be structured with definite objectives, in other words, when you begin to observe your students, you will select one or two previously taught skills or behaviors to observe and you will use some sort of written format to record your observations.

Important elements of observation are: informing students of exactly what behavior(s) will be observed and then, providing a nonevaluative, nonjudgmental report to them. The report is a frequency count of how often you observed the target behaviors.

Workshop participants often ask why we tell students what we're going to observe. The teachers believe that by telling them, their students will demonstrate these skills just because their occurrence is being counted. We agree. Your students w*ill* practice these behaviors just because you're drawing attention to them. But......it is only with intense practice that these behaviors, i.e., social skills, will be transferred to routine classroom, playground, and outside school behavior.

We also believe it is a disservice to "surprise" kids; that's like a *"gotcha."* We even believe in advising students of the specific areas to be covered on tests. This sends the message that we want to enhance learning of specific areas we consider important, to assess what they know rather than set them up to make errors.

Our college students *expect* to be told and become upset if we don't inform them, so why keep it a big secret from younger students? Tests are meant to measure a sample of a person's knowledge and understanding. Besides that, a test can, and should be, a learning experience. Students can leave a test with insight about their own level of knowledge and understanding as well as new ways to think about the material covered. This is particularly true when cooperative group tests are given.

WRAP-UP ACTIVITIES

Although they're called by many different names and differ slightly between models, "Wrap-Ups" are another critical element in Cooperative Learning.

Wrap-Ups have many benefits: can you think of just two from your reading of the chapter text?

You can use a Wrap-Up at the end of a social skills or an academic lesson, at the end of a period of time during the day, or at the end of the day. Wrap-Up activities also act as transitions.

Always use a Wrap-Up at the end of a cooperative activity.

SAMPLE ACTIVITIES

WRAP-UP ACTIVITIES

Title: **Small Group Discussion**
Grade Level: Kindergarten - Adult
Group Roles: Optional - Facilitator
Time: 5 - 10 minutes
Materials: None

Activity:

Each Group discusses among themselves a specific such as:

- One way our group worked well together to accomplish the task was..........

- I thought that the most interesting part of this assignment was.........

- One way we can improve as a group is.............

- How we're doing with...........(praising, listening, claiming own thoughts, etc.)

- One way the content of this assignment relates to real life is ....

- I liked this activity because...........................

- I didn't like this activity because.....................

and so on.

Students should be given a minute of "thinking time" before beginning group discussion. Allow about three minutes for group discussion, then, if time permits, ask each facilitator to share two or three of her group's responses with the whole class.

TITLE: **The Compliment**
GRADE LEVEL: Kindergarten - Adult
ROLES: None
TIME: 5 - 10 minutes
MATERIALS: None

Activity:

1. Within the Simple Cooperation Group, each member gives a compliment to the person on her right about how he has helped the group accomplish its task.

2. Compliments begin with one group member, for instance, the group member who is sitting closest to the wall clock, and then continues around the circle. Only one person speaks at a time. This allows each group member to hear all the compliments.

TITLE: **Feedback Cards**
GRADE Level: 1 - Adult
TIME: 3 - 5 minutes
MATERIALS: One 3 x 5 index card per student

ACTIVITY:

1. Feedback cards are used at the end of the group assignment and may be open-ended such as:

    a. Write your reaction to the lesson.
    b. Describe how you felt about this assignment.
    c. What was the best thing about this group activity.
    d. Write any concerns you have about this lesson.
    e. Write any questions you still have about the content of this lesson.

2. Feedback cards may be specific, such as:

    a. Rate your group on praising/sharing/asking questions/listening to others/or any other social skill you want to reinforce.

    b. Write one new thing you learned about......(whatever the lesson content is).

    c. How would you rate yourself on......(again, pick a social skill you've taught).

d. Write down the three most important facts in this lesson.

e. How can you use the information in this lesson outside this classroom.

f. How is ....(specific social skill) important in your life outside school.

Cards may be signed or left anonymous. You could collect and shuffle them and read them aloud to the class or use the information to adjust your next lesson.

TITLE: **The Wrap-Up Sheet**
GRADE LEVEL: 2 - ADULT
ROLES: None
TIME: 10 minutes
MATERIALS: Prepared Wrap-Up Sheet with one to five questions for each student.

ACTIVITY:

This is similar to the Feedback Cards except that the sheet with questions is prepared and distributed to students. Figure 18 demonstrates three of the many possible Wrap-Up sheets.

Questions must lend themselves to short responses.

1. Distribute prepared Wrap-Up Sheet to each student.
2. Allow two to five minutes for students to write their responses.
3. Teacher's option:

    a. Students read their responses aloud.
    b. Teacher collects responses and reads them aloud.
    c. Teacher collects responses for personal review.

Figure 18: Sample Wrap-Up Sheets

Sample #1

```
To me, the most important parts of this lesson were:
_____
_____
_____
```

* *

Sample #2

RATE YOURSELF -- Circle the number that best describes how much YOU contributed to your group's assignment today.

LOW   HIGH

1   2   3   4   5   6   7   8   9   10

* *

Sample #3

Complete the drawing that shows how you feel about today's group lesson.

TITLE: **The Fantasy**
GRADE LEVEL: 2 - Adult
ROLES: None
TIME: 15 minutes
MATERIALS: Paper and Pencil or Pen

ACTIVITY:

1. Students are asked to use their imaginations and to create new ideas relevant to the topic they have just been working with.

   For example: if they had been studying a unit on famous inventors, they would be asked to pretend they are famous inventors themselves, and imagine a fantastic invention they would like to create.

2. Students are given a minute or two of "thinking time" before writing the name and description of their invention on paper.

3. Students then share their new inventions with their small group, or with the entire class, as time permits.

SOURCES:

SMALL GROUP DISCUSSION: Adapted by Peggy and Jacquie from their many experiences as participants and leaders of workshops.

WRAP-UP SHEET: Adapted by Jacquie who first experienced a variation of this concept while enrolled in a sociology class.

THE FANTASY: Jacquie

ALL OTHERS: Original Source Unknown.

Chapter 8

GRADES & REWARDS

OVERVIEW: Grades and rewards are part of every classroom, in one way or another. On the next few pages we'll discuss the benefits and pitfalls of group grades and the value of rewards.

TOPICS INCLUDE:

1. The value of group rewards.
2. How to select and use individual and group rewards.
3. Examples of individual and group rewards.
4. The controversy of group grading.
5. Using bonus points.
6. Implementaiton Activities.

Chapter 8: Grades & Rewards

Grades and rewards, like cooperation, are not new to education. We grade our students every day. Most teachers have some sort of reward system for student effort and achievement and many teachers provide full class rewards for specific behaviors or accomplishments.

You do not need to abolish your present grading or rewarding system to implement Simple Cooperation. Your students will still be completing assignments individually, independent of any group, and you will grade that part of their work as you always have. The difference is that you will also include a grade, bonus points, and/or rewards based on group work.

Students will receive individual grades plus group grades or rewards.

Group grades and rewards provide incentive and motivation for all group members to "pull together" towards a common goal. Individual responsibility grows as each member of the group realizes that the group will not succeed if he does not do his part of the assignment. For many students, this will be the first time in their school career that they feel equally as important and valuable as their classmates. As each student internalizes her importance, the quality of both the individual and group work will increase.

Group grades and rewards are very powerful motivators to help students get into the cooperative spirit. Because this is a very new experience for most students they need an incentive to really work together, to help and cooperate with each other. Group rewards provide that incentive because unless the group members work effectively with each other, unless they help each other, they will not receive the reward.

Grades and rewards provide the initial motivation for students to cooperate.

As students begin to see the value of cooperation, reward systems can be decreased and nearly eliminated. But before you eliminate rewards entirely consider how it makes you feel to receive high praise and even some special treatment for doing a good job.

GROUP REWARDS

Group rewards place the focus on the group, as a whole, to meet the academic and/or social skills objective(s). With this focus, it becomes the ultimate responsibility of the group to ensure that all members participate, learn, and do their fair share.

When first implementing Simple Cooperation, there may be times when groups do not complete an assignment. At these times, it is important for group members to examine their behavior. They need to look at what went right and what went wrong in their group. Problem solving techniques and Wrap- Up activities will help this self-analysis process.

Students learn to be responsible.

These situations are simply part of the group growth process. Students are not accustomed to being responsible to each other nor are they accustomed to being responsible for their own learning. Structured teacher observations and skilled facilitation on your part will help students work through group difficulties.

Group rewards also help students learn to work cooperatively with each other. It's important, especially during the initial stages of implementing cooperative groups, to provide a reward for all groups who complete assignments successfully or who demonstrate social skills that have been taught.

The group reward must be desirable to every member of the group.

The most important factor to consider when determining what the group reward will be is that the reward must be meaningful to the group as a whole as well as to the individual members of the group. For example, extra physical education time would not be a reward for students who hate physical education or for students with some type of physical limitation which prohibits them from participating in the activity. This "reward" could well be seen as a punishment by these students and they may covertly (or even, overtly) block the group's progress. For these reasons, group rewards must be selected with care and consideration of the individual students comprising the group. One way to be sure the selected reward is important to each member of the group is to allow the group to choose their own reward.

While there are always some students who are rewarded simply by

While there are always some students who are rewarded simply by completing the task or doing a good job, many students need a more tangible reward system. That's why an effective reward system is often the key to full group participation. This is especially true when first implementing Simple Cooperation groups.

Our bias is that rewards are more fun when they aren't competitive; when each group has an equal opportunity to earn the reward. In other words, rewards are based on successfully completing the assignment or demonstrating specific social skills rather than which group does the best or finishes first.

SOME EXAMPLES OF GROUP REWARDS ARE:

- **_Certificates of Award_** — Each student in the group receives a certificate for outstanding achievement. Some samples appear in the Workbook section.

- **_Bulletin Boards_** — Each group is listed on the bulletin board. Whenever the group completes the assigned task a sticker is placed after the group's name.

- **_Free Time_** — The group receives free time to read or play a game together. This reward could be given immediately, or could be earned by accumulating a specific number of points.

- **_Computer Center_** —The group is allotted a specific amount of time to work at the computer together, playing games or doing extra credit assignments. As with Free Time, this could be an immediate reward or one that requires a specific amount of accumulated points.

- **_Edible Treats_** — The group would be given a healthy treat such as popcorn.

- **_Assignment Selection_** — The group would be given a choice of assignments or objectives for their next task.

- **_Extra Responsibility_** — As an example, groups could be in charge of distributing playground or physical education equip-

Examples of group rewards

- **_Helping the Teacher_** — Many young children like to help the teacher. If this is true in your class, you could allow the group to help clean the chalkboard, take messages to the office, straighten the shelves, etc. (On second thought, many students of all ages enjoy helping the teacher.)

- **_Library Time_** — Extra library time is given to the group members.

- **_Visiting the Principal_** — The group visits the principal to show their completed project.

- **_Special Art Projects_** — Group members are given extra time to select and complete various art projects.

- **_First in Line_** — Group members are allowed to be first to leave for recess, for lunch, at the end of the day.

Needless to say, there are an infinite number of possible group rewards. Your students could probably brainstorm a very long list.

IDEA: Have your students brainstorm a list of possible rewards

INDIVIDUAL REWARDS

Individual awards/rewards can also be helpful. You might want to provide each group member or specific individuals with certificates, personal notes, or other forms of recognition for successfully completing the assignment, for achieving a specified group goal, or for individual improvement and progress either academically or socially. A sample certificate is offered in Figure 19 in the Implementation section at the end of this chapter.

GROUP GRADES

Get administrator's support <u>before</u> you initiate group grades.

Group grades are very controversial so if you decide to use them, be sure you get the approval of your site administrator and inform the parents of what you're doing, how you're going to do it and why.

Group grading simply means that every member of the group receives the very same grade for the assignment. For instance, if the assignment were an essay researching the causes of the Civil War and the group paper earned 85 points, you would record 85 points for each and every member of that group.

Note that in the above example each individual member of the group receives a grade which is recorded in the grade book next to that individual's name, but the grade is based on the group product. Individual members of a group, regardless of the work they did or did not do, are not given a grade that is different than their fellow group members. The message must be clear that all members of the group are responsible for the group completing the assignment and that the individuals within the group will receive the same grade which is based on the quality and/or the completion of the assigned task.

Every group member receives the same grade

OTHER EXAMPLES OF GROUP GRADING INCLUDE:

- *GROUP GRADE AVERAGING:* This method may be used when each individual group member is assigned a specific task as part of the whole. The group function is to assist each member to complete the assigned task and to check each other's work.

  You would grade each individual's work, compute the total and divide by the number of group members. Each member would then receive the averaged grade. For instance, let's say there are four group members whose grades are: 80, 75, 84, and 90. The average of the four grades is 82, thus, each group member receives a score of 82 for that assignment.

- *TWO GRADES:* Using this method, you would give each member his own individual grade *and* the group average grade.

- *BONUS POINTS:* Each group member receives his own individual grade and the group average is used as bonus points.

  You can also use bonus points for assignments which do not have a grade attached to them. You would give group members a specified number of bonus points for simply completing the assignment.

IMPORTANT POINTS TO REMEMBER WHEN GIVING GROUP GRADES AND REWARDS

1. *Include some type of grade or reward for each lesson.*

2. *Be clear and precise.* Students should know exactly what they must do to receive the reward or grade. Provide a complete explanation before you begin the lesson.

3. *Be consistent.* Don't change the rules in midstream. Follow through on the reward or grading system that you established for the assignment. If it didn't work out quite the way you wanted, change the system *next* time.

4. *Rewards must be meaningful to each student in the group as well as to the group as a whole.* You may want to have students help establish the reward system. For example, you could give your students a list of possible rewards and each group, using consensus decision making techniques, would select its own reward.

5. *Stay fresh.* Vary the reward system to keep both you and your students motivated and interested.

6. *Reduce the frequency of extrinsic rewards.* As time goes by, many groups will become less dependent upon external rewards. When you notice this shift in motivation, you might consider omitting a specific reward for certain assignments. This is really a matter of personal preference and teaching style. We know teachers who include some type of reward or grade for each and every assignment throughout the entire year, while others begin decreasing extrinsic rewards as soon as possible.

SUMMARY

- *Group grades and rewards provide incentive and motivation for all group members to work together cooperatively.*

- *Group rewards can be offered for completing an assignment or demonstrating a specific social skill.*

- *Rewards must be meaningful to the group as a whole as well as to each individual student in the group.*

- *Individual awards could also be offered for improvement and progress in academic or social skills.*

- *Group grades are very controversial. It's a good idea to discuss group grading with your site administrator and students' parents before using them.*

- *Consider reducing the frequency of group grades and/or rewards as students become more internally motivated.*

Superteaching Workbook: Chapter 8 - GRADES & REWARDS

Self-Evaluation Quiz

1. Why are group grades or rewards important in the Cooperative process?

2. Why should the reward be meaningful to all students in the group?

3. What is one way you can make sure the selected reward is, in fact, meaningful to each group member?

4. What are two methods of group grading?

5. What do the authors suggest you do before using group grades?

IMPLEMENTATION ACTIVITIES

The following samples of awards and certificates can be presented to individuals or groups for academic or social skills. The "Good Work Award" can be copied on 3 x 5 plain index cards. The others can be copied and framed, attached to matting or presented on plain paper.

Students of all ages value these types of award certificates. An award is reinforcing and encouraging to students and parents.

Figure 19: Sample Achievement Certificates

GOOD WORK AWARD

To: _____

For: _____

_____

CERTIFICATE OF ACHIEVEMENT

Presented to: _____

On this date: _____

For Outstanding Performance In:

_____

signed: _____

GREAT   JOB!

_____

CERTIFICATE OF ACHIEVEMENT

Presented to: _____

On this date: _____

For outstanding performance in: _____

signed: _____

Chapter 9

THINKING SKILLS AND THE COOPERATIVE CLASSROOM

OVERVIEW: This chapter discusses how cooperative group activities inherently support the development of thinking skills, and how these activities can be structured to purposefully develop higher order thinking skills.

TOPICS INCLUDE:
1. Thinking skills defined
2. How thinking paths are developed.
3. Thinking paths and internal dialogue.
4. Mediation.
5. Higher level questioning and thinking.
6. How Cooperative lessons inherently enhance thinking skills.
7. Sample activities to develop thinking skills.
8. Self-Analysis.
9. Selected list of Thinking Skills Programs.

Research studies conducted during the last five to seven years have consistently suggested that most of our students are not developing the skills necessary for problem solving and decision making. Curriculum requirements mandated at the state and local levels appear to be increasing nation-wide. Getting through the required material in one year often seems to be an impossible task. The result is that students are seldom treated as thinking people. Instead, they seem to be viewed as "empty heads" to be filled with specific knowledge and facts for the purpose of regurgitation on tests and in class discussions.

Students learn at a very young age that to be successful in school, they must determine what the "right" answers are, then give those answers on tests, assignments and in class discussion. In most classrooms, there is little, if any, time to think about content areas in different ways. Yet, it's important to set aside time to teach thinking skills and to integrate these skills into daily activities because *teaching thinking skills teaches students how to learn,* the most powerful tool we can give our young people. Cooperative learning provides a natural opportunity to include the teaching of thinking into each lesson.

Learning how to learn.

Merely teaching facts alone is no longer as relevant as it once was. We are living in a rapidly changing world, a world where the body of knowledge in some fields is doubling and tripling in a matter of a few years or less. Information relevant today may very likely be obsolete tomorrow. We need only to look at the changes in our technology during the last five years for evidence of the significant changes occurring in our society. Consider, for example, *"talking"* cars and *"talking"* cash registers in grocery stores or robots building cars. Think about jobs that have become obsolete and the jobs that did not exist three to five years ago.

The recent focus on teaching thinking skills in our classrooms has resulted in an almost overwhelming amount of information on the subject. Teachers attempting to review all the literature for the purpose of determining the best approach to use in their classrooms would be faced with a near-impossible task. The issue is compounded by the fact that there is no

An overwhelming amount of information on thinking skills exists but there is still no single definition of "thinking skills."

common definition of "thinking skills." Different writers use the *same* words and phrases to express *different* ideas and they use *different* words and phrases to express the *same* concepts.

Why all the differences? Because, while it's true that we are gaining more and more knowledge about how the brain works and what thinking is and how it occurs, this field of knowledge is still in a stage of infancy. As in any field of study, eventually, a common vocabulary will be adopted. Until that time, however, we are each faced with the formidable task of deciding what "thinking" means to us and how to effectively teach thinking skills in our classrooms.

Working definition

It would be helpful to have a common definition of "thinking." Since thinking is an abstract, internal process which occurs differently in each individual, it is difficult, to say the least, to define it in concrete terms. For our purposes, we will say that:

> *"Thinking is a series of mental strategies used by an individual to organize and manipulate previous learning experiences and perceptions in order to assimilate new knowledge, to formulate new ideas, and to make judgments."*

To be able to understand new information, we need to be able to relate it to something

The ability to assimilate new information and to think about new concepts can be related to the "frame of reference" we discussed in the Successful Communication chapter: we need some sort of reference point to understand new information. A concrete example of this premise is the study of algebraic theory. If we have never been exposed to algebra, the equations are nothing more than a jumble of letter and numbers. It's a foreign language. Once we have studied algebra, however, the mystery is removed and the equations make perfectly good sense to us.

The same premise is true for developing thinking skills.

For new information to be relevant we must be able to either link it to past experiences or construct new meaning. Each time we are exposed to a new way to think about something, we add another strategy or path to our thinking abilities. If there is nothing in our past experience or if we are unable to construct new meaning, we will not be able to make sense of the information.

As teachers, we can create a classroom environment that promotes the development of more and more thinking paths. If we tell students the *"why's"* and elaborate on some of the "*how's,*" rather than just telling them *what* to do, we help them develop new paths of thinking.

For example.......if we tell students one of the class standards is that only one person can speak at a time, they will understand only that this is a rule in this room. Some students may not have any idea why only one person can speak at a time, so the standard makes no sense to them. This is particularly true for the child who comes from a family where two or more people seem to be talking simultaneously. **But**, if we explain: *"When two students speak at the same time, it is impossible to hear everything each student says; when only one person speaks at a time, everyone can hear the speaker and will gain the benefit of knowing what that person is thinking."* the standard begins to make sense.

Teachers can help students develop thinking paths.

Another example is one that frequently occurs in a home. Assume that it's winter and an eight year old child does not make sure he closes the door completely upon entering the house. The child can be told to close the door and nothing more: *"Joshua, close the door."* To the young child this is just another command to obey or get into some kind of trouble. But, if the parent takes the time to explain: *"Joshua, close the door; cold air is coming in."* the child begins to make a mental connection — if the door is open, cold air gets in the house. If the parent elaborates even further: *"Joshua, close the door; cold air is coming in. The house will get cold causing the heater to turn on more often and the heating bill will go up."* the child is able to make a series of mental connections. Joshua is learning about cause and effect which is a critical element in problem solving and decision making skills.

Explanations can help a child learn to make cause and effect connections.

We can illustrate both these examples by envisioning the sum total of our thinking paths as the trunk of a tree, which becomes our "THINKING BANK" from which we can draw upon experiences or past learning to assimilate new information and perceptions. Each limb or branch represents a thinking path. (see Figure 20)

The more thinking paths a person has, the more ways he or she has to deal with new perceptions, experiences and information. Our thinking

Thinking paths and internal dialogue.

paths are directed by our *internal dialogue,* the constant self-talking that goes on in our minds. When confronted with any situation, we begin talking to ourselves about how best to approach it. Our minds search through past experiences to find a similar situation. We then discuss with ourselves how we dealt with that situation in the past and how successful or unsuccessful our actions were.

Develop thinking paths vicariously..

Another way to gain internal dialogue and thinking paths is vicariously, by listening to how someone else approached various situations, arrived at conclusions, or solved problems. The other person is, in effect, *sharing his internal dialogue.*

We can also *observe the behavior* of others — how do they act in different situations? From observation, we can make some inferences about thinking processes. In other words, by looking at the successes and failures of others, we can learn new paths of thinking.

The concept of internal dialogue is analogous to a computer. The computer (and student) has the capacity to accomplish any given task. But, until it is programmed — given a way of sorting and putting the information together in a way that makes sense to him — the information available for input is useless. Until the student has learned how to manipulate the new information, he cannot complete the task.

Internal dialogue and mediation

Sharing internal dialogue is a part of the *mediation process* as developed by Reuven Feuerstein. He discusses the **mediated learning experience** through which the *mediator shares alternative thinking paths to enhance and expand a student's internal dialogue repertoire.* Feuerstein's studies working with identified "retarded" performers clearly demonstrate that individuals of any age or ability level can develop thinking strategies which enable them to function in a more efficient and productive manner.

Mediation will enhance an individual's thinking processes.

Feuerstein's studies dispel the assumption that intelligence is a static entity — you either have it or you don't. By providing specific kinds of experiences, an individual's IQ level can be raised by 20, 30, and more points. (This assumes there is no neurological deficit, chemical imbalance, or severe emotional disorder.)

Intelligence is dynamic and, as such, is subject to change

Other researchers have also concluded that not only is intelligence not static, the ability to perform higher order thinking tasks is not directly related

Figure 20: Examples of Thinking Paths/Patterns

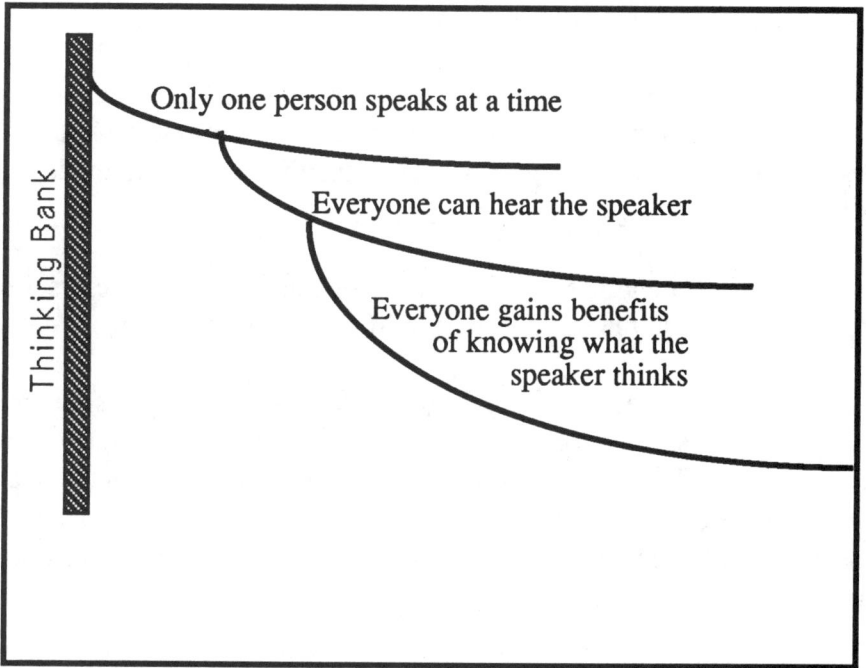

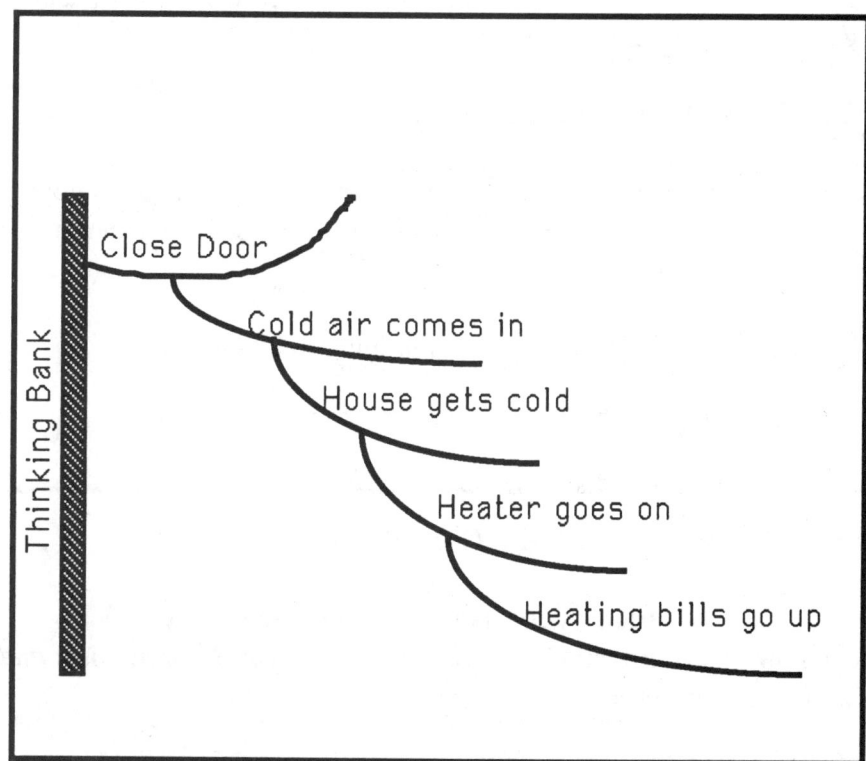

to an individual's IQ level. An individual's thinking strategies are developed through exposure to different information and situations. The discrepancy in thinking skills abilities from one individual to another is due largely to the thinking strategies that have been learned.

Higher order thinking skills are not directly related to IQ level

The lack of alternative thinking strategies is not limited to our low achievers. High achievers may arrive at the correct answer quickly but all too often, they do not know how they arrived at it; they're at a loss to explain the process involved in getting to the solution.

An inability to analyze thought processes may well become a serious handicap at the university level as well as in life and work situations.

Given the opportunity to think creatively, identified low achievers may surprise you

Sadly, it is assumed that it would be a waste of time to expose students who cannot perform simple operations or memorize basic facts to higher level thinking activities. When put to the test, however, we find that given the opportunity, some of the most creative thinking comes from these very students. We only have to look at Albert Einstein, Thomas Edison, Hans Christian Anderson and many others to demonstrate this point.

As teachers, we have the power to influence the development of any student's thinking skills; cooperative learning strategies will help students of all ability levels develop thinking skills.

Thinking skills can be developed:

How to develop thinking skills

1. *Vicariously* by listening to other people discuss what and how they thought about a problem and how they arrived at certain conclusions;

2. By infusing *higher level questioning* into lessons; and

3. Through *direct instruction,* i.e., a thinking skills program.

DEVELOPING THINKING SKILLS VICARIOUSLY

Three specific aspects of cooperative learning inherently provide exposure to how others are thinking: *group process; Wrap-Up activities; and teacher/student observation.*

GROUP PROCESS

Cooperative lessons require students to work together to complete assignments, study academic content, and/or agree on responses for a worksheet or test. As we have already discussed, when working in groups, a student may not simply state his answer, he must share how he arrived at the answer. *Explaining how he arrived at his answer helps students develop thinking skills because:*

1. The student must think about his thinking. Thinking about how one thinks is called **"metacognition"** and is an important attribute in effective thinkers.

    "Metacognition"

2. The student is sharing his **"internal dialogue;"** what he said to himself, when confronted with this specific question, problem or situation.

    "Internal Dialogue"

3. Sharing what he thought and how he actually arrived at his conclusion **"mediates"** the development of other students' thinking skills. It gives them alternatives to thinking about specific events, situations, problems, and content material. It provides new **"thinking paths"** increasing the student's "thinking bank" from which he can draw upon when faced with the same or similar situation or problem.

    "Mediation"

    "Thinking Paths"

Teachers should be alert to *aspects of metacognition* and heighten students' awareness of the process. This can be done by:

1. **Modeling metacognition** -- sharing thought process with students;
2. **Labeling spontaneous processes**, for example, verbalizing thoughts while observing a butterfly; and
3. **Encouraging students to metacognate** about concrete objects.

When explaining mediation and internal dialogue to students, its important to point out that we each have different ways of thinking and approaching problems. The more ways we have of thinking, the greater our chances of finding successful solutions to problems and making good decisions in the future. While there are no right and wrong ways to think, different strategies work better in different situations, so it's beneficial to

How to explain mediation and internal dialogue to your students

have as many thinking strategies as possible.

Self-talk

Then, discuss the fact that *effective thinkers talk to themselves continuously*. This is called self-talk, or internal dialogue. When we share how we arrived at our answers, we are sharing our internal dialogue. This, in turn, mediates the thought processes of other group members and gives everyone new ideas, new paths of thinking.

Thinking about our thinking is **metacognition**

In order to explain how we arrived at an answer, we must examine our own thinking process, i.e. we must think about what we thought and how we thought it. This is called "metacognition" and it helps us become more effective thinkers. (Art Whimbey. "Students Can Learn to be Better Problem Solvers." *Educational Leadership*. Vol. 37, #7. April 1980. Benjamin Bloom & L.J. Broder. *Problem Solving Processes of College Students*. Chicago: University of Chicago Press. 1950.)

Workshop participants have reported that explaining the process of mediation, internal dialogue, and metacognition to students reaps great rewards. Students of all ages seem to love this whole concept of thinking about thinking (they also love the word, "metacognition").

Students enjoy the prospect of helping each other learn how to think differently and approach their group discussions with enhanced enthusiasm.

WRAP-UP

The Wrap-Up activity which was discussed in depth in "Monitoring Student Progress," is a brief activity immediately following a cooperative group lesson.

A Wrap-Up activity asks students to analyze and discuss a specific aspect of the group lesson activity. In other words, it requires students to think about what they did, how they did it, what they learned, and/or how that learning relates to something else.

The Wrap-Up provides an opportunity for "transference" or "bridging" by asking questions such as *"When else in life do you have to think of your own thinking?"* or *"When do your Mom and Dad do this (think about thinking)?"*

Wrap-Ups provide a "bridge"

Whatever the specific content of the Wrap-Up activity, internal dialogue is shared and mediation and metacognition occur. You can structure the Wrap-Up activity to enhance any level of thinking that you want — from simple recall to analysis and synthesis of content information.

The opportunities to enhance thinking skills development through the Wrap-Up activity are infinite.

TEACHER-STUDENT OBSERVATION

Observation was discussed in different contexts in *"The Classroom as a Meeting"* and again in *"Monitoring Student Progress."* Those two chapters focused on the use of observation to heighten self-awareness of behaviors that enhance group and individual performance in social and academic skills. These observations can also help students become aware of how they are thinking.

To know exactly what a person is thinking, we would have to be mind-readers. Since we're not, we have to rely on two elements, one of which is definitely more valid than the other. The first is: *what students tell us they're thinking* both in writing and orally. Introduce thinking aurally by effective use of class and small group discussion, modeling by teacher, Wrap-Up activities and other verbal techniques. Thinking in writing can be encouraged by frequent use of journals, group assignments and Wrap-Up activites.

How to know what another person is thinking

The other is *overt behavior*. Obviously, making conclusions about another's thoughts based solely on his or her behavior would be nothing short of ridiculous. But....we can, through observation, help students become aware of their behaviors, which would provide them with the opportunity to explore their own thinking patterns (metacognition) and recognize the discrepencies, if any, between their thoughts and their behavior.

Through observation, we can also get an idea of the effectiveness of a student's thinking processes. Some theorists have written lists of behaviors that identify "effective" and "ineffective" thinkers. These lists certainly have some value but there is a danger in classifying or labeling any student as an "effective" or "ineffective" thinker. Labeling any individual as anything immediately sets up an expectation level which, in turn, will actually limit the individual's growth and progress. In truth, each individual's thinking behaviors will most likely fall somewhere on a continuum between effective and ineffective thinking, exhibiting strengths in some areas and weaknesses in others.

Thinking behaviors most likely resemble a continuum

A continuum of thinking skill behaviors can be a powerful diagnostic tool. Identifying areas of weakness in thinking processes can provide invaluable information which can be used to design specific lessons to enhance your students' thinking processes. And, Cooperative Learning techniques provide a natural vehicle for focusing on thinking skills development.

The following are examples of thinking behaviors that may be observed. Please remember:

a.) *This is a sample list.* There are many categories and ways of thinking. What is presented here is by no means an exhaustive list of thinking behaviors.

b.) *View thinking as a continuum, as a progressive scale* -- each of us exhibits strengths and weaknesses and most of us fall somewhere between "ineffective" and "effective." What is important is that we provide experiences through which our students can enhance and expand their thinking processes.

c. The following two pages reflect the sample continuum or scale of thinking berhaviors that might be associated with effective and ineffective thinking processes. It is based on the work of Louis Rath and others.

Chapter 9: Thinking Skills and the Cooperative Classroom

Inneffective Thinking	Effective Thinking
1. **Lacks clear goals.** Planning behavior is not evident. Seems to act without thinking. Acts impulsively. Does not seem to consider consequences of behavior.	1. **Goal-Oriented.** Plans short- and long-range goals and develops plans to reach goals. This is true of class assignments as well as other aspects of life. Before implementing plan of action, considers possible consequences.
2. **Speaks impulsively.** Seems to say first thing that comes to mind; speaks at "inappropriate" times. Comments are not relevant to topic of discussion or conversation.	2. **Thinks before speaking.** Speaks at times perceived as "appropriate." Comments are relevant to topic of discussion or conversation.
3. **Is dependent on others.** Needs help with every step of assignment. Requires constant prompting and encouraging. Questions are mostly irrelevant to task.	3. **Is a "self-initiator."** Completes assignments without prompting and constant encouraging. Asks only relevant questions.
4. **Dogmatic and Closed-Minded.** Students who believe they are always right. The only way to do something is their way. Rejects other people's ideas.	4. **Open to ideas of others and different ways of doing things.** Considers new ideas and examines their strengths and weaknesses. Seeks new ideas from others and from readings.
5. **Always know what to do.** When most people are in doubt they are certain about what to do and how to do it. Decisions are made immediately without seeking or accepting new information. Never uncertain about anything.	5. **Allows uncertainty to emerge regarding an issue.** Effective thinkers do not require themselves to always "know" the right answer or to choose a make a decision immediately. They take time to examine the issues involved, weigh the pro's and cons, consider many points of view and then select what they determine is the best answer from the alternatives available.
6. **Poor Comprehension.** Can't seem to follow directions. Don't understand what is meant in written, oral, or nonverbal messages.	6. **Good Comprehension.** Follows directions; understands written, oral and nonverbal messages.

211

Ineffective Thinking	Effective Thinking
7. **Rigid and Inflexible.** Cannot cope with change or new ideas. May withdraw or manifest other defensive-type behaviors.	7. **Flexible; Open to change.** Enjoys new experiences and seeks out new ideas.
8. **"Under Confident."** Afraid to express own ideas because they might be wrong. Seldom, if ever, volunteers ideas during class discussions.	8. **Confident.** Expresses own ideas freely; not afraid to be wrong. Enthusiastically participates in class discussions.
9. **"Anti-Intellectual."** Believes the process of thinking is a waste of time; dislikes work that requires creativity. Does not care about learning new things. Does not question self or others about thoughts or thinking process.	9. **Displays Questioning & Wonderment.** Seeks new information; questions others and self regarding the process and content of thoughts and thinking. Is "turned on" to creativity and learning.
10. **Oblivious of Environment.** Is not aware of what is happening in the world. Does not pay attention to what others are doing or saying. Is unaware of changes in environment.	10. **Aware of Environment.** Is conscious of what is happening around self. Aware of what others are doing and saying and of the changes in the environment.
11. **Does not recognize the relationship between the means and the ends, i.e., cause and effect..** Does not develop plans for reaching a goal. Does not seem to learn through observing others. Deals mostly with the concrete. Behavior is determined through trial and error.	11. **Recognizes relationship of means and ends, i.e., cause and effect.** Actively develops a plan to reach a goal and follows through with it. Also, can learn through study and observation. Understands abstract relationships.

While this list of behaviors can be helpful to you in assessing possible thinking skills weaknesses, it **should be used only as a guide. And,** as a continuum, a progressive scale. Few individuals "fit" into one column or the other. Our behaviors change in different situations and under different conditions. So, as with all lists, it must be used with caution; there are numerous reasons a student might exhibit or not exhibit any or all of these behaviors.

In all probability, we have each demonstrated some or all of the "ineffective thinking" behaviors at one time or another. Certainly, there have been occasions when you became very rigid about what you thought was right, and times when you were not confident enough in your own knowledge and ideas to express them in a group setting. And, haven't we all been in situations where we simply did not understand what was being said, where the concept presented in a class or the direction given to us just did not make any sense to us?

INFUSING HIGHER LEVEL QUESTIONING INTO LESSONS

If we are to help students develop effective thinking skills, we need to move beyond asking questions that require mere recall of facts. We're not saying that it isn't important for students to learn facts; it is. Knowledge provides a foundation for higher order thinking tasks. But, we need to take students beyond mere recall.

One taxonomy that can be used as a guide is Bloom's six levels:

1. **Knowledge**: to define, recognize, recall, identify, label, and collect. Example: "Name the last three U.S. Vice-Presidents."

2. **Comprehension**: to translate, interpret, explain, describe, summarize, and extrapolate. Example: "Explain the importance of the Civil Rights Act."

3. **Application**: to apply, solve, experiment and predict. E.g., "Construct a chart showing the inflation percentages of the last 10 years."

4. **Analysis**: to connect, relate, differentiate, classify, arrange, group, organize, distinguish, categorize, compare, and infer. E.g., "Listen to three TV commercials and determine which parts are facts and which are inferences."

5. **Synthesis**: to produce, propose, design, plan, combine, formulate, compose, and hypothesize. E.g., "Using real issues in the community, write a speech for a candidate for mayor."

6. **Evaluation**: to appraise, judge, criticize, decide. E.g., "Does the author support his main premise? Why or why not?"

Bloom's Taxonomy

Incorporating questions at levels 3 through 6 will greatly enhance student thinking ability

Designing lessons that include questions promoting higher level thinking skills should be a part of every teacher's overall plan. The following is just one example of how this can be accomplished easily without purchasing extra materials.

The "content" is a magazine ad showing a truck with this caption: "IT'S ALL TRUCK." Beneath this banner is a list of the selling points of the truck, including its load capacity, horse power, cargo load capacity, suspension, and so on.

Give each group a copy of the advertisement and ask them to respond to these questions:

1. **Knowledge** level: Identify the make of the truck.

2. **Comprehension**: Explain the significance of the caption, "It's all truck."

3. **Application**: How could a farmer use this truck.

4. **Analysis**: Some statements in the ad are factual and some are opinions. Write a list identifying which statement are facts and which are opinions.

5. **Synthesis**: Write an ad to sell your bike.

6. **Evaluation**: Based on your analysis of this ad, would you buy this truck? Why? or Why not?

These questions require the group to apply the skills of a good thinker, to be aware of their own internal dialogue, and to share their internal dialogue. The questions, combined with the group process, will promote effective thinking.

You'll find a form for infusing higher level questions into your lesson in the Sample Activities section at the end of this chapter.

DIRECT INSTRUCTION: USING A PUBLISHED PROGRAM

There are many good programs on the market. Their strength lies in the fact that they provide ready-made activities you can use with your class.

Thinking skills and activities are sequenced in these programs which may be a strength or a weakness. Very often there is no logical sequence in the way a person learns or thinks, a student may be able to successfully complete activities at level 6 before he can complete the activities at level 4. For this reason, any sequenced continuum should be used as a guide and modified to fit the needs and skills of your students.

At the end of this chapter, we've included annotated references for some of the thinking programs that have shown excellent results in various research studies. While many of these programs have been designed for individual use, they can easily be modified for use with cooperative groups.

Individuals do not necessarily learn in a "logical" sequence. (That's one of the fun things about human nature)

SUMMARY

- *Thinking skills are essential for a successful life.*

- *Different thinking strategies, or thinking paths, are needed to think about new concepts or situations.*

- *Thinking skills development can be enhanced through mediation.*

- *Some students, while not adept at mastering facts, may demonstrate very creative thinking skills when given the opportunity.*

- *Cooperative learning techniques inherently enhance the development of thinking skills through: group process; Wrap-Up activities and through observations.*

Superteaching Workbook:
Chapter 9 - THINKING SKILLS AND THE COOPERATIVE CLASSROOM

Self-Evaluation Quiz

1. What is meant by these terms:

    a. "internal dialogue"

    b. "mediating"

    c. "metacognition"

2. Why is it so important to help students develop effective thinking skills?

3. How do these aspects of cooperative learning enhance thinking skills:

    a. group process

    b. wrap-up

    c. observation

4. Why is it important for students to share how they arrived at an answer?

5. Identify three characteristics of an effective thinker.

SUPPLEMENTAL INFORMATION AND SAMPLE ACTIVITIES

THE FOLLOWING ACTIVITIES WILL ENHANCE THINKING SKILLS WITHIN THE *GROUP PROCESS*.

1. Give students "think time" before the group begins the task. Instruct students to individually think about how they will approach the task or problem for one minute before the group begins discussion.

2. Instruct group to develop a strategy before beginning the task.

3. Instruct the group to discuss the importance of the content before beginning the assignment.

4. Have the group talk about when, why, and how the information contained in the task is to be used.

5. Have the group review the questions and identify what is to be learned.

The above suggestions will help students prepare for a more successful cooperative group experience.

THE FOLLOWING LIST OF ACTIVITIES WILL ENRICH THE *MEDIATION PROCESS*.

While the mediation process occurs naturally in cooperative groups, you can broaden and enrich the process by planning group activities to encourage the sharing of internal dialogue.

1. Include concrete examples and tasks in group activities. For example, provide materials such as newspaper and paper clips, and instruct students to develop a plan for building the tallest tower possible and follow that plan to build the tower. The plan must be developed within a given amount of time (around 10 minutes). Only after the plan is completed may the building begin and students must build exactly as planned. This forces *"thinking before doing."*

2. Discuss the meaning of words. For example, have groups agree on a common definition of the word *"surplus"* when discussing government subsidy in relation to farming.

3. Have groups verbally "walk through" the thinking strategies they used in finding a solution to a problem.

4. Practice brainstorming. Have groups brainstorm as many ideas as they can for using an object in a way that is different than its intended use. Any object will work — pencils, chalk, erasers, paper clips, and so on.

5. Ask groups to generate questions for a passage they have just read.

6. Ask groups to determine how many different ways the quality of a lesson can be evaluated. For example, how many factors could be graded in an English composition or a term paper.

7. Have students paraphrase sections of required reading passages. In other words, they would write the meaning of the passage in their own words.

8. Synthesize reading material. After reading an assignment, each group would write what they determine to be the essence of the material in the fewest words possible.

9. Students can explore and discuss the consequences of their behavioral choices. Examples...."*What happens if I don't complete my homework?*" "*What are the consequences if I decide to take drugs?*"

10. Self-evaluation. Group members are asked to evaluate their social or academic performance in the group.

11. Giving feedback. Groups are asked to share their reaction to the information you present in the lesson.

12. Sharing points of view. Groups are required to develop a point of view about a current political event and to share it with other groups. (Or, individuals within each group share their points of view with each other.)

13. Role playing. Each group is assigned a specific behavior or social skill to "role play"

Chapter 9: Thinking Skills And The Cooperative Classroom Workbook

for the other groups.

14. Elaborate on an idea. After hearing or reading a concept, each group must expand on the idea and write as much as they can that directly relates to the concept.

15. Discuss "what if...." For example, have groups discuss: "What if the South had won the Civil War?"

16. Describe how objects or events relate to each other. Examples...how does learning to read relate to future income; or, how does our national deficit relate to the value of the dollar; or, how does a penny relate to a nickle.

17. Placing events in sequential order. Almost any content area can be used: provide students with a mixed up list of the daily schedule and have them rearrange it to reflect the class schedule; present the major wars in which the U.S. has been involved and require them to list the wars in sequential order.

18. Relate past and present to future, such as: how will learning the Pythagoras theorem today be useful in the future, as adults?

19. Predict the future. Examples include: envisioning what school will be like in 2005. Expand on this by having groups draw or build a model of what the school would look like, or what transportation vehicles might look like.

20. Identify the pro's and cons of current issues, such as listing reasons why they should or should not vote for specific political candidates.

These activities foster self-awareness of thinking strategies and provide a mechanism for sharing internal dialogue with others.

THE FOLLOWING ARE EXAMPLES OF *WRAP-UP ACTIVITIES* THAT WILL PROMOTE THE DEVELOPMENT OF EFFECTIVE THINKING STRATEGIES, ENHANCE METACOGNITION, ENSURE SHARING OF INTERNAL DIALOGUE, AND PROVIDE MEDIATION.

Have students discuss each of the following either in their cooperative group or in a whole class discussion.

1. After completing this assignment, one question I have is....

2. I can use the information I learned today in the future by....

3. One way I contributed to my group was....

4. One new thing I learned was....

5. I disagree with...because....

6. A better title for this book is....

7. I felt the greatest strength of the character in this story was....

8. If ...had happened, the outcome of the story would have been....

9. I discovered ... in this lesson.

10. I disagree with the author about...because....

11. If I had written this story, I would have....

12. If I had lived in that time era, I would feel....

13. If I were..., I would....

14. I am concerned about....

15. If I were (a particular figure in history or character in a story), I would have....

16. One frustration I felt during this activity was....

17. One good feeling I had during this activity was....

18. I received help from my group in....

19. If we were to do this activity again, I would suggest....

20. Our strategy for accomplishing this task was....

21. What I thought about when we were solving this problem was....

22. I think a better approach to the task would have been....

23. The way I reached my conclusions was....

24. I would like to have more information about....

25. One idea I really liked was...because....

26. One idea I'd like to compliment a group member on is....

27. I can compare this information to....

28. Given this information, I predict....

29. I think this idea will work because....

30. If I were to change something, it would be....because....

Wrap-Ups place a demand on the group and the individuals within the group to be aware of their own internal dialogue and to share that with others. The Wrap-Up can be a powerful activity in helping students establish effective thinking strategies.

THE FOLLOWING LIST OF BEHAVIORS CAN BE USED WHEN *OBSERVING* THE DEVELOPMENT OF THINKING STRATEGIES.

1. Contributing ideas.

2. Listening to the ideas of others.

3. Giving noncritical feedback.

4. Elaborating on ideas.

5. Verbally exploring the consequences of a decision before acting.

6. Examining the pro's and cons of issues.

7. Summarizing ideas.

8. Sharing thoughts behind an idea or suggestion.

9. Taking time to think before attempting to solve a problem.

10. Developing and discussing a strategy before beginning work on a problem.

11. Asking others how they arrived at a decision or solution.

THE FOLLOWING LIST OF BEHAVIORS CAN BE USED WHEN *OBSERVING* THE DEVELOPMENT OF THINKING STRATEGIES.

1. Contributing ideas.

2. Listening to the ideas of others.

3. Giving noncritical feedback.

4. Elaborating on ideas.

5. Verbally exploring the consequences of a decision before acting.

6. Examining the pro's and cons of issues.

7. Summarizing ideas.

8. Sharing thoughts behind an idea or suggestion.

9. Taking time to think before attempting to solve a problem.

10. Developing and discussing a strategy before beginning work on a problem.

11. Asking others how they arrived at a decision or solution.

SAMPLE ACTIVITES TO DEVELOP THINKING SKILLS

TO REINFORCE INTERNAL DIALOGUE AND MEDIATION:

TITLE: **Alternative Solutions**
GRADE LEVEL: 2 - Adult
GROUP ROLES: Recorder
MATERIALS: Paper and pencil.

ACTIVITY:
Assign groups of 3 - 4 students each.

Write the following problem on the chalkboard (Increase or decrease the difficulty to match the ability level of your students.):

```
  234
  568
  462
+ 128
```

TASK: List as many ways as you can think of to arrive at a solution to this problem. Note: we are not looking for the correct answer but for methods to arrive at the answer. Example: add the numbers from bottom to top.

Step 1: Have each student work individually for three to four minutes. At the end of this time, students should tally the number of ways they have thought of.

Step 2: Provide an equal amount of time for groups to combine their individual ideas into one list and generate additional ideas.

Step 3: Discuss the activity with the class. Ask how many new ideas were generated when they worked together in their groups. Point out that when our minds are put together, we gain new ideas and learn from each other. Also point out, that during their group activity they were actually teaching each other new strategies for thinking. By sharing ideas, they have mediated each other's thinking processes; they have expanded their internal dialogue by gaining new ways to talk to themselves when approaching a problem.

TO REINFORCE THE CONCEPT OF "EFFECTIVE THINKER."

TITLE: **Qualities**
GRADE LEVEL: 1 - Adult
GROUP ROLES: Recorder
MATERIALS: Paper and pencil

ACTIVITY: Assign students to groups of three to four students each. Groups list as many qualities of a good thinker they can think of in five minutes. Each recorder shares his group's list with the class. Write the lists on the chalkboard.

(Since younger students may not be able to write a list of responses. A group discussion followed by a sharing session may be substituted for written responses.)

Following the activity, discuss with the whole class the benefits of effective thinking strategies.

DEVELOPING HIGHER LEVEL THINKING ABILITIES

TITLE: **Writing Higher-Level Thinking Questions**
GRADE LEVEL: 5 - adult
GROUP ROLES: Recorder
MATERIALS: Bloom's taxonomy (or whichever taxonomy you use); paper and pencil.

ACTIVITY:

Step 1: Explain the differences among Bloom's six levels, providing examples for each category.

Step 2: Give students a reading assignment.

Step 3: Assign students to groups of three to five students each.

Step 4: Groups write questions about the reading assignment for each of Bloom's six levels.

Step 5: Groups each share and discuss their questions with the rest of the class.

TO INFUSE HIGHER LEVEL QUESTIONS INTO LESSONS

The following guide sheet will help you infuse higher level questioning into your lessons. Write the specific content of the lesson, then write an appropriate question for each thinking level related to that content. Use the completed example in the Chapter as a guide..

Figure 21: Preparing Higher Level Questions

Content: _____

Questions:

Knowledge (recall, identify, recognize, label):

Comprehension (translate, interpret, explain, describe, summarize, extrapolate):

Application (apply, solve, experiment, predict):

Analysis (connect, relate, differentiate, classify, arrange, organize, categorize, compare)

Synthesis (produce, propose, design, plan, combine, formulate, compose, hypothesize):

Evaluation (appraise, judge, criticize, decide):

TO REINFORCE THE CONCEPT OF INTERNAL DIALOGUE

TITLE: **Why?**
GRADE LEVEL: 3 - Adult
GROUP ROLES: Recorder
MATERIALS: Paper and pencil

ACTIVITY:

Assign students to groups of three or four students each.

Step 1: Groups develop a list of reasons it's important to develop internal dialogue.

Step 2: Groups then develop another list of reasons for why it's important to share their internal dialogue with others.

Step 3: Each group recorder shares his group's lists with the rest of the class.

Step 4: Whole class discusses ideas they gained from other groups.

SELF-ANALYSIS OF QUESTIONING STRATEGIES USED IN YOUR CLASS

This simple analysis will give you a good idea of which levels of thinking you are emphasizing in your classroom.

1. Review your lessons over the past several days.
2. Write a list of the questions you have asked students.
3. Then, place a check mark (√) after each question that was at the knowledge or comprehension level and a plus mark (+) after each question that was at a higher level of thinking, i.e., application, synthesis or evaluation.
4. Add up the check marks and plus marks and translate the sums into percentages.

There are no "right" answers but we would hope that your percentage of engaged time in higher level thinking activities far outweighs time spent with lower level questioning.

Also, it is important to recognize that just asking the questions is not enough--you must insure that students are *actively* engaged in seeking the solutions.

SELF-ANALYSIS OF YOUR OWN THINKING STRATEGIES

If we are going to teach effective thinking skills, we must model effective thinking strategies in our classrooms.

Complete the following questionnaire by rating yourself on a scale of 1 to 5; "1" is low or never, "5" is high or always.

1. I demonstrate the skill I'm teaching and share my inner dialogue with students as I am demonstrating. _____

2. I use a wide range of questioning levels (per Bloom's or other taxonomy of thinking skills) _____

3. I encourage students to share ideas. _____

4. I encourage students to search for alternative methods to reach a solution. _____

5. I include a structured Wrap-Up activity after each cooperative activity. _____

6. I observe and give feedback to students frequently. _____

7. I frequently require students to explain how they have arrived at an answer. _____

8. I encourage students to think out loud. _____

9. I include thinking skills activities in group assignments. _____

10. I value ideas that are different than my own and encourage students to share their divergent views _____

11. I encourage students to consider many points of view before making a decision. _____

12. I often provide "think time" before requiring students to begin work on an assignment. _____

13. I provide students with many opportunities to evaluate their own behavior. _____

14. I explain to my students how the information being presented to them will be of value to them in the future. _____

15. I relate past events to the present and discuss their possible impact on the future. _____

© 1988 Rhoades & McCabe; Permission to reproduce is granted.

SCORING FOR "SELF-ANALYSIS OF YOUR OWN THINKING SKILLS QUESTIONNAIRE"

67 - 75 = Great Job
60 - 74 = Need to work a little
51 - 59 = Need to work a lot
50 & below = Reread the chapter on thinking skills.

THINKING SKILLS PROGRAMS

The following is a list of a few of the many excellent thinking skills programs available. Further information about these and other programs may be found in the publications listed in the reference section of this book.

INSTRUMENTAL ENRICHMENT: Developed by Reuven Feuerstein.
Curriculum Development Associates, Inc.
1211 Connecticut Ave, NW
Washington, DC 20036

The core of the Instrumental Enrichment program is a three year series of problem solving tasks and exercises that are grouped in 14 areas of cognitive development. They are called "instruments" rather than "lessons" because they are virtually free of any specific subject matter.

CoRT (COGNITIVE RESEARCH TRUST) : Developed by Edward DeBono
Pergamon Press, Inc.
Fairview Park
Elmsford, NY 10523

The CoRT program is designed to be used easily by teachers. Although training is available, the program can be used without it. This program has been used with great success in many countries of the world.

CALIFORNIA WRITING PROJECT Developed by the U. of California, Irvine
University Extension
University of California
P.O. Box A 2
Irvine, CA 92716

The California Writing Project integrates basic principles of learning theory, current research on the composing process and practical strategies in a developmental approach to fostering critical thinking skills through writing.

PHILOSOPHY FOR CHILDREN Developd by Matthew Lipman
Institute for the Advancement of Philosophy of Children
Montclair State College
Upper Montclair, NJ 07043

The goal of Philosophy for Children is to promote creative as well as critical thinking. Students read novels with inquisitive children as characters. This is followed by teacher-led discussions, using structured discussion plans, exercises and games.

PROJECT IMPACT
Center for Teaching of Thinking
21412 Magnolia Street
Huntington Beach, CA 92646

Project Impact seeks to improve student performance in mathematics, reading and language arts by infusing critical thinking instruction into content areas.

STRUCTURE OF THE INTELLECT Developed by Mary Meeker
SOI Institute
343 Richmond St.
El Segundo, CA 90245

Based on Guilford's theory of intelligence, SOI is designed to teach creativity as well as reasoning and higher level critical thinking skills.

TACTICS FOR THINKING
ASCD Order Processing Department
Dept. 1242
125 N. West Street
Alexandria, VA 22314-2798

This is a 22 unit program based on the "22 tactics for thinking" as identified by Bob Marzano. Daisy Arredondo then developed this implementation model. This program can be used by districts to train teachers (of all grade levels and subject areas) in the teaching of thinking skills.

BONUS:
HOW TO ORGANIZE FOR SUCCESS

One of the problems many students have is organizing their assignments and their time.

The following format, developed by Rhoades and McCabe, will help your students learn to think through an assigned task. Through this process, students will learn how to organize their thinking, their time and their assignments for success.

There are six steps:

1. ***Define*** *the task.*
2. ***Identify*** *today's date.*
3. ***Specify*** *the assignment's due date.*
4. ***List*** *the requirements, e.g., length of speech/number of pages or words for an essay/ sections in a research paper/pages or chapters to be read/number of math problems to be solved/steps in a math problem/etc.*
5. ***List*** *the subtasks in order.*
6. ***Develop and write a schedule*** *for completing the assignment; specify dates, times and locations for completing the work.*

The **"Organizing for Success"** Worksheet is easy to teach:

- Provide each student with a copy of the blank form, completed sample, and list of steps.

- Explain the sections of the worksheet — this will only take 10 minutes.

- Help your students work through the worksheet with an actual assignment.

- Monitor the student's progress in planning and organizing skills by requiring them to turn in the "Organizing for Success" Worksheet with their assignment.

Figure 22.1: ORGANIZING FOR SUCCESS WORKSHEET
Completed Sample

TASK Deliver a speech on "Freedom of Speech"   **TODAY'S DATE** 11/20/87

REQUIREMENTS

1. DUE 11/29
2. Can use cue cards but may not read speech
3. LENGTH: 5 Minutes
4. May use illustrations

SUBTASKS NEEDED TO COMPLETE ASSIGNMENT

Research "Freedom of Speech"
Make cue cards
Write speech
Practice speech with friend
Draw illustrations
Write outline of main points

ORDER OF SUBTASKS

1. Research subject
2. Outline main points of speech
3. Write speech
4. Draw illustrations
5. Make cue cards
6. Rehearse speech
7. Give speech on 11/29

SCHEDULE FOR COMPLETION

Wed. 11/20 - Research during class period

Th. 11/21 - Research during class

Fri. 11/22 ——————————

Sat. 11/23 - write outline main points, begin writing speech

Sun. 11/24 ——————————

Mon. 11/25 - Finish writing speech, draw illustrations after dinner.

Tues. 11/26 - Make cue cards

Wed. 11/27 - Rehearse with Tom, his house, 5:30

Th. 11/28 - Rehearse with Tom, my house, 4:00

Fri. 11/29 - Deliver speech to class.

© 1985 Rhoades & McCabe. Permission to reproduce is granted.

Figure 22.2: ORGANIZING FOR SUCCESS WORKSHEET

| TASK | _____ | | TODAY'S DATE _____ |

_____

REQUIREMENTS: (Due date; Length; # Chapters, etc.)

1. _____   4. _____

2. _____   5. _____

3. _____   6. _____

SUBTASKS NEEDED TO COMPLETE ASSIGNMENT

_____   _____
_____   _____
_____   _____

ORDER OF SUBTASKS

1. _____   4. _____

2. _____   5. _____

3. _____   6. _____

SCHEDULE FOR COMPLETION

©1985 Rhoades & McCabe. Permission to reproduce is granted.

Chapter 10

PUTTING IT ALL TOGETHER

OVERVIEW: Each component of Simple Cooperation has been explained. Now, it's time to discuss how to arrange your room, and how to plan, design and deliver a lesson. In other words — how to put it all together.

TOPICS INCLUDE:
1. Review of the components of Simple Cooperation.
2. Physical arrangement of the classroom.
3. A model lesson plan format is offered which integrates academic and social skills objectives and includes all the components of a Simple Cooperation lesson.
4. An example of a completed lesson plan.

This final chapter discusses the final "how-to's" of designing a Simple Cooperation lesson. A lesson plan format with instructions and a sample lesson plan are offered. One important element in planning your lesson is how your room will be arranged.

ROOM ARRANGEMENT

How your room is arranged, where the furniture is placed and where student groups work are important factors in designing and conducting cooperative lessons. A little bit of planning goes a long way in reducing chaos and providing an organized "set" for your class. We have found the following arrangements to be most successful:

- Clusters of movable desks.
- Small round tables (square is okay, round is better).
- Sitting in circles on the floor.

Successful room arrangements

Since school budgets don't usually allow teachers to go out and purchase ideal furniture for different grouping patterns, we have to make do with what we have. Consider these factors when planning where to have students work together:

Factors to consider

√ *Students must face each other.* It's important for the members of each group to be able to see and hear each other. Each group member should be able to maintain eye contact with each of the other group members.

Eye contact

√ *There should not be any empty places or chairs* within the group setting. Empty spaces or chairs divide the group. If a student is absent, his or her chair should be removed and the other chairs moved to take up that space.

Empty spaces

√ *Group members should be close enough to each other* to speak softly and hear each other, and to be able to see whatever material they are working on together.

Proximity

Distractions

√ *The area in which each group is working should be void of any distracting materials.* For instance, if the group members have moved their desks together, the only material on top of the desks should be related to their group assignment.

When informing students of where they are to congregate to work, it is important to:

√ *Give very clear directions*; posting signs at each work area is helpful.

Wait 'till I say "Go"

√ *Have each group move immediately after you advise them of their work location and before you tell the next group. OR, tell your class that no one is to relocate until you give a signal, such as saying "go"*, then inform each group of their work location. We have found it very helpful to actually walk and point to each group's area as we give instructions.

√ *Keep the actual movement of furniture at a minimum.* This lowers the noise level and reduces confusion.

DESIGNING A LESSON

Each component of the Simple Cooperation method was discussed individually. To allow you to review these components without returning to previous chapters we have duplicated the charts here: Figure 23: Major Components of Simple Cooperation and Figure 24: Social Skills Components.

Two new charts follow: Figure 25 reflects the Academic Components and Figure 26 shows the the different aspects of a Simple Cooperation Lesson Design.

Figure 23: Major Components of Simple Cooperation

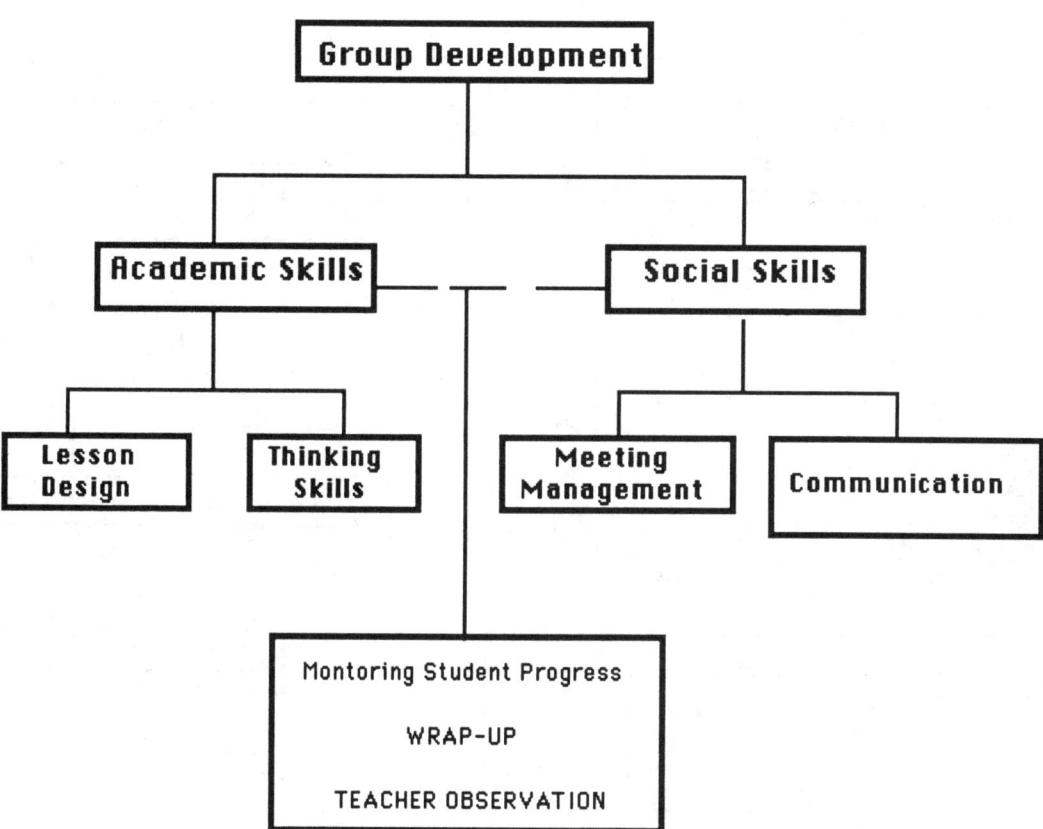

Figure 24: Social Skills Components

```
                    SOCIAL SKILLS ───── Social Norms & Values
                         │                      │
                         │               Classroom Standards
              ┌──────────┴──────────┐
      MEETING MANAGEMENT - - - - COMMUNICATION
              │                          │
              │                   ┌──────┴──────┐
              │                Sending      Receiving
              │                   └──────┬──────┘
              │                          │
              │                    Congruence
              │                    Verbal
              │                    and
              │                    Nonverbal
   ┌──────┬───┴────┬──────────┬──────────┐
  Group  Group  Observation  Problem  Decision
  Size   Roles               Solving   Making
```

Figure 25: Academic Skills Components

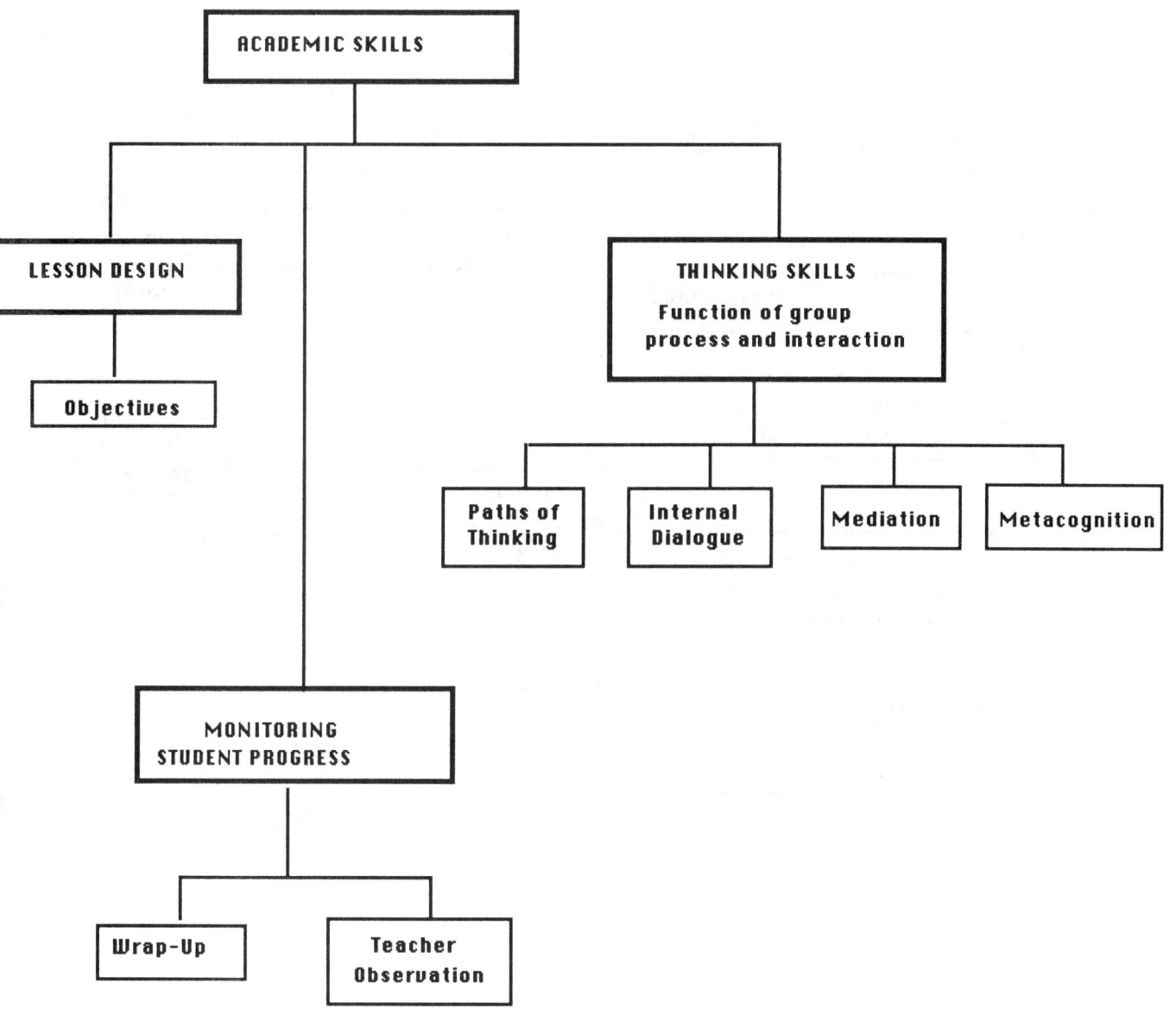

Figure 26: Lesson Design

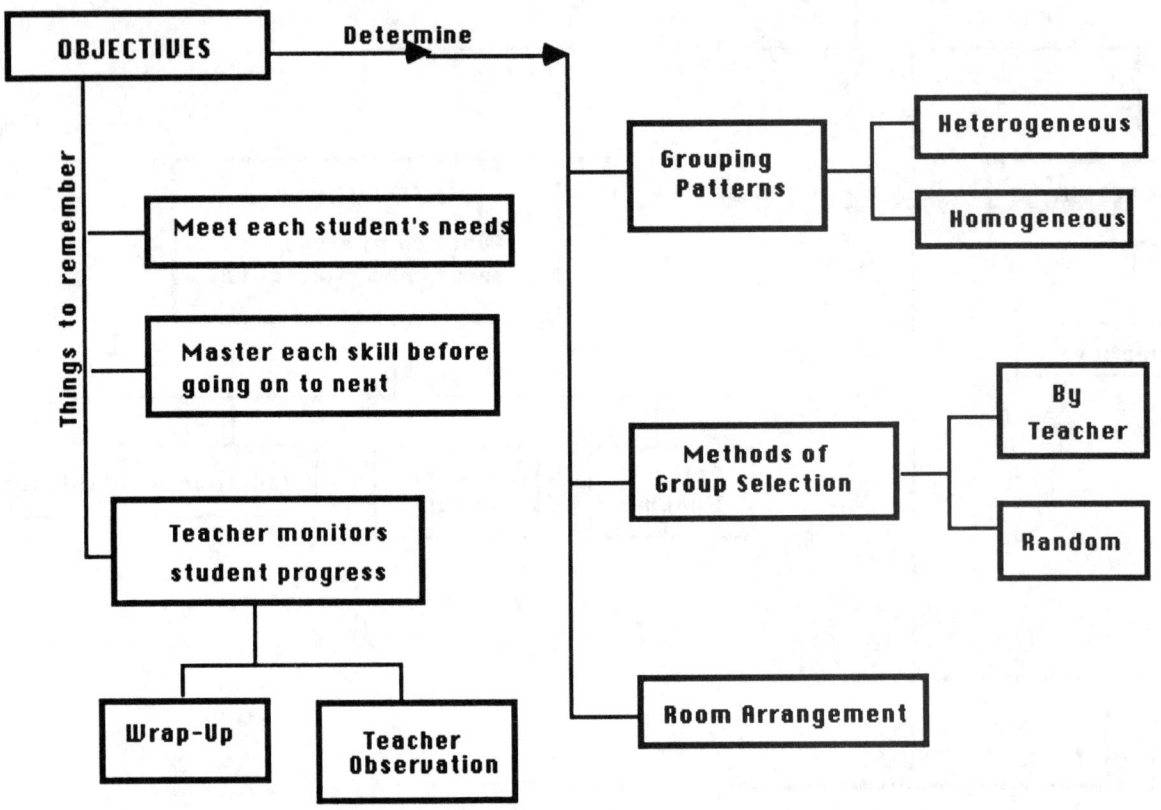

PLANNING YOUR LESSON

Points to remember when planning your cooperative lessons:

1. Group membership is never left to chance when planning academic activities.

2. Academic objectives should be appropriate for each member of the group.

3. Lesson objectives must be clear for teacher and students. It's always a good idea to check student understanding of the objective as well as what they are to do. There are any number of ways to check understanding including:

    a. Ask for a volunteer to paraphrase your instructions.

    b. Ask questions regarding your instructions such as: "What's the first thing you're going to do?" "What's the next thing you're going to do?" and so on through the steps. OR, "The first thing you'll do is move to your group work area. What will you do when you get there?" And, "What's the purpose of the activity you're going to do; what's the objective for this lesson?"

    c. You can also check individual understanding — As you move from group to group during the lesson/activity, you can ask different group members, "What's the objective for this lesson?" or "What are you supposed to do now?"

4. Be sure the lesson activities are congruent with your objectives.

5. Teach each social skill separately before integrating it into a Simple Cooperation lesson. The Social Skills Continuums are provided (see Figures 28 and 29) to help you plan the sequence of instruction. Because the initial group roles may be

When planning a cooperative lesson, remember these

How to check for understanding

Congruence

> The continuums are only guidelines; modify them for your students.

The Nurturing Classroom

Figure 27: Integration of Social and Academic Objectives

```
                    ┌─────────────────────┐
                    │ Teacher Sets Standards │
                    └──────────┬──────────┘
                               ▼
         ┌─────────────────────┐           ┌─────────────────────┐
         │  Getting Acquainted │ - - - - - │ Students Set Standards │
         └──────────┬──────────┘           └──────────┬──────────┘
                    ▼                                  │
    ┌───────────────────────────────┐                  │
    │            START              │                  │
    ├───────────────┬───────────────┤    ┌─────────────────────────┐
    │   Academic    │ Social Skills │    │  CONTINUOUS ACTIVITIES  │
    │  Objective #1 │ Objective #1  │    │                         │
    │               │  e.g. Get     │    │   Getting Acquainted    │
    │               │  Listener's   │    │      Transitions        │
    │               │  Attention    │    │       Energizers        │
    ├───────────────┴───────────────┤    │        Wrap-Ups         │
    │           MASTERY?            │    └────────────┬────────────┘
    ├───────────────┬───────────────┤                 │
    │  No: Return,  │  No: Return,  │                 │
    │    Review,    │    Review,    │                 │
    │    Adjust     │    Adjust     │                 ▼
    ├───────────────┼───────────────┤
    │    Yes,       │    Yes,       │
    │  Go to Next   │  Go to Next   │
    ├───────────────┼───────────────┤
    │   Academic    │ Social Skills │
    │  Objective #2 │ Objective #2  │
    ├───────────────┴───────────────┤
    │           MASTERY?            │
    ├───────────────┬───────────────┤
    │  No: Return,  │  No: Return,  │
    │    Review,    │    Review,    │
    │    Adjust     │    Adjust     │
    ├───────────────┼───────────────┤
    │    Yes:       │    Yes:       │
    │  Go to Next   │  Go to Next   │
    └───────┬───────┴───────┬───────┘
            ▼               ▼
```

introduced simultaneously with other social skill instruction, a separate continuum for group roles is provided.

6. Each objective will have a life cycle. In other words, an academic objective may be completed before mastery is gained for the social skills objective. In that case, the next cooperative lesson would have a different academic objective but the unmastered social skills objective would become the social skills objective again. This situation is graphically represented in Figure 27.

Figure 28: Social Skills Continuum

1. Teacher Sets Standards
2. Get Acquainted
3. Speaker Get Attention of Listener
4. Speaker Look at Listener
5. Listener Look at Speaker
6. Claim Own Thoughts and Feelings
7. Clarify by Asking Questions
8. Students Set Standards
9. 3 C's - Be Clear, Concise, Complete
10. Identify Own Feelings
11. Clarify by Paraphrasing
12. Nonverbal Awareness
13. Congruence: Listener
14. Congruence: Speaker
15. Perception Checking
16. Feedback
17. Decision Making
18. "I-Messages"
19. Problem Solving

Figure 29: Group Roles Continuum

1. Group Member
2. Facilitator as Monitor
3. Beginning Recorder
4. Praiser
5. Time-Keeper
6. Checker
7. Observer - must have skill and awareness of nonverbal messages
8. Advanced Recorder for Problem Solving and Brainstorming.
9. Advanced Facilitator - must have excellent skills in all aspects of effective communication.

A sample lesson plan format and instructions for completing the form are provided in Figures 30.1 and 30.2. You may want to modify the sample lesson plan format to better meet your own personal needs.

Appendix III includes completed sample lesson plans and some academic activities that workshop participants (and/or we) have used and found successful.

Figure 30.1: SIMPLE COOPERATION SAMPLE LESSON PLAN FORM

DATE(S):   TIME(S):   CLASS/SUBJECT:

ACADEMIC OBJECTIVE:

SOCIAL SKILLS OBJECTIVE:

MATERIALS:

ROOM ARRANGEMENT:

GROUP SIZE: GROUPING PATTERN:

GROUP ROLES:

GRADE/REWARD:

STUDENT OBSERVATION:

LESSON ACTIVITY:

WRAP UP:

TEACHER OBSERVATION:

Figure 30.2: INSTRUCTIONS FOR COMPLETING LESSON PLAN FORM

1. **Date(s) and Time(s):** Write the date(s) and time(s) you are planning to present the lesson.
   Class/subject: Write the grade or class and subject area.

2. **Academic Objective:** Write the academic objective for the lesson.

3. **Social Skills Objective:** Write the social skills objective for the lesson.

4. **Materials:** List the materials needed for the lesson.

5. **Room Arrangement:** How will the room be arranged? Clustered desks? Tables? Or?

6. **Group Size:** Write the number of students you want to be in each group.

7. **Grouping Patterns:** Write grouping pattern to be used. If not enough space, make a check mark (√) or an "X" and write grouping information on the back of the lesson plan form, i.e. method of group selection, which students assigned to each group, etc.

8. **Group Roles:** Note the group roles to be used and how students will be selected for roles.

9. **Grade/Reward:** Note if completion of the assignment will result in a grade, bonus or reward and the criteria for receiving it. Example: "Each group that completes the assignment by the end of the period will receive ten minutes of free time on Friday" OR, "The group product will receive a grade and each member of the group will receive that grade as bonus points."

10. **Student Observation:** If you will appoint a student observer for each group, specify how that person will be selected and what behaviors the student will observe. If each group will have a student observer, attach an observation form for each group to your lesson plan.

11. **Lesson Activity:** Describe the specific step-by-step procedure you will use to present the lesson, including (as appropriate):
    a. How you will introduce the lesson to your students for motivation, establishing relevance and meaning, etc.
    b. How the new content will be presented - will you model it? How? How will you check to be sure students understand the new skill or content? How will students practice the skill? When and how will the groups work on the skill independently?

12. **Wrap-Up:** List the specific Wrap Up activity you will use. If a Wrap Up sheet is to be used attach it to the lesson plan.

13. **Teacher Observation:** List the behavior(s) you will be observing; attach observation forms.

Note: It may not be necessary to include each element of this lesson plan format in every lesson. Include only those elements which are appropriate for the specific lesson content you are presenting.

Chapter 10: Putting It All Together

COMPLETED SIMPLE COOPERATION LESSON PLAN - SAMPLE #1

DATES: **TIMES:** 1:00 - 2:00 daily   **CLASS/SUBJECT:** Grade 2 Social Studies

ACADEMIC OBJECTIVE: Each group will complete one section of the "Our School" mural.

SOCIAL SKILLS OBJECTIVE: Each group member wlll "be on time," i.e. in the classroom immediately after lunch and with his group at the directed times during the lesson.

MATERIALS: Poster paint; butcher paper; construction paper; crayons; scissors. Materials will be placed at each group's working space during lunch hour.

ROOM ARRANGEMENT: No change.

GROUP SIZE: 3   **GROUPING PATTERN:** X

GROUP ROLE: Group Member

REWARD: Each group that has each group member seated in the assigned working space after lunch, and at other teacher-designated times will receive one sticker to be placed after the group name on the bulletin board.

STUDENT OBSERVATION: None

LESSON ACTIVITY:

   Day 1 — Lead whole class discussion about why we have schools and what is supposed to happen in schools. Take a walking tour of the school pointing out specific buildings and classrooms.

   Day 2 — Introduce mural concept, including what is to be included in mural. Divide students into groups, assign each group a specific building, classroom, playground equipment, to draw. Students discuss and begin drawing.

   Day 3 — Groups complete drawing, color and cut out assignment. One group will paint the background for the mural.

   Day 4 — Conduct whole class discussion about where the different drawings should be placed on the mural. As each building, classroom, playground and equipment are discussed, make a notation on the mural showing where each group is to place their assigned drawings.

   Day 5 — Invite visitors, principal, another class, librarian, secretary, custodian, to the classroom to see the mural. If time allows, each group may discuss, one at a time, their section with the visitors. Conduct Wrap Up.

WRAP-UP: One sentence WHIP...."One new thing I learned about my school is....."

TEACHER OBSERVATION: Using observation form, check those groups where all members are in their assigned work spaces after lunch and at other times as appropriate.

> **REVERSE SIDE OF LESSON PLAN FORM**

Heterogeneous groups of three, each group includes one identified high achiever, one middle range, and one low achiever.

Groups will be preassigned with names written on wall chart.

Group names will be consistent with the assigned task:

Cafeteria Group: Suzanne, Cynthia, Clarence

Auditorium Group: Michael, Mike, Cleo

Wing 1 Group: Jenna, Margaret, Bill

Wing 2 Group: David, Gregory, Pat

Wing 3 Group: Billie Jo, Robert, Anthony

Tree Group: Tom, Mellissa, Billy

Flower Group: Heath, Dawn, Tommy

Primary Playground Group: Jose, Jessica, Kim

Mural Group: Joshua, Jason, Kathy

COMPLETED SIMPLE COOPERATION LESSON PLAN: SAMPLE #2
(NOTE: This activity involves a test. Preassigned groups study together from several days to six weeks, as appropriate for the material.)

DATE: **TIME:** 10:00 - 11:00   **CLASS/SUBJECT:** Grade 9 History

ACADEMIC OBJECTIVE: Each group will successfully complete one knowledge level test covering Chapters 9 and 10 of the text.

SOCIAL SKILLS OBJECTIVE: Each group member will practice "Claiming own thoughts, ideas and feelings," by beginning sentences with phrases such as: "I think/I feel..." or "My idea is..."

MATERIALS: Text book, tests.

ROOM ARRANGEMENT: Move desks into clusters of four.

GROUP SIZE: 4   **GROUPING PATTERN:** √

GROUP ROLES: Group Member, Praiser, Facilitator as Monitor, and Beginning Recorder for each group.

REWARD: Each group scoring 90% or better on the test will receive 20 minutes extra computer time (five minutes per group member). Group grade will be used as bonus points in grade book.

STUDENT OBSERVATION: None

LESSON ACTIVITY:
     a. Ask students to be seated with their study group.

     b. Opening: Ask each group to determine the most important reasons for studying the material found in Chapters 9 and 10; <u>give two minutes</u> for individuals to think about the question, <u>five minutes</u> for group discussion and <u>three minutes</u> for the group to make its decision. Then, have the Facilitator in each group share their decision with the rest of the class (maximum of <u>one minute per group</u>).

     c. Review testing process and group decision making rules. (<u>five minutes</u>)

     d. Students take test. (<u>25 minutes</u>)

WRAP-UP: Each individual student to complete Wrap Up sheet which will ask students to:

1. Identify the most important things you learned in these two chapters.

2. Write a one sentence response to the following question: How do you feel when you claim your own thoughts, ideas, and feelings?

3. Share responses with study group.

TEACHER OBSERVATION: Observations of individual students claiming own thoughts, ideas, feelings, i.e., statements beginning with "I" or "My idea is..." Use observation form.

(Note:This same observation process has occurred during group study sessions on previous days.)

REVERSE SIDE OF LESSON PLAN FORM

Heterogeneous groups of four. The groups were formed using information from the pretest administered at the beginning of the unit.

SUMMARY

- *Furniture needs to be arranged so that students can hear and see each other easily.*

- *Physical movement of furniture should be kept minimal.*

- *Introduce Simple Cooperation to your students in a sequential and clear manner.*

- *Although a Social Skills Continuum is provided, it is suggested that you modify it to fit the needs and skills of your students.*

- *A sample lesson plan format was also provided; however, all elements are not necessary for each and every lesson.*

- *The social skill objective and the academic objective in each lesson are each separate entities. If mastery is not gained in one or the other, repeat that objective until it is mastered.*

Superteaching Workbook Chapter 10 - PUTTING IT ALL TOGETHER

Self-Evaluation Quiz

1. What are the important factors to consider when planning student group work areas?

2. Why is it important to plan your room arrangement?

3. What are the factors to consider when planning your cooperative lesson?

4. Is it necessary to complete all parts of the lesson plan for every lesson?

Appendix I

INTRODUCING SIMPLE COOPERATION TO YOUR STUDENTS

It is finally time for you to lead your first complete Simple Cooperation lesson. You've laid the ground work by setting standards and getting acquainted. You've taught the social skill you're integrating in your academic lesson and you have written your lesson plan.

It's possible that you're feeling a bit nervous right now, asking yourself, "How can I make this all come together smoothly? How am I going to introduce this new way of learning to my students? and What will I do if my lesson bombs?"

The first thing to be aware of is that most people feel some pangs of anxiety when they are about to do something new or different. This is especially true when we've been successful doing our job another way.

The second thing to know is that it takes time and practice to implement a new process. You and your students need time to get used to it..

More often than not, students of all ages respond to cooperative lessons with enthusiasm — they actually look forward to their group assignments.

The following sequence should help you when first introducing Simple Cooperative Lessons to your class:

- a. Tell your students what the academic and social objectives of the lesson are in terms that are appropriate to the age group.

- b. Check for understanding. Make sure your students know what they are supposed to do.

- c. Explain individual and/or group rewards or grading systems.

- d. Let students know which group they are to join and where their group will work.

e. If teacher or student observation is included in the lesson, tell students about it; tell them what behaviors will be observed.

f. Before the lesson begins, tell students what wrap up activity will be used at the end of the lesson. This will heighten their awareness of the objectives and reinforce the fact that they are accountable for specific behaviors and/or content areas of the lesson.

g. Direct students to join their groups.

h. When students have moved to their work areas, direct them to begin the activity.

i. While students are working, move from group to group, facilitating discussion and problem solving.

j. When the allotted time is up, conduct the planned wrap up activity.

k. When evaluating the lesson, remember: if things didn't work out exactly as you planned, analyze what happened and try again. Simple Cooperation will work for you and your students.....it just takes a little time to get going.

Appendix II

SAMPLE IMPLEMENTATION SCHEDULE

Appendix II: Sample Implementation Schedule

This sample implementation schedule spans six weeks. It is meant only to give you a starting point and should be adjusted and modified for your particular grade, age, and/or subject area.

To begin, select one subject area or time period in the day and use cooperative activities only at that time. Cooperative learning strategies are not intended to replace direct instruction and too much of anything (even cooperative activities) will wear very thin, very quickly with your students.

Regardless of the age group you are working with do not assume your students know any of the social skills outlined in the book. In other words, don't skip anything because it seems too elementary to you. An example are the first three skills on the social skills continuum: "Get the attention of your intended listener before speaking;" "Look at your intended listener;" and "Listener look at speaker." Observe your students in conversation; do they get the attention of their intended listener before they start talking? And, where is the speaker looking? Where is the listener looking? Do they have eye contact every so often and spend the rest of the time looking down, at the wall, out the window, or someplace else? Or do they really look at each other and show interest and attention for each other?

Always check for mastery, i.e. consistent and appropriate use of a skill before moving on, no matter how elementary it seems to you.

OK; let's begin implementing Simple Cooperation in your classroom.

WEEK 1

This week you will:

1. Establish and explain GROUP STANDARDS.
2. Conduct GETTING ACQUAINTED activities.
3. Teach the role of GROUP MEMBER.
4. Teach the initial skills for effective communication:
   SPEAKER GET ATTENTION OF LISTENER BEFORE SPEAKING.
   SPEAKER LOOK AT LISTENER.
   LISTENER LOOK AT SPEAKER.
5. **Group students in pairs** or triads for 10 - 20 minute cooperative activities.
6. Conduct TRANSITION ACTIVITIES.
7. Conduct WRAP-UP ACTIVITIES.
8. Teach the role of FACILITATOR AS MONITOR.
9. Do OPENING activities.

Week 1, Day 1

This will be the first day of school OR the first day you decide to establish a cooperative classroom.

1. Begin the day (elementary) or class period (secondary) with a *Getting Acquainted* activity.

2. Review the *Class Standards* that you have developed. Be sure students really understand what you mean, e.g. what does a "clean" area mean? Explain, demonstrate, model, role-play, as necessary for clarification. If there are any exceptions to the rule, tell your students about it.

   Remember: if a new student is enrolled after the standards have been explained, it is necessary to explain to the new student.

3. Discuss the role of *"Group Member"* -

   "Beginning today, we are going to be establishing a cooperative classroom which means that students will be completing some of their work in small groups. Some of the

Appendix II: Sample Implementation Schedule

time, you, the teacher, will be assigning students to groups and some of the time they will be able to select their own groups. When students are preassigned to groups, they will work together for the entire assignment. Groups will change during the year which will give each student the opportunity to work with every other student in the class during the year."

Tell students they *"will be learning and experiencing lots of new things."* A discussion about the work world will be helpful for secondary students. For instance, *"In the work world, employees are often required to work in small teams to complete a project or resolve a problem. In any case, employees must be able to get along with each other, resolve differences, and work together towards the company's goals. Employees must also be able to actively participate in meetings. Employees who demonstrate these kinds of skills will have a greater chance at promotions and raises. Cooperative learning will give students the opportunity to gain and practice these skills."*
(Also, see Appendix I for an example of introducing cooperation to your students)

Further explain to your students that:

You and your students *"will consider your time together as a meeting. Students should also consider their time in small cooperative groups as "meetings." The reason the classroom is a meeting is because you are all meeting there for the purpose of accomplishing something in specific: learning. Everyone in the class is a member and each member must do his or her part in order for the group to succeed. The group/class simply won't be as successful unless each and every member completes his or her part of the work."*

EXPLAIN: THE RESPONSIBILITIES OF EACH GROUP MEMBER ARE TO:

- Be on time to class/school

- Move quietly and quickly to their assigned areas;

- Actively participate; in other words, share their ideas and help their group complete its assignments. Each member of the group is responsible for helping each of the other members of the group. The group is not finished until each member has learned the material;

- Follow-through on agreements, in other words, when your agree to do something for the group, do it;

- Listen to the other members of their group;

- Take turns speaking-don't hog the discussion, give everyone a chance to say

The Nurturing Classroom

> what he or she is thinking or feeling;
>
> - Encourage other members of the group share their ideas and feelings; do this by asking what others think; and
>
> - Praise and compliment each other for good ideas and a job well done.

It will be helpful to write the responsibilities on a large piece of butcher paper and hang it on the wall.

Encourage students to ask questions to clarify the responsibilities.

4. **Discuss and model** the first sending and listening skills on the communication continuum: <u>Speaker get attention of the listener; Speaker looks at listener; Listener looks at the speaker</u>.

   Demonstrate. Give younger students the chance to "practice" these skills.

5. **Group students** in dyads or triads for a nonthreatening activity - a short assignment which needs only 10 to 20 minutes to complete.

6. Check students' use of these skills during the day.

Week 1, Day 2

1. Begin day or period with a **Getting Acquainted** activity.

2. **Observe** students' use of the communication skills you explained yesterday: Speaker getting attention of listener; Speaker looking at listener; Listener looking at speaker.

3. Check students' understanding of class Standards.

4. Conduct at least one **Transition** activity during the day.

5. **Group** students for a short activity/assignment; the assignment should need only 10 to 20 minutes to complete.

6. Conduct a **"Wrap-Up"** - perhaps a written form like:

   "The best thing about working in the group today was_____"

Week 1, Day 3

1. Begin day or period with an **Opening** activity such as:

   "Everyone walk around the room slowly and quietly, walk as tall as you can, walk as short as you can, walk back to desk."

2. **Group students** in pairs or triads for a short social skills activity, such as sharing what they did last night.

3. **Check students' use of social skills** taught thus far: speaker get attention of listener; listener and speaker look at each other.

4. Inform students that you are introducing a specific group role today: **"Facilitator as Monitor"** is the person in each group who will get the materials the group needs to complete its assignment and will also return them.

5. **Group** students pairs or triads and appoint a Facilitator as Monitor.

6. **Monitor** the new roles as well as the communication skills you've taught thus far.

7. Conduct a **"Wrap-Up"** at the end of the activity; again a written form such as:

   "One thing I learned in my group today was.................."

8. Do at least one **Transition** today. Check the samples for ideas.

Week 1, Days 4 and 5

Follow the same format for these two days as for Day 3.

Be sure you begin the day or class period with an Opening or Getting Acquainted activity and a Transition after lunch.

End each cooperative lesson with a Wrap-Up activity.

WEEK 2

This week you will:

1. Conduct OPENING activities.
2. Teach the role of BEGINNING RECORDER.
3. Review responsibilities of GROUP MEMBER and FACILITATOR AS MONITOR.
4. **Prepare** short knowledge level cooperative lessons.
5. Conduct WRAP-UP ACTIVITIES at the end of each cooperative lesson.
6. Conduct informal and formal OBSERVATIONS.
7. Lead TRANSITION and ENERGIZER activities.
8. **Review** class Standards.

WEEK 2, Day 1

<u>Prepare a short knowledge level cooperative lesson for today with both social skills and academic objectives.</u>

1. Begin day or class period with an **Opening** activity: this may be one of the Getting Acquainted or Transition activities outlined in the book.

2. Review the responsibilities of the **Group Members**. Ask students to demonstrate what each one might look like. Draw some pictures for younger students.

3. Review responsibilities of **Facilitator as Monitor.**

4. **Group** students according to your plan. Appoint a Facilitator as Monitor for each group.

5. Conduct your lesson. Your **Wrap-Up** today could be a verbal one asking each student to share one thing they learned in their group activity.

6. During the individual cooperative group work, informally observe how each person is performing their assigned responsibilities, including group members.

7. Provide the class with general comments about your informal observations; if you noticed some areas that really need work, tell the students you'll be concentrating on those area during the next few days.

Appendix II: Sample Implementation Schedule

8. Use the Lesson Analysis Form to analyze each of your cooperative lessons.

Week 2, Day 2

Repeat Day 1, with different academic material, of course.

Week 2, Day 3

1. Opening/Transition Activity.

2. Explain **Beginning Recorder** role. This student completes the written work that the group will hand in to the teacher.

3. **Explain** to your students that you'll be conducting **formal observations** during their group work beginning today. That means that you'll sit or stand outside each group during a few minutes of their group meeting and you will be counting how many times group members demonstrate specific behaviors.

   Today you'll be observing students "Getting attention of the listener before speaking." It'll be a *group observation* so you'll report how many times you observed this behavior in the group without regard to the individual members.

3. Assign groups and conduct the lesson. Don't forget a Wrap-Up.

4. Transitions and energizers should be conducted during the day, every day now.

Week 2, Day 4

Basically, repeat Day 3, with different academic material.

Today, tell students you'll be observing how often the "Speaker gets the attention of the intended listener(s) before beginning to speak" as well as how often each "Listener" looks at the speaker."

265

> **Week 2, Day 5**

1. Opening Activity

2. **Review** the class Standards and Group Member responsibilities. Conduct this session by asking students what they are rather than telling them.

3. **Group** students in pairs or triads and appoint a Facilitator and Recorder for each group.

4. Select one of the Group Member responsibilities to observe today.

5. Conduct a Wrap-Up.

6. Don't forget to do some Transitions and Energizers today.

> **WEEK 3**

This week you will:

1. Develop **longer cooperative learning lessons**, lasting from one class period to the full week. Lessons will formally **integrate both social and academic skills objectives.**

2. Teach **"Claiming own thoughts, feelings, ideas"**.

3. Make **formal observations**.

4. Discuss and observe **"on-task" behavior.**

   This week your cooperative lessons may begin lasting for the full class period or longer -though no longer than one week, for now. This means that students will remain in the same group for the duration of the assignment whether that's one day or the full week.

Appendix II: Sample Implementation Schedule

Week 3, Day 1

1. Opening Activity (Transition for departmentalized schedules)

2. Teach **"Claiming your own thoughts, ideas, feelings and opinions."** tell students this means they begin their sentences with "**I** think/**my** idea is/**I** feel, etc." (see Chapter 3.)

2. Group students, assign roles, conduct lesson.

3. **Observe** "Claiming own thoughts, ideas, feelings and opinions." Again, conduct a <u>group</u> observation without regard to individual students.

4. Don't forget the Wrap-Up.

5. Transitions and Energizers during the day.

Week 3, Day 2

Repeat Day 1.

Week 3, Day 3

1. Opening/Transition activity

2. Cooperative Lesson - observe "Claiming own thoughts, ideas, feelings." Tell students that you'll be observing their use of these skills.

3. Transitions and/or energizers during day, as appropriate.

Week 3, Day 4

1. Opening or Transition Activity - A getting acquainted activity could be used..

2. Conduct Cooperative Lesson — Observe a class standard, one of the Group Member's responsibilities or one of the social skills previously taught.

3. Transitions and Energizers during day, as appropriate.

Week 3, Day 5

1. Opening activity.

2. Review group members' responsibilities. Be sure students understand each one.

3. If you have not previously discussed what **"on-task"** behavior means, discuss it today and tell students you'll be conducting a group observation of "on-task" behavior.

4. Conduct Cooperative Lesson and report back to each group the number of times you observed "on-task" behavior.

5. This is the last day these particular groups will be together. A good Wrap-Up could be: *"What's the best thing that happened in our group this week?"*

6. Transitions and Energizers during day.

WEEK 4

This week you will:

1. Teach **Praising**.
2. **Review** social skills previously taught.
3. Teach **"Clarifying by asking questions."**
4. Conduct **individual observations**.
5. Group students for a **week-long academic unit**.

Week 4, Day 1

1. Opening Activity.

2. Teach PRAISING - begin by asking students if they know what a compliment is. Ask for examples. Explain that praise is similar to compliments - the difference is that praise is for something very specific a person has done. Have students brainstorm some "praising" statements and write them on the board.

Discuss how people frequently react to receiving a compliments and praise and what an appropriate response to praise might be, i.e. a simple *thank you."* (Chapter 2 outlines in greater detail how to teach praising.)

3. Give students time to practice Praising.

4. Assign students to groups and appoint a Facilitator and Recorder, if appropriate. Tell students you'll be observing Praising in the class (you won't count by group or individual, just the number of times you hear Praising in the classroom during this activity.

5. Transitions and Energizers during day.

Week 4, Day 2

1. Opening or Transition Activity

2. Remind students that yesterday you discussed praising and even observed praising that occurred in the classroom. Today you will assign a praiser in each group. Be sure students understand what they are to do in this role.

   Again, write some "praising" comments on the board to cue students such as: *"Good job," "Nice work," "Great idea," "All right!"* etc.

3. Group students; appoint a **Praiser** and **Facilitator as Monitor** for each group.

4. Continue cooperative lesson from yesterday. Observe "Praising" - be sure you tell students what you're observing.

5. A good Wrap-Up today might be to have each group discuss what went right in their group today.

Week 4, Day 3

1. Opening activity.

2. It's time to teach a new communication skill: **"Clarifying by asking questions."**

   Explain that *"As listeners, we cannot be sure we really understand what the speaker* *really means unless we check it out somehow."* Older students may enjoy the *"words don't mean the same thing to you as they do to me"* activity.

Demonstrate by asking triads of students to decide what's meant by "honest" and "friend" - or any two words you think are more appropriate for your students.

Give the groups two or three minutes to reach their group decision, then ask each group how they defined the two words; point out the differences among the definitions. Also point out that when two people mean different things when they each say the same word, arguments and hurt feelings can result. That's why we need to make sure we really understand what a speaker is saying.

Following the demonstration, explain that *" one of the easiest ways to check our own understanding is to ask questions."* It's important, however, to ask the *right* questions - otherwise, we won't get the information we want. (Chapter 3 gives more ideas for teaching this skill. There are also sample activities for learning how to ask good questions.)

3. Continue cooperative lesson from yesterday - tell students you'll be observing groups for **"Clarifying by asking questions."**

4. Following lesson, report back to each group your observations.

5. Transitions and Energizers during day.

Week 4, Days 4 & 5

Continue cooperative lessons with group roles: Facilitator as Monitor and other roles you've taught.

Observe "Clarifying by asking questions" and/or "Praising" each day.

WEEK 5

THIS WEEK YOU WILL:

1. Review PRAISING
2. Review CLARIFYING BY ASKING QUESTIONS.
3. Review CLAIMING OWN THOUGHTS, FEELINGS, IDEAS, OPINIONS.
4. Teach TIME-KEEPER role
5. Conduct **individual observations** of social skills previously taught.
6. GROUP STUDENTS FOR **WEEK-LONG COOPERATIVE ACADEMIC ACTIVITY.**

Week 5, Day 1

1. Opening or Transition Activity.

2. Ask student to explain what it means to "Claim your own feelings, ideas, thoughts and opinions."

3. Group students (groups of 2 - 4) for cooperative academic lesson. Appoint Facilitator and Beginning Recorder, if appropriate, for each group.

4. Tell students you'll *be conducting individual observations of "Claiming your own thoughts, ideas, feelings, opinions" which means that you'll go to as many groups as possible during the activity and note how many times you observe each student "claiming own ideas, etc."* You'll then stop the group work just long enough to give them a frequency count. (see Chapter 5 for how to report observations back to group.)

5. Wrap-Up Activity.

6. Transitions and Energizers during day.

Week 5, Day 2

1. Opening (Transition for departmentalized schedules) or Getting Acquainted activity.

2. Review "Clarifying by asking questions" by asking students what this means.

3. Groups continue lesson. Rotate roles from yesterday.

4. Tell students that today you'll be conducting individual observations of "Clarifying by asking questions." Report back to group immediately following your observation.

5. Wrap-Up activity.

6. Transitions and Energizers during day.

Week 5, Day 3

1. Opening or Transition

2. Review Praising.

3. Teach role of Time-Keeper. (see Chapter 5)

4. Groups convene for lesson. Rotate roles and appoint a Time-Keeper for each group.

5. Conduct individual observations of Praising.

6. Wrap-Up

7. Transitions and Energizers during day.

Week 5, Day 4

1. Opening or Transition

2. Explain that today you'll appoint a Praiser for each group. That doesn't mean the other group members should stop praising, it just means that praising is one student's specific responsibility.

3. Groups continue lesson. Rotate roles from yesterday. For groups of two or three students, the Facilitator can also be the Praiser.

Appendix II: Sample Implementation Schedule

4. Tell students you'll be conducting individual observations of "on-task" behavior.

5. Report back to each group immediately following your observation.

6. Wrap-Up.

7. Transitions and Energizers during day.

Week 5, Day 5

1. Opening

2. Continue lesson; rotate roles, including Praiser.

3. Decide which social skill to observe and inform students.

4. Wrap-Up. Idea: Each group rate itself on "on-task" behavior.

5. Transitions and Energizers.

WEEK 6

This week you will:

1. Conduct STUDENT SETTING STANDARDS session.
2. Teach the **3 C's**.
3. Teach the role of CHECKER.
4. GROUP STUDENTS FOR **WEEK-LONG STUDY** ACTIVITY.

The role of Checker is used only when there are definite right and wrong answers. Activities most appropriate for using this role include studying for spelling, vocabulary, math facts, etc. quizzes.

Grouping your students for the purpose of studying for a quiz on Friday would be an excellent cooperative activity for teaching the Checker role.

Week 6, Day 1

1. Opening

2. Review Class Standards.

3. *Explain that tomorrow, students will have the opportunity to modify or supplement the class Standards. They should begin thinking about what standards they believe would be beneficial for their class.*

4. Introduce role of **Checker**. Explain that this is the person in the group who will have the "key" to the correct answers. (see Chapter 5)

5. Assign new groups; appoint Facilitator as Monitor and Checker; after distributing assignment to Facilitators, provide answer sheet to Checker. As students get the correct answer, they should explain to the group how they arrived at their answer.

6. Don't forget to do a Wrap-Up.

7. Transitions and energizers, as appropriate during day.

Week 6, Day 2

1. Opening

2. Conduct Student Setting Standards Session (Chapter 5)

3. Wrap-Up for session: WHIP — *"How I feel about being involved in setting standards?"*

4. Groups continue study. Rotate roles.

5. Informal observtion of Checkers.

6. Wrap-Up

7. Transitions and Energizers

Appendix II: Sample Implementation Schedule

Week 6, Day 3

1. Opening (or Transition)

2. Teach the "3 C's: Part 1 — Being Clear." (see Chapter 3)

3. Cooperative study groups.

4. Informal observation of "being clear."

5. Wrap-Up

6. Transitions and Energizers

Week 6, Day 4

1. Opening

2. Teach "3C's: Part 2 — Being Concise" (see Chapter 3)

3. Cooperative study groups.

4. Informal observation of "being concise."

Don't forget "Wrap-Ups," "Transitions," and "Energizers."

Week 6, Day 5

1. Opening: Focus Worksheet (see Sample Activities, Chapter 2)

2. Teach the "3 C's: Part 3 — Being Complete" (see Chapter 3)

3. Cooperative groups; rotate roles.

4. Informal observation of "being complete."

5. Wrap-Up

6. Quiz

7. Transitions and Energizers.

Appendix III

SAMPLE LESSON PLANS

&

ACADEMIC ACTIVITIES

SAMPLE LESSON PLANS

The following lesson plans were developed individually and in cooperative groups by workshop and class participants.

| DATE(S) | Begining of School | TIME(S) | 20 minutes | CLASS/SUBJECT | K-1; Colors |

ACADEMIC OBJECTIVE Relate correct color to ice cream flavor. Each group will identify their ice cream choices for a graph—identifying appropriate color for flavor.

SOCIAL SKILLS OBJECTIVE Learning other students' names; sharing materials.

MATERIALS Large class graph with cones in place, prepared paper ice cream scoops to be colored, crayons, scissors, and glue stick.

ROOM ARRANGEMENT Groups sit on floor

GROUP SIZE 3   **GROUPING PATTERN** Random Selection - "Count-off" by teacher

GROUP ROLES None

GRADE/REWARD Praise and ice cream sticker at completion.

STUDENT OBSERVATION None

LESSON ACTIVITY

1. Teacher and aide will model introducing self and favorite flavor of ice cream: "I am Betty and I like chocolate."
2. Teacher will then count off three students and direct them to their working space where materials will be available.
3. Students will tell each other their names and favorite ice cream flavors.
4. Students will color their "ice cream cones" and decide who will introduce whom.
5. Teacher will act as time-keeper.
6. Each triad of students will introduce each other by name and favorite ice cream flavor.
7. Students will then place their "scoops" on the graph.

WRAP-UP Following all introductions, teacher will lead a discussion about the graph and working together. Stickers will be distributed.

TEACHER OBSERVATION General observation of sharing materials behavior.

DEVELOPED BY: Linda Marschall; Erma Johnson; Stella Winckler; April Nichols; Barbara Corrillo; Suzanna Hogan; Deanne Zysomski; and Sara Hoefer.

The Nurturing Classroom

| DATE | | TIME | 30 minutes | | CLASS/SUBJECT | K - Math |

ACADEMIC OBJECTIVE 1. Students will form number sentences with sums to six using concrete objects.
  2. Students will copy number sentences on paper.

Social Skills Objective Giving and receiving compliments.

Materials *For each two students -*
  1. Ziploc bag containing 15 tiles marked with numerals
     0, 1, 1, 2, 2, 3, 3, 4, 4, 5, 5, 6, 6, +, =.
  2. One pencil
  3. One worksheet.

```
┌─────────────────────────────────────┐
│                    Team Members:    │
│                    _____  │
│  □  □  □  □  □     _____  │
│                                     │
│  △△ + △  =  ____                    │
│       △△                            │
│                                     │
├─────────────────────────────────────┤
│                    Team Members:    │
│                    _____  │
│  □  □  □  □  □     _____  │
│                                     │
│  △  +  △△  =  ____                  │
│  △△    △                            │
│  __  __  __    __      __           │
└─────────────────────────────────────┘
```

ROOM ARRANGEMENT Tables arranged to enable each pair of students to sit side by side.

Group Size 2   **Grouping Pattern** Teacher selection

Group Roles Member

Grade/Reward Each group, having completed the task, will receive two stickers. Oe sticker will be placed on each half of the worksheet. The worksheet will be cut in half and each team member will receive one half to take home.

Student Observation None

Lesson Activity Seat students in groups of 2. Assign each group the following tasks:

Appendix III: Sample Lesson Plans & Academic Activities

1. Write your names under the "Team Member" headings.
2. Decide between yourselves who will do each task.
3. One member will, after looking at the picture: Δ Δ = Δ Δ Δ = ___, place the correct tiles above the number sentence "2 + 3 = 5". The second member of the group will then write, on the worksheet, the sentence which was formed with the tiles.
4. Roles should be reversed for the second number sentence.

Wrap-Up Group discussion about the task with volunteers doing more sample sentences on the chalk board. OR WHIP: *"One way I helped my group."*

Teacher Observation Whole class observation for participation.

Developed by: Yvonne Grimm

DATE(S)   **TIME(S)** 15 minutes per day   **CLASS/SUBJECT** 1 - 3; P.E.

ACADEMIC OBJECTIVE Gain ability to perform sit-ups.

SOCIAL SKILLS OBJECTIVE Practice group roles of Recorder and Facilitator.

MATERIALS Watch; One 3 x 5 index card for each student.

ROOM ARRANGEMENT Floor space for students

GROUP SIZE 3   **GROUPING PATTERN** Self-Select

GROUP ROLES Facilitator/Praiser; Recorder; Time-Keeper

GRADE/REWARD Certificates or Ribbons at end of week.

STUDENT OBSERVATION None

LESSON ACTIVITY This lesson takes place over the course of one week Students are to do as many sit-ups as they can in the allocated time each day: Day 1 = 30 seconds; Day 2 = 60 seconds; Day 3 = 90 seconds; Day 4 = 120 seconds; Day 5 = 150 seconds.
- The "Facilitator" assures each student actually does sit-ups and praises effort and achievement.
- The "Recorder" writes each student's number of sit-ups on the student's index card each day.

The Nurturing Classroom

- The Time-Keeper keeps time for the group.
- At the end of the week, total the number of sit-ups for each student.
- Each student who was able to do progressively more sit-ups (even one more) each day receives a reward.

WRAP-UP WHIP each day - "how I helped my team today...."
Class Disscussion about the value of physical fitness.

TEACHER OBSERVATION Two types of observation should occur: First, assure the proper manner in which to do sit-ups, thereby, securing each child's physical safety. Second, observe praising and other helpful behaviors.

Developed by: Connie White

DATE(S) **TIME(S)** 10 - 20 minutes per day for several weeks **CLASS/SUBJECT** 1 - 3 Horticulture

ACADEMIC OBJECTIVE Gain knowledge of how vegetables grow.

SOCIAL SKILLS OBJECTIVE Contributing to group product

MATERIALS Seeds; Small plot of land; Garden tools (hoe, shovel); Hose or Watering Pots; Charts

ROOM ARRANGEMENT N/A

GROUP SIZE 3   **GROUPING PATTERN** Teacher select

GROUP ROLES Recorder; Facilitator as Monitor; Praiser (Roles to rotate within groups)

GRADE/REWARD Intrinsic -- Eating vegetables

STUDENT OBSERVATION None

LESSON ACTIVITY
1. Introduction to plant unit.
2. Discussion about specific plants that will be grown and how to plant and care for the seeds, such as depth of row, watering, weeding, etc.
3. Each group is assigned specific seeds with discussion about group's responsibilities: a. Dig row in which to plant seeds.
   b. Plant seeds and record data on chart: when planted, depth
   c. Must water and weed regularly.
   d. Must chart days and time when watered and weeded.

Appendix III: Sample Lesson Plans & Academic Activities

      e. Chart progress of growth of plants.
    4. Plants are to be harvested and eaten at appropriate time.

| WRAP-UP | Weekly discussions about how each group's plants are progressing.

| TEACHER OBSERVATION | Observe Praising and rotation of roles within groups.

Developed by: Connie White

| DATE(S) | | TIME(S) | 15 - 20 Minutes | CLASS/SUBJECT | 1 - 3: Vocabulary

| ACADEMIC OBJECTIVE | To learn weekly vocabulary words.

| SOCIAL SKILLS OBJECTIVE | To practice praising.

| MATERIALS | 3 x 5 Index cards, each with one vocabulary word and meaning written on it. One set for each group.

| ROOM ARRANGEMENT | Desks or tables arranged for groups of 3.

| GROUP SIZE | 3 | GROUPING PATTERN | Teacher selects based on previous performance; heterogeneous groups; written on wall chart.

| GROUP ROLES | Facilitator as Monitor; Time-Keeper; Praiser

| GRADE/REWARD | Stickers for groups with the most members standing after "vocabulary bee."

| STUDENT OBSERVATION | None

| LESSON ACTIVITY | **Part I.** Groups meet in assigned places to study words.
    1. Facilitator holds cards with word and definition.
    2. Beginning on his/her right, Facilitator quizzes each member.
    3. If respondent is wrong, Facilitator provides correct answer.
    4. Practice continues for 15 minutes. Roles of Facilitator rotates each 5 minutes. Time-Keeper keeps time.
  Part II. Class have "vocabulary bee" between groups. Groups stand together around room. Teacher asks vocabulary words. If student is incorrect, he/she sits down. At the end of specified time, e.g. 10 minutes, OR specified number of rounds, e.g., three times around the room, the groups who have the most members left standing receive stickers for each group member.

The Nurturing Classroom

WRAP-UP Group rates themselves "thumbs up" or "thumbs down" on how well they worked together.

TEACHER OBSERVATION Teacher observes praising by group and provides feedback between study session and "vocabulary bee."

NOTE: Can be adapted to spelling words or Dolch word list.

DEVELOPED BY: Connie White

DATE(S)   **TIME(S)** (50 minutes)   **CLASS/SUBJECT** Grade 3; Language Arts

ACADEMIC OBJECTIVE The Learner will correctly match 7 out of 8 objects with the object's name.

SOCIAL SKILLS OBJECTIVE To work cooperatively in pairs, i.e. sharing dictionary, recording responses

MATERIALS Ditto sheet and dictionary for each pair.

Ditto sheet is entitled: "Dictionary Object Match Game" and has a space for the date and each student's name.

Visually interesting collection of 8 objects, e.g. mortar and pestle; trumpet and mute; large quartz crystal, picture of a loon; awl; rattan basket, placed on a table in the room.

The objects are listed by name with a blank space on the left for student to write identifying letter and a space on the right side to write in the definition. Example:

```
_____ trumpet _____
_____ loon _____
_____ quartz crystal _____
_____ awl _____
```

ROOM ARRANGEMENT Desks side by side or small tables

GROUP SIZE 2   **GROUPING PATTERN** Random, student select

GROUP ROLES Alternating Recorder

GRADE/REWARD Smelly Stickers for each person where group scores 7 of 8 correct

Appendix III: Sample Lesson Plans & Academic Activities

| STUDENT OBSERVATION | None

| LESSON ACTIVITY | (**Important**: Students have already been introduced to dictionary work and have completed individual worksheet requiring them to look up five words and write each word's definition. Set up materials during recess.)

1. Each item on the table has a tag with a letter on it.

2. Teacher explains that students are to work with one partner and are to match the word on the worksheet with the appropriate object on the table. They must write in the identifying letter on the object's tag.

3. Students will then look the word up in the dictionary and write its definition in the correct space.

4. Teacher: models the process with the first word;
   instructs students to select a partner;
   instructs students to take turns recording the responses.
   explains he or she will be observing "sharing recording and dictionary search"

5. Allow 20 - 30 minutes for actual activity.

6. Following activity: Teacher reports observation. Then provides correct responses; students self-correct responses.

| WRAP-UP | Each pair states one benefit from working as a cooperative pair.

| TEACHER OBSERVATION | Sharing dictionary search and alternating recording responsbility

| DEVELOPED BY: Daniel Konigsberg |

| DATE(S) | | TIME(S) | 15 minutes | CLASS/SUBJECT | 3 - Adult; Group Cooperation

| ACADEMIC OBJECTIVE | Thinking skills practice; Brainstorming & Classifying

| SOCIAL SKILLS OBJECTIVE | Create an awareness that as a resource, a group is often more powerful than an individual working alone.

| MATERIALS | Large sheet butcher paper; felt pens, pens or pencils; binder paper

The Nurturing Classroom

ROOM ARRANGEMENT — Open floor space, tables, or desk arrangement for 5 - 6 groups.

GROUP SIZE 4 - 6   **GROUPING PATTERN** Random by Birthday Line

GROUP ROLES — Recorder for single assignment; Time-Keeper; Facilitator as Monitor; Praiser

GRADE/REWARD — Tangible reward (pencils, gum, stickers) or bonus points for group with the most material/information at the end of task.

STUDENT OBSERVATION — None

LESSON ACTIVITY — Student Activities - Task: How many ways do we work in groups in our lives?

Step 1 - Explain "groups," elicit three to four examples; Model the information

Step 2 - Individuals make a list of all the groups they have worked in since their earliest memory.

Step 3 - Meet in randomly selected groups.
Pool lists, add new information, classify information (e.g. do these group activities fall into certain categories such as family, sports, school, etc.)? Recorder writes lists and categories on butcher for all to see.

Step 4 - Facilitator posts butcher paper on front wall for entire class to see.

WRAP-UP — WHIP - *"What I learned about cooperating in this activity is....."* OR *"During this cooperative activity, I experienced............."*

TEACHER OBSERVATION — Participation, i.e. contributing ideas

** Spin-Offs from this activity:
1. Discussion of value of cooperation.
2. Watch newspaper, TV, and daily activities for examples of cooperation.
3. Writing: Write one page on the best/worst/funniest/weirdest group experience I've ever had.

DEVELOPED BY: Dick Bevacqua; Millie Pease; Carol Richwine; Carol Treu

---

DATE(S)   **TIME(S)** (45 minutes)   **CLASS/SUBJECT** 4th Grade - Language

ACADEMIC OBJECTIVE — Write Haiku Poetry

Appendix III: Sample Lesson Plans & Academic Activities

SOCIAL SKILLS OBJECTIVE — Practice claiming own ideas & sharing ideas

MATERIALS — 1 Teacher-prepared idea card per group with topics such as spring, summer, snow, etc.
1 sheet of binder paper and pencil per student
1 dictionary per group

ROOM ARRANGEMENT — Desks clustered into groups of 3

GROUP SIZE 3   **GROUPING PATTERN** X

GROUP ROLES — Facilitator as Monitor; Time-Keeper

GRADE/REWARD — Library or Office Display of Haikus

STUDENT OBSERVATION — None

LESSON ACTIVITY

1. The teacher will define Haiku (A form of Japanese poetry, usually about nature, that has three lines):
   - the first line has five syllables
   - the second line has seven syllables
   - the third line has five syllables
   - rhyming is not a factor

2. The teacher will model a number of Haikus by writing them on the chalkboard leaving "5-7-5" noted on the left side as a reminder of the required syllables. Example.....

   <u>*SNOW*</u>
   5   White, peaceful, pretty
   7   Cold, wintery, fun, outside
   5   Ski, sled, snowman, brrr!

3. Check for understanding

4. Each group will then write three Haikus with each group member being responsible for one line of each Haiku.

5. The Facilitator for each group will get an idea card for the group, e.g., "spring."

6. Each group member will then select a topic related to spring such as "flowers", write the title and first poetry line.

7. The papers will then be exchanged for the second line and again exchanged for the third line — each group member will have written one line for each Haiku.

The Nurturing Classroom

WRAP-UP Oral or Written group discussion about "which Haiku written by our group do I like best and why?"

TEACHER OBSERVATION Rotate among groups noting individual students sharing ideas and claiming their own idea.

REVERSE SIDE OF LESSON PLAN

GROUPING PATTERN Heterogeneous grouping with one high achiever, one mid-range and one low achiever per group. Preselected groups will be listed on chalkboard.

DEVELOPED BY: Teresa Brown

DATE(S)   **TIME(S)** 10 - 15 Minutes   **CLASS/SUBJECT** 4 - 5; Math

ACADEMIC OBJECTIVE Students will practice and improve math-fact recall by using numbers and mathematical operations to achieve a given numerical solution.

SOCIAL SKILLS OBJECTIVE To improve and practice praising group contributions.

MATERIALS "Krypto Cards" Numbers 1 - 25 on cards (Available from Creative Publications); Paper and pencil for each recorder.

ROOM ARRANGEMENT Desk Clusters or students in groups on floor.

GROUP SIZE 5   **GROUPING PATTERN** √

GROUP ROLES Recorder, Time-Keeper, Praiser praises praising

GRADE/REWARD Bonus points towards earned "free time"

STUDENT OBSERVATION None

LESSON ACTIVITY

1. Teacher selects one student to draw one "Krypto Card" from the stack. This is the "answer" that all groups will try to arrive at.

2. Another student draws 5 Kryptocards from the stack (5 more numbers).

3. These six numbers will be used for all groups. All 5 numbers must be used with any or all of the mathematical operations in order to arrive at the given solution.

4. All members of each group must be able to understand and give solution to class

5. At the end of the allotted time, the teacher randomly calls on a member from each group to report their solution.

6. Teacher then gives a full class report on his or her observations.

| WRAP-UP | Each group discusses one new thing each member learned from the activity.

| TEACHER OBSERVATION | Full Class Praising — report at end of activity

Reverse Side of Lesson Plan

| GROUPING PATTERN | Random with teacher-selected criteria

Example: Each group must have the following represented:
- √ boy
- √ girl
- √ someone wearing blue
- √ someone who walks to school
- √ someone who has attended this school fewer than three years

| DEVELOPED BY: Krista Sievers-O'Connor; Carol Edwards; Jim McElroy; Sue Storc; Shirley Banellis; Edith Smith; Barbare Maire Stewart; Janette Witte.

| DATE(S) | | TIME(S) | 1 1/4 hours | CLASS/SUBJECT | Grades 4 - 8; READING/MATH

| ACADEMIC OBJECTIVE | Review geometric shapes and transfer written descriptions to a concrete structure.

| SOCIAL SKILLS OBJECTIVE | Practice roles of group member and praiser

| MATERIALS | 50 straight plastic straws (non-bending);
25 straight pins; and
1 (HBJ bookmark, Level 12) reader for each group.

| ROOM ARRANGEMENT | Floor space for each group |

| GROUP SIZE | 4 | | GROUPING PATTERN | √ |

| GROUP ROLES | Praiser practiced by all; Facilitator as Monitor; Reader |

| GRADE/REWARD | Straw towers will be kept on view all week. Tallest tower will support class flag as week's "mascot." |

| STUDENT OBSERVATION | None |

| LESSON ACTIVITY |

1. Seat students in assigned groups

2. Identified "Reader" in each group reads story on Towers to group while others follow along.

3. Teacher discusses the different geometric shapes seen in story, and draws them quickly on the chalkboard.

4. Facilitator gets materials for groups.

5. Groups given 40 minutes to construct a tower; they may use only materials provided.

6. Highest score given to group who constructs tallest free-standing tower.

7. Teacher gives observation report

| WRAP-UP | 4-question sheet to be completed by each group:

1. What activities did your group members do to cooperate with each other?

2. Give your group a score from 1 to 10 on "praising" during the activity.

3. What are the strongest points in your tower?

4. What are the weakest shapes in your tower?

| TEACHER OBSERVATION | Praising by group.

Appendix III: Sample Lesson Plans & Academic Activities

REVERSE SIDE OF LESSON PLAN

GROUPING PATTERN   Heterogeneous - 1 high, 1 low, 2 middle achievers on same task; Use wall chart to identify groups.

DEVELOPED BY: Stephanie Urbanie

DATE(S)   **TIME(S)** 1 class period   **CLASS/SUBJECT** 6 - 8; Social Studies

ACADEMIC OBJECTIVE   Understanding the political connection between Panama and U.S.A.

SOCIAL SKILLS OBJECTIVE   Reaching consensus.

MATERIALS   Pencils & paper; Access to current events bulletin board, maps.

GROUP SIZE   4   **GROUPING PATTERN**   Birthday Line

ROOM ARRANGEMENT   Desks or tables arranged for groups.

GROUP ROLES   Facilitator; Recorder; Time-Keeper; Praiser

GRADE/REWARD   15 bonus points or early dismissal for lunch.

STUDENT OBSERVATION   None

LESSON ACTIVITY   Each group will take one of the following roles: President Reagan, Noriega; Senate; and Duvalier and develop a consensus about the group's character's viewpoint about why the conflict exists.

WRAP-UP   Each group will share with the class their character's thoughts and feelings about this conflict.

TEACHER OBSERVATION   Listening to each other's opinions while reaching consensus.

Follow-up Activity: Form new groups of 4 that include each "character." The new groups must work out an agreeable solution to the problem in Panama.

DEVELOPED BY: Debbie Dee; Gary Stanley; Cathy Parker; Mary Lee Jones, and Anne Percelay.

(**Note: *This is an excellent example of how to use current events in a cooperative activity.*)

The Nurturing Classroom

DATE(S)   **TIME(S)** 1 class period   **CLASS/SUBJECT** Remedial 7th grade Reading

ADADEMIC OBJECTIVE Through a prereading activity, students will relate themes found in the book, *The Red Pony*, to their own lives. (Written by John Steinbeck in 1937.)

SOCIAL SKILLS OBJECTIVE Group Members will practice "claiming and sharing their own thoughts, feelings and experiences.

GROUP SIZE 4   **GROUPING PATTERN** Teacher selection

GROUP ROLES Recorder (group member with first letter of name closest to the letter "R;") Time-Keeper (Name closest to the letter "A.")

LESSON ACTIVITY
1. Write this Statement on board: "The boy in *The Red Pony* begins to realize that grownups are human and that they make honest mistakes."
2. Explain and give examples of what an honest mistake is -- and is not.
3. Ask students for examples.
4. Distribut one work sheet per group.
5. Instruct students that they are to:
   a. give at least four examples of honest mistakes adults make.
   b. give 4 examples of how grown-ups' mistakes make you feel.
6. Check student understanding of task.
7. Allow 5 minutes for activity.

WRAP-UP
1. Group WHIP: Each group identifies one mistake that adults most often make.
2. Individual WHIP around entire class: "How do you feel when an adult makes a mistake?"

Teacher Observation Group observations of "claiming and sharing own feelings, thoughts, and experiences.

DEVELOPED BY: Irene Meehan; Ken Byster; Gail Abbott; Meg Wallach; Sonja Erickson.

Appendix III: Sample Lesson Plans & Academic Activities

| **Date(s)** | | **Time(s)** 20 - 30 minutes | **Class/Subject** H.S. English |

Academic Objective Create derivative words from root words.

Social Skills Objective Increase verbal communication skills.

Materials
1. Lists of derivatives from six root words
2. Root word, suffix and prefix cards to create words.
3. Computer program in which the root word is highlighted when the word is keyed in.

Room Arrangement Clusters of desks or small tables for six groups

Group Size 4   **Grouping Pattern** √

Group Roles Recorder; Time-Keeper

Grade/Reward Intrinsic reward of increasing vocabulary.

Student Observation None

Lesson Activity Instruction has been given on prefixes, suffixes, and root words.

1. Groups of four work together to create as many words as possible using the root, prefix and suffix cue cards.

2. Students must also use the dictionary to check the correctness of their words.

3. At the end of the allocated time, each group's recorder will read the group's words.

Wrap-Up WHIP - "Two new words I learned during this activity were....."

Teacher Observation Individuals giving praise; report given to each group after observation.

REVERSE SIDE OF LESSON PLAN

Grouping Pattern Heterogeneous; teacher selected based on past performance. Groups identified on wall chart.

Developed by: Bob Whitney, Karen Olberg, Charline Ford, Greg Schindel

The Nurturing Classroom

| **Date(s)** | | **Time(s):** 30 minutes | **Class/Subject** | H.S. Life Science |

Academic Objective — Given 15 pictures of animals representing 5 different classes, student will be able to arrange the animals by group in chart form, and list three major characteristics of each class with 87% accuracy (13 out of 15 correct).

Social Skills Objective — Share ideas; consensus decision making

Materials — 3 completed charts for introduction to activity
 For each of eight groups:
 a. envelopes: each will contain 15 pictures of animals representing 5 different classes
 b. White glue or glue stick
 c. Poster board
 d. Fine point felt tip pens

Room Arrangement — 2 - 3 students on each side of one rectangular table

Group Size 4 - 5   **Grouping Pattern** X

Group Roles — Facilitator; Recorder; Time-Keeper; Praiser
(Roles assigned by drawing numbers)

Grade/Reward — *Individual* - 20 points lab assignment (Neatness, accuracy and spelling all count)
Group - 10 points extra credit for cooperation/participation in group

Student Observation — None

Lesson Activity

1. Teacher will review classes of animals, giving reference information. Sample charts from other classes will be presented, along with discussion about quality of charts.

2. In 20 minutes, students are to arrange in chart form the photos of animals by class.

3. Students will then list 3 distinguishing characteristics of each class of animal.

(**Note:** Textbooks may be used for reference. No specific chart format is required - creativity is encouraged.)

Wrap-Up — Each group will share its chart with entire class.

a. Discussion of the distinguishing characteristics each group listed for each animal class.

b. Discuss methods used to facilitate identification of specific traits in physical or behavioral patterns of animals.

c. Briefly ask each group member to describe, in one word, how they personally felt the group worked together.

TEACHER OBSERVATION: Individual observations of sharing ideas; Performance of specific group roles; Group consensus decision making

REVERSE SIDE OF LESSON PLAN

GROUPING PATTERN Preselected groups, including high, middle and low achieving students based on previous quiz scores in the same subject matter. Identify groups on wall chart.

DEVELOPED BY: Betty Hartnett

DATE(S)   **TIME(S)** ONE PERIOD   **CLASS/SUBJECT:** High School -- U.S. History

ACADEMIC OBJECTIVE To learn the products and industry in various States in the U.S.A. This is accomplished by studying one State per week and creating a bulletin board reflecting different aspects of that State.

SOCIAL SKILLS OBJECTIVE Sharing and claiming own ideas

MATERIALS One lined piece of paper per student
6 - 10 rectangular pieces of construction paper (2" x 6") per group
One felt tip marker per student

ROOM ARRANGEMENT Clustered Desks

GROUP SIZE 4   **GROUPING PATTERN** Random using Birthday Line

GROUP ROLES Facilitator as Monitor; Beginning Recorder; Time-Keeper; Praiser (Selected by initial letter of first name)

The Nurturing Classroom

GRADE/REWARD: Group grade; intrinsic reward for having work displayed.

STUDENT OBSERVATION: None

LESSON ACTIVITY:

1. Discuss diversity of industry and products in U.S.A.

2. Introduce "State of the week" as weekly overview of a U.S. state.

3. Motivate interest by explaining that we will be creating part of the bulletin board for this weekly experience *right now* (the product/industry section).

4. Groups spend five minutes listing as many products and industries in "this week's State" as they can think of.

5. Groups report their lists.

6. Eliminate duplications. Each group will then design a label for each product or industry assigned to it, providing an illustration, if possible.

7. The finished labels will be placed on the bulletin board section for that State. (Display will also include a map, other important facts, illustrations, current events, etc.)

WRAP-UP: WHIP......"Did you learn of any product or industry you hadn't thought of before? Other reactions to the group activity?"

TEACHER OBSERVATION: Sharing and claiming own ideas.

DEVELOPED BY: Mathew Metrock

DATE(S): **TIME(S):** One Class Period **CLASS/SUBJECT:** H.S.— Spanish III

ACADEMIC OBJECTIVE: Students will be able to verbally express personal opinions using the conditional and present subjunctive verb tenses correctly.

SOCIAL SKILLS OBJECTIVE: Students will practice verbally expressing personal thoughts, ideas and feelings.

MATERIALS: Written group instructions on chalkboard.
3 x 5 Cards for Wrap-Up activity.

ROOM ARRANGEMENT: Desks in clusters of six.

Appendix III: Sample Lesson Plans & Academic Activities

GROUP SIZE: 6   **GROUPING PATTERN:** X

GROUP ROLES: Advanced Recorder; Praiser; Time-Keeper; Advanced Facilitator
Roles to be assigned by drawing titles from envelope.

GRADE/REWARD: Group Grade

STUDENT OBSERVATION: None

LESSON ACTIVITY: In preceding lessons, students will study Spanish vocabulary necessary to complete this assignment.

Each group will take the parent role in a family. The family has two children: boy, age 18; girl, age 15.

1. The group task is to agree upon a list of five rules by which the teenagers are expected to abide. Group members must also develop a rationale for each rule.

    a. Rules may be made for each teenager or the same rules may apply to both.

2. Discussion must occur in Spanish.

3. 20 minutes will be given to complete this phase of the task.

4. At the end of the allotted time, each group will present its list and the rationale for each rule to the rest of class. The presentation is also to be made in Spanish.

5. Teacher will grade presentation based on list of rules, rationalization for each, and correct use of Spanish.

WRAP-UP: Each student will write on a 3 X 5 card what they thought was the most important element that had to be considered when establishing the rules. Cards will be collected, shuffled, and read aloud to class.

TEACHER OBSERVATION: Individuals within groups expressing own personal thoughts, ideas, and feelings during group discussion.

REVERSE SIDE OF LESSON PLAN

GROUPING: Heterogeneous based on conversational ability (2 high, 2 middle, 2 low performers);

The Nurturing Classroom

Use of colored name tags, one color per group - students' names will be written on name tags prior to class.

DEVELOPED BY: Karen Olberg

DATE(S):   **TIME(S):** (30 minutes)   **CLASS/SUBJECT:** Secondary Special Day Class Science

ACADEMIC OBJECTIVE: Classification

SOCIAL SKILLS OBJECTIVE: Group Participation

MATERIALS: Assortment of objects, e.g. marbles, buttons, coins, pebbles, etc.

ROOM ARRANGEMENT: Clustered desks or tables

GROUP SIZE: 3 - 4   **GROUPING PATTERN:** √

GROUP ROLES: Facilitator as Monitor

GRADE/REWARD: Bonus points for all groups finishing assignment within 15 minute time allotment

STUDENT OBSERVATION: None

LESSON ACTIVITY: Prior instruction on classifying objects has been given. Students have also previously practiced classifying.

1. An assortment of 24 items will be placed in a small box for each group;

2. Facilitator for each group will go to a central area and get one box of items and eight pieces of yarn for his group.

3. Each group will decide how to sort the objects into 3 to 8 categories with at least 3 items in each category.

4. Groups will place a piece of yarn around each category of items.

WRAP-UP:

1. Within each group, students will discuss how each student contributed to the completion of the assignment.

2. Class discussion - Each group will share how and why they sorted the items as they did. For example......One group may place a button, coin, and marble in a category because each one is round; another group might sort them the same way but because each one can be rolled on its side.

TEACHER OBSERVATION: Individual contribution to group product

REVERSE SIDE OF LESSON PLAN

GROUPING PATTERN: Random self-selection within these parameters - each group must include one person who is:
- wearing tennis shoes
- has an odd number birthday
- under 15 years old.

DEVELOPED BY: Sue Short based on a lesson developed by Sue Short, Annette Morrison, Dick Hobson, Geri West and Linda MacDonald.

DATE(S):   **TIME(S):** 20 minutes   **CLASS/SUBJECT** Teacher Inservice

ACADEMIC OBJECTIVE: How to Integrate Literature and Science

SOCIAL SKILLS OBJECTIVE: Participation and sharing of ideas. Consensus decision making.

MATERIALS: *Aesop's Fables* or *Grimm's Fairy Tales*

ROOM ARRANGEMENT: Chairs in circles in separate areas of room.

GROUP SIZE: 4 - 5   **GROUPING PATTERN:** X

GROUP ROLES: Facilitator; recorder (Facilitator is person with curliest hair; Recorder is person with shortest hair)

GADE/REWARD: Intrinsic

STUDENT OBSERVATION: None

LESSON ACTIVITY: Inservice topic is new language arts curriculum and the incorporation of reading (literature) into other subject areas.

1. "Semantic webbing" will be demonstrated with progression to a science or history lesson.

2. Groups will be assigned one fable or tale.

3. The Facilitator will play teacher.

4. Recorder will synopse the proceedings.

5. Other group members will be age-appropriate students for a 10-minute lesson.

6. Group must reach consensus about a grade-appropriate science or history topic that would follow the literature reading.

7. At the end of the allotted time, Facilitator for each group will share name of Fable or Tale and the history or science lesson idea group decided upon.

WRAP-UP: WHIP- Around entire group - "One new idea I gained from this exercise is................."

TEACHER OBSERVATION: Whole group use of consensus decision making. Also, available to assist and answer questions.

REVERSE SIDE OF LESSON PLAN

GROUPING PATTERN: Heterogeneous; Self-Select based on following criteria: group must include 3-4 Members of same grade level plus one "support person."

DEVELOPED BY: Geri West

Appendix III: Sample Lesson Plans & Academic Activities

ACADEMIC ACTIVITIES

The following activities can be modified to use in most subject areas. They can also be easily put into the lesson plan format. The amount of time necessary for each activity varies depending on the content, student skill level and how long you and your students have been involved in Cooperative Learning.

Title: Cooperative Drawing
Grade Level: Preschool - 2
Roles: None
Materials: Construction or drawing paper, crayons or marking pens

Activity:
- Group students in pairs. Each group decides on a subject for their drawing and tells teacher what they will draw.
- Pairs work together for a specified amount of time to complete drawings
- Drawings are hung on bulletin board.

• •

Title: Matching
Grade Level: Preschool - 2
Roles: None
Materials: Two-piece jigsaw puzzles.

Activity: Group students in pairs or triads and assign to workspace. Each group receives the pieces needed to complete one puzzle per student. The pieces are mixed up and placed face-down in front of each group. Students are given a specific amount of time, e.g., five or ten minutes, to turn the pieces face up and assemble the puzzles correctly.

• •

Title: Building the Alphabet
Grade Level: Preschool - 2
Roles: Checker
Materials: Alphabet tiles (or write the alphabet on construction paper squares.)

Activity: Assign students to groups of two or three. Each group is given a complete set of "mixed-up" alphabet letters. Students must arrange the letters in correct order from A to Z within a specified amount of time (five to ten minutes).

At the end of the allocated time, an answer sheet is given to the checker in each group and the group checks its answers for accuracy.

NOTE: Any sequencing task may use this same format.

• •

Title: Murals (This activity can be used after a series of lessons on any subject that lends itself to visual representation, such as: farms; gardens; maps; inventions; botony; and so on.)

GRADE LEVEL: Preschool - 9

ROLES: None

MATERIALS: Varies, depending upon the type of mural the class is to make. Commonly used materials include: butcher paper; poster paint; marking pens; paste; scissors; sample pictures or stencils of objects to be put on mural.

ACTIVITY: Assign students to groups of two to four. Each group is given the assignment to complete one section of the mural. For instance, if the assignment is to make a mural of a farm, one group would complete the background, including the sky, grass, dirt, and trees; another group would make the chickens; another group, the cows; another, the buildings, if any; and so on.

Students need to receive instructions about the relative size of the objects to be included on the mural.

After each group has completed the assignment, the teacher assists the class (as necessary) in attaching all the component parts to the background.

• •

Title: Group Worksheet
Grade Level: 1 - Adult
Roles: Facilitator, Recorder, Timekeeper
Materials: Worksheets

Activity: Assign students to groups of 3 - 5 members each, depending on grade level and lesson objective.
Assign a Facilitator, Recorder, and Timekeeper for each group.

Steps:
1. Distribute worksheets to each student. It is important that each student in a group has the same worksheet, though worksheets may differ between groups.

2. Provide one group answer sheet to each group.

3. Students first work individually on their own worksheets for a specified amount of time.

4. Group members discuss each question one at a time, sharing their individual answers and how they arrived at them. The Facilitator makes certain that each group member has the opportunity to share responses.

5. Group members determine the correct response which the Recorder writes on the clean answer sheet. It's important for the Recorder to read back the response for each question to verify accuracy.

6. Each group member signs the answer sheet to indicate agreement with the responses. The Facilitator then hands in the group's work to the teacher.

• •

Title: Study Groups
Grade Level: 2-Adult
Roles: Checker, Test-Taker, Challenger
Materials: 20 Index cards, numbered 1 - 20; a list of 20 questions with answers. These should be short answer questions with a definite right answer.

Activity: Assign students to groups of three to five, depending on grade level and students; social skills ability Groups may be homogeneous or heterogeneous, depending on the lesson objective.

Three roles are assigned in each group: Checker; Test-Taker; Challenger. These roles are rotated in a clockwise direction after each question.

A specific amount of time is allocated for the study session (10 - 20 minutes works well).

Steps:

1. The index cards are shuffled and placed in a stack face down in the center of the table.

2. The Test-Taker draws a card, states the number, and places it face up on the table.

3. The Checker locates the corresponding number on the question/answer sheet and reads the question.

4. The Test-Taker responds.

5. The Checker asks if there are any challenges. This is asked whether the Test-Taker gave a correct or incorrect response.

6. If there are any challenges, the Challenger sitting closest to the Test-Taker's right side may provide an answer.

7. The Checker then states the correct answer. The person who gave the correct response, the Test-Taker or the Challenger, keeps the numbered index card.

8. If neither the Test-Taker nor the Challenger were correct, the index card is placed at the bottom of the stack.

9. Roles are then rotated one person to the right (clockwise). Study continues until the end of the time.

Hints: 1. Study questions and answers must be clear and concise. There must be a very definite "right" answer. Spelling, vocabulary, math facts and other knowledge level questions are most suited for this activity.

2. To avoid confusion, require students to give the precise answer that is on the answer sheet.

3. When first initiating this activity, write the group roles on index cards. The cards can be rotated clockwise after each question. This helps students remember what role they are.

VARIATION: Include a penalty for incorrect challenges. This helps deter students who simply like to challenge others. When challenger are incorrect, they must place a previously won card back in the stack. This means, that a student may not challenge until he or she has "won" a card.

• •

Title: Writing Assignments
Grade Level: 2-Adult
Roles: Recorder; Optional: Facilitator and/or Timekeeper
Time: 30-45 minutes
Materials: Paper and pencils

Activity: Assign students to groups of two to three.

Assign a topic on which they are to write.

1. Groups should each discuss the assigned topic and decide what they will include in their group paper. Brainstorming may be a useful techniques for the groups to use. A facilitator and timekeeper would be appropriate for the problem solving part of this assignment.

   Discussion about what to include in the paper should only last five to fifteen minutes.

2. Each group should decide how they will approach the writing assignment. Will each person complete a sentence, paragraph, section? Will they work together to write each sentence?

3. No matter what approach the group uses, the recorder will write the final product on one sheet of paper.

4. The actual time for writing the paper will be 15 - 30 minutes.

5. Each group reviews its paper and makes any desired changes or necessary corrections.

6. Each group member signs the finished paper to indicate agreement with the finished product.

7. Paper is handed in to teacher and/or read to class.

• •

Title: Group Testing (Takes longer but students learn a lot more.)
Grade Level: 2 - Adult
Roles: Facilitator, Time-Keeper and Recorder
Time: Depends on the test; Plan a 15 minute test.
Materials: <u>Short</u> Group Test, Text Book and/or other appropriate information; Paper and pencils.

Activity: Assign students to heterogeneous or homogeneous groups of 2 - 5 students each, depending upon your objectives, the content of the test, and the structure in which your students have been working.

This is an open book test and may be used as an study session, or you can give your students bonus points for their performance. It would be appropriate to follow up with an individual test to evaluate mastery of the content material.

Test should be short and simple, especially the first few times students are asked to participate in a group testing situation.

Steps:

1. Distribute a copy of the test to each student.

2. Each group discusses each question and decides what the correct response is. The group Facilitator will help keep the group on task and will also help the group reach a consensus decision for each question.

3. The group's recorder writes the response on a clean copy of the test.
   The Timekeeper should give the group half-time, ten and five minute warnings.

4. The recorder will read the responses a final time to be sure its been written as the group intended.

5. All group members sign the test to indicate agreement with the responses.

6. Tests are submitted to you for grading.

••

Title: Group Research Projects and Reports
Grade Level: 3 - Adult
Roles: Facilitator and Recorder
Materials: Group assignment sheet, reference materials, paper and pencils.

Grading: A single group grade or bonus points.

Activity: Assign students to heterogeneous groups of 3 - 5 members each.
Each student is given an assignment appropriate to his ability level.

Assign a Facilitator and Recorder for each group.

Sample schedule for multi-day assignment:

Day 1: Facilitator reviews assignment with the group to ensure understanding. Each member should be aware of his or her own part in the complete project, the components of the assignment as well as the content and location of various reference materials.

Days 2 and 3: Team members work independently on their respective assignments, gathering information, taking notes and constructing outlines for their own sections.

Day 4: Team members meet and discuss what they have each learned; each member gives a progress report.

Day 5: The group report is written, following the teacher's guidelines. The Facilitator keeps the discussion "on track" and moving; the recorder writes the report. When the report is completed, the recorder will need to read it aloud to the group to verify the content is as the group wants it.

All group members sign the report to indicate their agreement with the finished product.

The *Group Project/Report* is an ideal way to use the strengths of each group member because each student is assigned a part of the task appropriate to skill and ability level; Reference materials at the student's reading and comprehension levels are also provided

Example: The research project focusing on the Westward Movement is assigned. One group member might be assigned to research famous scouts and to make a list of names and their famous deeds. Another member might analyze the economic impact of the Westward Movement on the country. A third student might research the impact of of this movement on the Native American Indian population. One student might even build a model of a calistoga wagon or draw a scene the people might have seen at that time.

Each and every student may make an important contribution to the project.

• •

Title: Forming an Opinion
Grade Level: 4 - Adult
Roles: Facilitator, Recorder, Timekeeper
Time: 1 - 2 hours
Materials: Information sheets, Film (or lecture) about controversial issue relevant to the curriculum or a current event.

Activity:

1. Form heterogeneous groups of 3 - 5 students each; assign a Facilitator, Recorder and Timekeeper for each group.

2. Show film or give lecture.

3. Groups have 10 - 20 minutes to discuss pro's and cons of the issue. Recorder

writes the major points of discussion, noting pro's in one column and cons in another column. Facilitator assures each group member has opportunity to state thoughts and opinions.

4. Another 10 - 20 minutes are provided for students to reach a consensus decision on where their group "stands" on the issue. (It may be helpful to review the problem solving/decision making processes described earlier.)

5. At the end of the time period, the Facilitator of each group reports the group's decision and rationale behind their decision.

If the group has been unable to arrive at a consensus decision, the Facilitator shares that fact and discusses the problems they encountered in their decision making process.

• •

Title: The Great Debate
Grade Level: 4 - Adult
Roles: Facilitator and Recorder (Optional: Timekeeper)
Time: 35 - 50 Minutes
Materials: Information sheets, film or lecture on controversial issue.

Activity: Divide the class in half, forming two debate teams. Each team is assigned a position they will take regarding the issue. For example: providing classes in school about drugs and their effects. One team would support providing such classes regardless of the individual team members' own opinions; the other team would debate against providing such instruction in schools.

Assign a Facilitator and Recorder for each team. A Timekeeper may also be assigned for each team or the teacher may act as Timekeeper.

STEPS:
1. Show the film or deliver an orientation lecture about the issue.

2. Allow 20 - 30 minutes following the film/lecture for the teams to discuss the critical factors involved in their assigned positions and how they will support that position. The team's Recorder writes the key points on the chalkboard, chart paper, or notepaper.

3. Place two chairs facing each other at the front of the room (or in the middle, whichever works best for your classroom setting). All other chairs are placed on the sides of the room.

4. Team members sit together. Teams face each other.

5. *The Great Debate begins!*
   15 to 20 minutes are allowed for the debate. The rules are:

   a. *To speak,* a team member must sit in the chair.

   b. *Teams alternate speakers* with each speaker limited to one (1) minute. The teacher may choose to be the Timekeeper OR assign a student to be Timekeeper <u>before</u> assigning teams.

   c. Each team member *must* speak during the debate.

   d. A team member *may speak more than one time* but only for one minute at a time.

   e. There *must always be a team member* in each debate chair.

   f. *To get into the debate chair, the team member must walk up to the person sitting in the chair and tap him on his shoulder.* The present speaker may continue speaking for the rest of his minute, if he wants, then moves out of the chair to allow the other team member to be seated.

   g. If more than one team member wants to take the debate chair at the same time, the *team Facilitator establishes a waiting line.*

   h. It is part of the Facilitator's job to make sure *each team member sits in the debate chair and contributes at least once during the debate.*

Following The Great Debate, the ***Wrap-Up*** will be a general discussion about the strongest points presented on each side.

SOURCES:

Matching; Murals; Building The Alphabet: Jacquie

Forming An Opinion: Peggy & Jacquie

Cooperative Drawing; Study Groups; Writing Assignments; Group Testing; Group Research and Project Reports; The Great Debate; Group Worksheet: Original Source Unknown. Jacquie and Peggy have adapted some of these from different experiences — each of these activities seemed ideal as a cooperative group learning activity.

The Nurturing Classroom

The following pages describe a cooperative testing activity at the Community College level. It was developed and implemented by Judith Hummer who was teaching an introductory class on microcomputers.

This example may easily be adapted for use at the high school level.

Date: Mid-Term   **Time**: 3 - 4 hours   **Class/Subject**: Junior High School - Adult Introduction to Microcomputers Exam

ACADEMIC OBJECTIVE: Assess students' knowledge and ability to use computer and word processor.

SOCIAL SKILLS OBJECTIVE: Consensus decision making; sharing ideas; para phrasing

MATERIALS: Computers, Printers and Word Processing Program.

ROOM ARRANGEMENT: Computer Lab

GROUP SIZE: 3   **GROUPING PATTERN**: Teacher-Selected; one high, one mid-range and one low performing student per group. (Groups listed on chart paper)

GROUP ROLES: Advanced Facilitator and Recorder

GRADE/REWARD: Group Grade

WORK COMPLETED BEFORE TEST: Lecture and lab on word processor. Home-work that required each student to demonstrate all the capabilities of the word processor as well as each student's ability to use the computer.

PURPOSE OF TEST:

- To observe each student's ability with the computer and word processor.

- To encourage students to work together to solve problems.

- To demonstrate a more natural working environment with the computer, rather than the usually quiet lab with lots of help available from aides.

- To demonstrate expanded uses of the word processor. In this instance, the word processor will be used for creative writing.

• Mid-Term Grade

TEST: A Writing Project

INSTRUCTIONS GIVEN AT CLASS MEETING PRIOR TO EXAM:
Remind students there will be an exam at the next class meeting. They need to know how to use the word processor. Additionally, they are to:

1. Bring a hat.
2. Dress like a writer.
3. Decide what kind of writer to be.
4. Choose a pseudonym.

Students will probably ask questions; simply tell them it will be fun and don't tell them anything more.

TEST DAY:

Arrive dressed like a writer (whatever that means to *you*) - but give careful consideration to your attire. Your students will take their cues from you at the beginning of this exercise. If you dress too conservatively, it will set the wrong tone. If you dress relaxed, your students will relax. Remember - they're probably nervous; you have all the information and they don't know what's going on.

Take time to look at how everyone is dressed and let them know you noticed. Comment on the "distinguished group of writers" present. This should help to relax them a bit.

EXPLAIN THE PROJECT:

The project is a creative writing assignment; each class member is responsible for writing a specific part of it. The specific mode is up to you but it should be something each student will be comfortable with. Some possibilities include:

EXAMPLE #1:

Writing a book. Each student writes a chapter. Chapters can range in length from a couple of paragraphs to more than a page. The length depends as much on the student's typing ability as it does on his ability to use the computer and word processor. There are also time constraints - each student will have a limited amount of time to use the computer.

EXAMPLE #2:

A series of letters written to "Dear Abby" which span a character's lifetime. Each letter is dated so that they can be printed in sequential order.

EXAMPLE #3:

    <u>Writing a diary for a character</u>. Each entry would be dated chronologically.

EXAMPLE #4:

    <u>Writing a series of lies</u> told by a member of the Liar's Club. These would be written on April Fool's Day year after year.

Notice that each of these examples requires a single character to be the focal point. That makes the class assignment easier and creates continuity among aall individual student's work.

EXPLAIN THE PROJECT:

"This is a cooperative test — you are all in it together and need each other to complete the assignment."

Emphasize the fact they their writing ability is not important; writing skills are not being tested. Ability to use the computer and word processing program are being tested.

Discuss the specific project on which they will be working (the following sample is a book) and the fact that their individual parts will be put together to form a whole. It's okay if the story digresses or rambles, passing from one topic to another. The project can be a collection of vignettes or sketches. What will tie the whole thing together is the character who is developed.

CHARACTER DEVELOPMENT:
Character development is the first part of the exam.

1. The first step will be to decide upon the character's age and sex. This will be accomplished using consensus decision making with the entire class.

2. Instruct students to assemble in premarked locations according to group.

   3. Each group will develop particular aspects of the character's life:

Group 1: Physical description; habits and unusual aspects of character's personality and lifestyle.

Group 2: Occupation and hobbies; major events in character's life at different ages.

Group 3: Family and friends, i.e., central cast of characters.

Group 4: Where character has lived and at what ages; where character lives now; schools attended; organizations character belongs to; where he or she vacations.

(Note: Adjust these assignments to fit your population of students.)

4. Groups will have 15 minutes to complete thia section of the project. (teacher acts as time-keeper).

5. At the end of the time, each group's recorder writes their information on the chalkboard or chart paper to share with rest of class.

6. Class then: - gives the character a name;
   - entitles the book;
   - determines page headings - each student will be responsible for one page heading which will describe something about the character and/or events in the character's life.

THE TEST:
(You will have to predetermine the amount of computer time that will be available for each student.)

Students will now write an individual page about the character based upon the information determined in the group session.

One student needs to be responsible for creating a title page, table of contents, and overseeing the merging of the sections/stories. This could be a student who is simply intimidated by "creative writing" or a particularly fast student.

1. Advise students of the maximum number of minutes available for each student to individually work on a computer. Since the project must be completed by the end of the class period, no time extensions are possible. Also, each student must time himself.

2. Inform students that everyone will stay in class until the project is completed. This will avoid having the faster students complete their sections and leaving, causing other, slower students to feel incompetent. It also avoids having those "worker" students staying alone until the very end, putting things together for the rest. Those who finish early can help others and oversee the completion of the project.

3. Each student's work is to be transferred to the teacher's disk. Saving a file to a

different disk may be a new experience for them, but it's important. When students transfer their completed files to the teachers disk, they need to sign a sheet that stays with their disk. The sheet should identify the student's pseudonym, date of writing, and the name of the file. Students will need to check with each other to avoid duplicate file names.

4. Students will also print out their own sections, write their real names on the paper, and give it to you. This, along with the index to the disk will be your record of who wrote what.

5. Students may use their notes on operating the word processor or another student my offer verbal suggestions and information (the helping student may not touch the keyboard). If a student does help another, she must explain why the student needs to do something as well as what to do.

6. Toward the end of the exam time, when a majority of students have completed their sections, temporarily stop the exam and demonstrate chaining files together for print-out, with continuous pagination, format, and headings. Those who are finished can begin working on this process while the others complete their sections.

THE RESULTS:
You will have:

1. A printed sheet from each student containing the section she wrote signed with her real name.

2. A disk containing each student's file, along with a companion sheet that lists file names, date of file, and student's real name.

3. A print-out of the entire project. The pages should be numbered sequentially, have page headings, and continuous formatiing.

COMMENTS FROM JUDY:

This test works because of the way it is set up. If you asked a group of adults if they'd like to go to a costume party and write a book, most of them would say "no," even if they were intrigued by the idea. But the smiles and jokes and incredible story lines that were created when this test was given attest to its success.

A major part of the success was because the test was cooperative. Everyone was in the same boat and they paddled together. The tone of the test was set in the first 15 minutes. When the teacher is relaxed, students are relaxed. If the teacher explains that writing style or skills will not be graded, amazing things will be written. People who believe they can't write at all suddenly begin writing fabulous stuff.

The costuming and uncertainty before the test adds to the atmosphere. Dressing differently put students "off-guard." They become more creative because they are "not themselves." Students are curious about what will happen and can hardly wait to see what others have written.

Seeing all the parts printed out in one final product is very exciting. There is magic in creation under pressure. The time limit forces decisions to be made about what will be written. Perfectionism is impossible which makes it more realistic.

A lab aide paid my class what I considered to be the highest compliment, "Your students have gone past the mechanics of using the word processor." By concentrating on the creativity of the project, how to do it becomes less important than why to do it.

Observing students during the test provides an extremely accurate picture of how they are doing. It's easy to see if anyone is having problems.

Finally, students learned two new "tricks" during the test: how to transfer a file to a different disk and how to chain files together — there's no reason why a test can't be an opportunity to learn.

Most of all, everyone had fun; there were lots of smiles; and.........the other instructors and students enjoyed the "book."

BONUS:

ORGANIZING FOR SUCCESS WORKSHEET

One of the problems many students have is organizing their assignments and their time.

The following format, developed by Rhoades and McCabe, will help your students learn to think through an assigned task. Through this process, students will learn how to organize their thinking, their time and their assignments for success.

There are six steps:

1. *Define the task.*
2. *Identify today's date.*
3. *Specify the assignment's due date.*
4. *List the requirements, e.g., length of speech/number of pages or words an essay/ sections in a research paper/pages or chapters to be read/number of math problems to be solved/steps in a math problem/etc.*
5. *List the subtasks in order.*
6. *Develop and write a schedule for completing the assignment; specify dates, times and locations for completing the work.*

The **"Organizing for Success"** Worksheet is easy to teach:

- Provide each student with a copy of the blank form, completed sample, and list of steps.

- Explain the sections of the worksheet — this will only take 10 minutes.

- Help your students work through the worksheet with an actual assignment.

- Monitor the student's progress in planning and organizing skills by requiring them to turn in the "Organizing for Success" Worksheet with their assignment.

Completed Sample

TASK Deliver a speech on "Freedom of Speech" **TODAY'S DATE** 11/20/87

REQUIREMENTS

1. DUE 11/29
2. Can use cue cards but may not read speech
3. LENGTH: 5 Minutes
4. May use illustrations

SUBTASKS NEEDED TO COMPLETE ASSIGNMENT

Research "Freedom of Speech"
Make cue cards
Write speech

Practice speech with friend
Draw illustrations
Write outline of main points

ORDER OF SUBTASKS

1. Research subject
2. Outline main points of speech
3. Write speech
4. Draw illustrations
5. Make cue cards
6. Rehearse speech
7. Give speech on 11.29

SCHEDULE FOR COMPLETION

Wed. 11/20 - Research during class period

Th. 11/21 - Research during class

Fri. 11/22 —————————

Sat. 11/23 - Write outline main points, begin writing speech

Sun. 11/24 —————————

Mon. 11/25 - Finish writing speech, draw illustrations after dinner.

Tues. 11/26 - Make cue cards

Wed. 11/27 - Rehearse with Tom, his house, 5:30

Th. 11/28 - Rehearse with Tom, my house, 4:00

Fri. 11/29 - Deliver speech to class.

©1985 Rhoades & McCabe Permission to reprint granted

Organizing for Success Worksheet

Task: _____   Today's Date: _____

_____

Requirements: (Due date, Length, etc.)

1. _____   4. _____

2. _____   5. _____

3. _____   6. _____

Subtasks needed to Complete Assignment:

_____   _____

_____   _____

_____   _____

Order of Subtasks:

1. _____ _____   4. _____

2. _____   5. _____

3. _____   6. _____

Schedule for Completion:

_____   _____

_____   _____

_____   _____

_____   _____

Appendix IV

COOPERATIVE STUDENT STUDY TEAMS

COOPERATIVE TEAM STUDY TECHNIQUES

INTRODUCTION TO STUDENT STUDY TEAMS

The Jigsaw approaches are primarily designed to be used with any narrative material but they can each be adapted to art projects, math and science assignments, and various problem solving lessons.

Team Study Teach Games and Pair 4 Check Help are designed for Level 1, Knowledge material only, that is, material that has a single definite correct answer such as spelling and math.

SUGGESTED USES:

Jigsaw:
    Literature: Development of characters
    Social Sciences, including Psychology, Sociology
    Social Studies
    Specific Aspects of Science

Team Study Teach Games:

Spelling	States and Capitals
Vocabulary	Science Elements
Math Facts	Historical Places, Dates
Punctuation Marks	Parts of Speech
Primary: Shapes	
Colors	
Letters	

Pair 4 Check Help:

Math: four basic functions	Advanced Syntax
Algebra	Geographical Evolution
Geometry	Science

COOPERATIVE EXAM
(Peggy McCabe and Jacquie Rhoades. 1983)

Here's a way to monitor student progress that promotes learning, enhances thinking skills and retention and deters any possible thoughts of cheating.

A cooperative exam or quiz is a group exam; team members must use a consensus decision-making process to decide upon the answer to each question. The answer is written on the response sheet, each member signs the test responses to indicate agreement with the response and each member receives the same number of points for the exam/quiz. We use the score as bonus points as opposed to using the results towards the grade.

STEPS:

1. Rank students high to low based on prior performance in this subject area in the same manner as Team Study Teach Games described on the following pages.

2. Heterogeneously group students in three to five member teams.

3. Tell teams where in the room they are to sit together.

4. Team members decide upon a team name. (You could allow students to make a logo or write their team name on some sort of mobile that can be hung from the ceiling or set on the desk/table.)

5. Administer a pretest on the subject content to be taught.

6. Write the team pretest scores on chalk board or large chart paper on wall.

7. Provide instruction for as many days as needed for lesson.

8. Allow teams to study together each day for 5 - 10 minutes. The Team members' task is to help each other learn the material; no team member is finished "studying" until all members of his or her team know and understand the content.

9. Write scores next to pretest scores.

10. Note highest scoring team and the team with the greatest improvement.

11. Use team scores for rewards and/or bonus points.

12. Give individual quiz to determine mastery of material. If individuals are not performing well, their teams are responsible for helping them learn the material. (If students need additional incentive to help each other, you could average individual scores for each team and give rewards or bonus points for teams that had high averages, e.g. 80% average team score = 15 minutes computer game time or no homework one night).

JIGSAW

The Jigsaw technique is one of the most powerful methods to use when teaching and studying narrative material, such as literature, specific aspects of science, social studies, social sciences, and related areas where concepts rather than specific skills are the objective. Jigsaw may also be used successfully for art and problem solving activities. By using the Jigsaw approach, the teacher can cover large amounts of material in less time with greater learning and retention.

The first jigsaw process that was published (1978) was developed by Elliot Aronson and colleagues at the University of Texas.

In 1980, Dr. Robert Slavin and his colleagues at The Johns Hopkins University, modified Aronson's Jigsaw.

Without a doubt, teachers have been using different forms of the "Jigsaw" approach for many years. For example, as early as 1974 one of the present authors was using forms of this approach and simply called it group collaboration, in other words, "survival" — a way to get more information to college students and workshop participants in less time with less work and time on the student's part. College students historically have initiated study teams, breaking up the reading assignments among group members, having each synopse parts of the texts, then sharing the information and studying together. We should, however, be grateful to both Dr. Aronson and Dr. Slavin for formalizing the process and providing a data base proving the Jigsaw's validity as a learning technique.

Careful attention to certain logistics will enhance the jigsaw experience for your students:

1. <u>Goal or Objective</u> - Informing students of expected outcome (goal or objective) of the jigsaw activity will enhance their learning experience. State your objective clearly, in fact, write it on the board and briefly discuss it with your class.

2. <u>Materials</u> - Each jigsaw team needs materials; the type of materials depends on the jigsaw model you are using and the lesson you are teaching. Whatever materials are used, it's important to continually convey the message that teams are exactly that - TEAMS - and their members must help each other learn the content. Materials needed will be discussed within each model of Jigsaw.

3. <u>Group Size</u> - Three to six members in the group is best. And remember, the less skilled students are in communication and problem solving skills, the smaller the group should be (Chapter 6).

4. <u>Group Membership</u> - Heterogeneous groups almost always work and this type grouping gives students more opportunity to increase thinking paths, thus enhancing higher level thinking skills. Teachers should group students carefully based on variables discussed in Chapter 6. (Also, review Chapter 9)

5. <u>Group Roles</u> - Assign group roles as appropriate for the lesson. Remind students they are always "Group Members." (Chapter 5)

6. <u>Group Member Seating Arrangement</u> - Group members should be able to sit close enough to see and hear each other but not so close as to threaten "personal space" or "territory." (See Chapter 3: Proximity.)

7. <u>Room & Furniture Arrangement</u> - As discussed in an earlier chapter, teachers rarely have the luxury of selecting their own furniture so you must make what you have work; students can sit on the floor,

on counter tops, on chairs in small circles, clustered at the end of a rectangular table, at round tables, at movable desks turned so that four desks are clustered together or in any other arrangement that allows for small group cooperative activities.

8. Required Time - The amount of time required to complete a jigsaw is also dependent upon the type of jigsaw and the lesson content. This will also be discussed within the description of each Jigsaw model.

Jigsaw emphasizes team building activities before and during the activity. It is also one of the most useful approaches to cover massive amounts of material in the shortest possible time because the content to be learned is divided into sections. Students read individual sections which may be entirely different from the parts read by their team-mates. Thus, **each team member becomes valuable to the team as a whole. Students also develop a sense of responsibility for their own learning as well as that of their team-mates.**

ORIGINAL JIGSAW

(The original Jigsaw was developed by Elliot Aronson who is a professor at the University of Santa Cruz. Reference: Aronson, Elliot, et al. *The Jigsaw Classroom*. Beverly Hills: Sage Publications. 1978. What follows is a slightly modified version of the original Jigsaw)

Students are assigned to two groups: a "home" team and an "expert" team. The home team is usually a heterogeneous grouping of 3 - 6 students. Each member of the home team is assigned a specific part of the material to learn. In other words, the entire material is divided into the same number of sections as there are members in the team. (Each section must make sense in and of itself. Depending upon the material, we often find it helpful to provide an introduction or overview of the content which all students read prior to reading their assigned section.) Each home team then has a member responsible for a specific section of the material. After reading their respective sections individually, each home-team member meets with his counterparts from the other teams; this forms the "expert" group. "Expert" groups study their material and together decide how best to teach this to the other members of their "home" team. When each home team member shares his or her information, the group members will have all the information they need to pass the subsequent test.

FOR EXAMPLE: IF YOU WERE STUDYING A UNIT ON ANY foreign country, one member of the team might read a study sheet or chapter about its industry, another about its climate, another member could study the general politics of the country, another could study its geography, and so on. Each home-team member would be assigned a number which would correspond to the section he or she was responsible for learning, for example: #1s = industry; #2s = climate; #3s = politics; #4s = geography.)

MATERIALS: You can develop your own materials assuring that each section is at the appropriate ability level for students (example...if the #1s were high performing readers, # 2 and 3 average performers and the #4s were low performing readers, you would design the reading assignments at each student's reading ability level; the section for number 1's could be more difficult OR it could be greater in quantity than that for the number 4's.

Appendix IV: Cooperative Student Study Teams

TIME REQUIRED: you will have to determine three different amounts of time:
1. the amount of time needed to read the assigned material in home groups;
2. the amount of time the "expert" groups will have to study their sections and determine how to teach their home team members; and
3. the amount of time each student will have to share their part of the information.

The allocated times will vary based on your students' age level and the complexity of the material. On an average, allow about two to three minutes per page to read, two minutes per page to study in the expert groups and one and a half minutes per page to share the information. Always allow just a little less time than your student think they need; this helps students learn to synthesize <u>and</u> keeps them on task.

SEQUENCE:

1. Assign home teams and tell them where in the classroom they should sit together.
2. Distribute individual sections of the material to students within home teams.
3. Students read their section.
4. Assign expert teams to specific locations in the room.
5. Expert teams discuss, study and determine how best to teach their material to the rest of their home team members.
6. Experts return to their home team and teach their section to the other members.
7. General class discussion of the entire material.

SAMPLE SCHEDULE:

Day 1. Assign home teams and distribute reading material. Students read their sections.
Day 2. Expert teams meet to discuss and study their sections.
Day 3. Expert team members return to their home group and teach their unique material to the other members. General class discussion of all material and/or quiz to determine learning.

SOME ALTERNATIVES we use:

1. Have students read material at home.
2. Instead of preparing reading material, assign chapters or parts of chapters to each member.
3. Give each expert team a specific topic and have them research that area in the library.
4. Use Jigsaw for group writing projects with each member responsible for a specific section of the essay.
5. Jigsaw can also be used for other types of activities such as designing and constructing/painting/drawing murals, collages, other art projects; spelling or vocabulary words; math facts.

JIGSAW II

(Developed by Robert Slavin at The Johns Hopkins University. Reference: Slavin, Robert E. U*sing Student Team Learning*: The Johns Hopkins Team Learning Project. Maryland. The Johns Hopkins University. 1980.. What follows is a slightly modified version of Slavin's model)

Jigsaw II, like the original Jigsaw by Aronson, can be used whenever the material to be studied is written in narrative form. It is most beneficial for subjects such as social studies, literature, parts of science and related areas in which the concepts rather than skills are the learning goals.

The basic material for Jigsaw II can be a chapter, story, biography or any other narrative material.

Again, as in the original Jigsaw, students are assigned to two groups: a "home" team and an "expert" team. The home team is usually a heterogeneous grouping of 3 - 6 students. Students all read the same material. However, each member of the "home-team" is given an "Expert Worksheet" which lists specific topics, aspects, or questions for the student to focus on during the reading. After reading the chapter, section, story, etc., students get together with their counterparts from the other "home-teams" study their specific assignments and decide how best to share/teach their topics to the rest of their home-team members. After the allotted time (depending on the material, this might be anywhere between 15 minutes and several class sessions) "Experts" return to their original home-teams and share/teach their information with the rest of their team.

For example: If a story were read, one member of each home team might focus on how the main theme is developed throughout the story, another might focus on the development of the main characters, another on what part the minor characters play in the sequence, etc.

STEPS:

1. Decide what material will be used for the Jigsaw. The quantity can be as much as the teacher would cover in two - three days.

2. Select four or five themes or topics that are central to the reading material.

3. Develop "Expert Worksheets" for each topic or theme. The worksheet will tell students exactly what they should focus on while they are reading the material. The selected themes should recur during the reading rather than be something that is mentioned only once.

4. Determine the student group assignments....these should be as heterogeneous groups of four to five students each and should represent a cross-section on your class.

5. Determine the "expert" group assignments..these may be more homogeneous. Again, rank your students from high to low relative to performance in this subject area in your class.

6. Introduce Jigsaw II to your students. Example......."For the next several weeks we are going to be using a new way of learning. It's called Jigsaw II. In Jigsaw II, you will be working in teams, in fact, you'll be working in two teams: your home team and an "expert" team — it's called "expert" because you will study specific material together and will become an "expert" in that specific material; then, you'll return to your home team and teach that material to the rest of your team members.

7. Tell students which home team they'll be on and designate a spot for them to sit together. They can then select a name for their team.

Appendix IV: Cooperative Student Study Teams

8. Distribute the reading material. Tell students: "The first step in this process is to read the "expert worksheet" I'm about to give you, then read the material looking for the information identified on your "expert worksheet."

9. When all students have finished reading, introduce the "expert" groups. Designate the area where each group should convene. Explain they should now discuss the information and decide how to best share/teach it to their other group members.

10. Following this study session (which could last from 15 minutes to two or three class sessions depending upon the material), the "experts" return to their home teams and take turns sharing/teaching their specific topics.

11. Following the sharing, hold a general class discussion and/or give a quiz.
    (If a quiz is given, the team's score is the average of the individuals' scores.

SEQUENCE of JIGSAW II ACTIVITIES:

1. Assign home teams and distribute reading material. (10 min.)
2. Distribute Expert Worksheets and assign topics. (5 min.)
3. Students read material. (Time varies.)
4. Students meet in "expert" groups. (usually about 30 minutes but can range   between 15 min and two or three sessions.)
5. Students return and teach their info to rest of home group. (Usually about 10 minutes per topic area but ranges between 5 minutes and longer.)
6. Discussion and/or quiz.

Note: We've often found it more efficient to have students read the material at home as part of their homework assignment.

MODIFIED JIGSAW
(Developed by Jacqueline Rhoades & Margaret E. McCabe 1974)

The modified Jigsaw is very similar to Aronson's Original Jigsaw. The difference is that only expert groups are formed. Each expert group studies the material and then teaches that material to the rest of the class as a whole.

The modified Jigsaw is very useful for all narrative-type material as well as for any problem or question that has more than one right answer. For example...a problem may be presented to the class such as: "After reading the events surrounding the Boston Tea Party determine how else the citizens might have resolved their problems" or "After reading Chapter 10 in the Science text (or the Algebra or Geometry text) determine what mnemonic devices you can use to remember the formulas" (Each team could actually be responsible for certain formulas and teach those to the entire class) or "What do you think the three most significant results of [some current news story] will be?" You can even use this process for math problems, each group working on specific problems, then sharing the problem, the answer and the process for reaching that answer with the rest of the class.

This model, like the original Jigsaw, emphasizes group cooperation and social skill development.

Homogeneous or heterogeneous groups may be formed dependent upon the topic to be discussed. As always, groups of 3 - 6 members would be assigned.

STEPS:

1. Determine the assignment and its objective.
2. Assign students to groups.
3. Tell groups where to convene.
4. Allow groups to choose a group name.
5. Assign group roles as appropriate to the lesson.
6. Give a mini-lecture about the material.
7. Give students their assignments (having them read the assignment as homework often works well.)
8. Provide class time for students to study their part of the assignment and prepare to teach it to the rest of the class.
9. Student teams present to class.
10. Class discussion or individual quiz to check mastery.
11. Student rewards.

TEAM STUDY TEACH GAMES

(Adapted from Teams-Games-Tournaments (TGT) developed by Robert Slavin at The Johns Hopkins University 1980)

Team Study Teach Games can be used for any instructional material that has a definite correct answer, such as vocabulary, spelling, math or geography.

A. THERE ARE EIGHT COMPONENTS IN TEAM STUDY TEACH GAMES
1. Pretest
2. Instruction
3. Team Assignments
4. Team Study Games
5. Cooperative Competition
6. Team Score
7. Team Recognition
8. Post-Test

1. Pretest - On the Friday before you begin Team Study Teach Games, administer an individual pretest on the material to be covered. This establishes a base score to use when grouping students.

2 Grouping Study TEAMS - Using the pretest scores, group students in three to five member study teams. The teams should reflect a cross-section of the class as a whole. In other words, the class proportion of boy/girl ration; ethnicity, race and performance on the pretest would be reflected in each team. You will need to emphasize to students that the purpose of the study team is for students to help each other prepare for the games which is when they have an opportunity to earn points for their team, and for the individual post-test.

3. INSTRUCTION - Beginning on Monday, present your lesson in a clear and concise manner. Be sure to explain the objective of the lesson, i.e., what you expect your students to learn. Eliminate any unrelated or irrelevant material. You want students to realize they must pay attention to your presentation because they will be held accountable for the content.

4. Team Study - These are the Team Practice sessions. During this time, team members study the skill or information introduced by the teacher. Students must not only master the material themselves, they are responsible for being sure other team members know the material.

5. COOPERATIVE COMPETITION Games- The Games usually occur on Friday. This is the time each team member has the opportunity to earn points for his or her team. Students compete against other students of like performance on the pretest.

6. Team Score - Following the competition games, calculate the total score for each team and divide by the number of members on the team.

7. TEAM RECOGNITION - Teams can be recognized and rewarded for greatest improvement or highest score with "Good Job" certificates, bonus points, free time, bulletin board announcements, or in any other way that is meaningful to the members of the team.

8. Post-Test - Also on Friday following the cooperative competition games, an individual post-test is administered to determine individual mastery. This is the score that is entered in the grade book. Individuals can also be rewarded for improvement, etc.

B. PREPARING TO USE TEAM STUDY TEACH GAMES

1. MATERIALS - You will need study sheets, an answer key, and index cards numbered from 1 to whatever

The Nurturing Classroom

number of items are on the pretest, for each team. an alternative to making your own worksheets is to number items in prepared texts, such as spelling and math books.

2. ASSIGNING STUDENT TO TEAMS

a. Rank students from high to low based on a pretest of the material to be taught. Divide the ranking into fourths (see Figure 1.)

b. Determine the number of teams you will have by dividing the total class population by 4. If your class population is not evenly divisible by four, you will have one, two or three, five-member teams. Example.....a class of 30 students would have five four-member teams and two five-member teams.

c. Assign students to heterogeneous study teams. Each team should include one high performer, one medium high, one medium low and one low performer as determined by the pretest.

Each team should be a microcosm of the classroom reflecting, as closely as possible, the ratio of boys/girls and race or ethnicity as the class as a whole.

Each team member is assigned a number. Example....low performing students are assigned the number "1", medium high performing students are assigned the number "2," medium low are "3" and high performing students are assigned the number "4." The numbers are important because they identify which students will participate at which competitive tables.

3. ASSIGNING STUDENTS TO COOPERATIVE COMPETITION GAME TABLES - Each Game tables are made up of students of similar academic performance based on the pretest for this particular unit. The numbers previously assigned to students become the numbers of the tournament tables at which they will compete. In other words, all the "1's" will participate at the same tournament table, all the "2's" will compete at another table, and so on.

(Note: The study teams and the competition game table members are reassigned regularly based on post-test scores; the regrouping can be as often as weekly but no less frequent than every six weeks.)

4. Study Team Practice - In their Study Teams, each student is provided with a study sheet representing part of the total material to be studied. Students study their section and teach it to their fellow-team members. They may teach in any way they want, for example, they can draw pictures, use mnemonic devices, use charts, quiz each other ,etc. The important point is that they are responsible for each other knowing all the material. They will later compete with like-ability groups to earn points for their team.

5. Team Score - Team members earn points for their respective teams during the cooperative competition games. Study Teams can be rewarded for highest score or best improvement.

6. Post-Test - Following the competition, individual post-tests are administered to determine individual mastery of lesson content.

C. INTRODUCING TEAM STUDY TEACH GAMES TO YOUR CLASS

You will need:
1. Your lesson plan — be sure lesson objectives are congruent with pretest and study sheets.
2. Separate study sheets for each student.
3. Answer key and numbered index cards for each cooperative competition game table. - one copy for each three students.

Appendix IV: Cooperative Student Study Teams

SUGGESTED SCHEDULE:

Day 1: Friday - Pretest; rank students and decide teams
Day 2: Monday - Tell students what groups they're in; Teach Lesson
Day 3: Tuesday - Teach Lesson, if necessary; Team Study time.
Day 4: Wednesday - Team Study, need study sheets
Day 5: Thursday - Team Study
Day 6: Friday - Cooperative Competition Games; Tally Team Scores; Team Recognition; Individual Post-Test

STEPS:

Step 1: Pretest on the unit you intend to teach - Friday before beginning unit

Step 2: Study Team Assignments, following pretest rank students and determine groups

Step 3: Monday -

1. Explain the concept of teams and teamwork. Tell students this is a new way to learn and it's called Team Study Teach Games. Explain that being on a team will help each student learn more.

2. Explain about the weekly Competitions which is when students earn points for their teams. Be sure to tell them that it is their responsibility to make certain each of their fellow-team members fully knows and understands the material.

3. Give students their team assignments. When making the assignments, it's a good idea to tell and show teams where they will sit together. When they have moved to the area, have them rearrange furniture so they can face each other.

4. Teach the first lesson of a new unit. What you teach must be congruent with the objectives of the games. Eliminate, or at least minimize, irrelevant or unrelated material. Students must get the idea that they are responsible for everything you teach.

Spend as much time as you deem necessary for teaching the unit — one, two, three, or more class periods.

STEP 4: TEAM PRACTICE - MONDAY THROUGH THURSDAY

You need: One copy of Worksheet which contains part of the information for this unit for each student. Each Study Team will possess all the information needed but the information will be divided in sections so that each student will have part of the whole, for example, if you were studying for a 25 word spelling unit and your study teams each had four members, three members of the team would have six words each and one member would have seven words.

1. Explain that the purpose of team practice is to prepare each student for the Cooperative Competition Games. Team-mates must help each other learn all the material so each can do well in the Games and on the individual post-test. One way to study together is to quiz each other on the material. Emphasize that:

   a. No on is finished studying until everyone knows the material.

   b. If students have questions, they must first ask their teammates before asking the teacher.

c. Instead of simply giving the answer, students should explain how they arrived at their answer.

2. The first thing the team will do is select a team name. While they are deciding upon their name, you can distribute the worksheets to each team. (Be sure to give the appropriately numbered sheet to the student with that number; this allows you to design material suitable to each ability level represented in the team.)

3. Students spend the rest of this class period practicing in their teams. You should walk around the room during this time, monitoring how well students are working together and assisting, when necessary, with content-related questions.

STEP 5: CONTINUED TEAM PRACTICE - TUESDAY THROUGH THURSDAY

Students should immediately assemble in their teams at the beginning of this period. Remind students that their study is not finished until each member of the team knows the material.

STEP 6: COOPERATIVE COMPETITION GAMES - FRIDAY

You will need one copy of the Game Sheet and one deck of numbered cards for each Game table.

a. Introduce the Competition Games

Tell student that this is the time they have the opportunity to show how much they have learned in team study sessions. Each student plays in a competition with other students who have done about as well as they have in this subject area. The points each student wins will be points for their team.

b. Assign students to their tournament tables; four to five students at each table; remember all the 1's will compete at one table, all the 2's at another, and so on.

c. Give each table a deck of numbered cards and a game answer sheet. The answer sheet is a composite of the study sheets given to each team; like the index cards, the answer sheet is numbered 1 through however many items are included in the unit, for example 25 spelling words.(We usually have the questions and answers on the same sheet.) If this is a math lesson, you might also want to give each student some scratch paper on which to work out the problem.

d. Discuss the competition game rules:

There are two roles: the "Player" is the student whose turn it is to answer a question; the "Checker" is the student to the immediate left of the "Player." The Checker has the Game Sheet with Answers.

1.) The numbered index cards are placed face down in the middle of the table.
2) The "Player" picks a card and says the number aloud.
3) The "Checker" finds the corresponding number on the question sheet and reads the question aloud.
4) The "Player" responds to the question.
5) The "Checker" acknowledges the correctness of the question, or if incorrect, states the correct answer.

If the player responds correctly, he keeps that card; if the response in incorrect, the card is placed at the bottom of the deck.

e. To Start the Competition Games — You will arbitrarily select which student at each table will be the first "Player" with the student on his immediate left assigned as first "Checker." (Some ways to select: person sitting closest to clock; person with name beginning closest to the letter "D;" etc.)

f. The Competition Game is played for a predetermined number of minutes, or until all the questions have been answered, whichever comes first. Students then count the number of cards, i.e. points, they have earned. Each Player's points are recorded on their team chart.

g. Determining Team Scores - Total team members' individual points, i.e., number of cards earned at Game table, and calculate the average by dividing the sum total by the number of members in the team. That becomes the Team's score for that Cooperative Competition Game.

h. Post-test - An individual post-test is administered to check each student's understanding and knowledge of the material. This score can be used in your grade book. (Team scores can be used for bonus points or some sort of reward and recognition.)

i. Reassigning students to teams and Competition Game tables - Reassignments are made following each Competition Game..Using the individual post-test scores, reassign students to teams and Competition Game tables for the next unit in that particular subject area.

FIGURE 1: SAMPLE STUDENT RANKING - VOCABULARY PRETEST SCORES

```
 1. Juana 97
 2. Gerry 97
 3. Margie 95
 4. Suzie 94        { high performers
 5. Marilyn 93
 6. Pete 92
 7. Pat 91
 8. Evelyn 90
 9. Marie 89
10. Jackie 88
11. Julieta 88     {medium high performers
12. Jack 87
13. Karen 86
14. Juana 86
15. Jason 85
16. Patsy 82
17. Frank 81
18. Bob 79
19. Nancy 77
20. Laurie 74      {medium low performer
21. Lin 72
22. Joseph 68
23. Scott 63
24 Carol 62
25. Julio 60
26. Dottie 56
27. George 55
28. Manny 53
29. Kim 50         {low performers
30. Rich 47
31. Tomas 44
32. Vickie 39
```

To group students, take one from the top, one from the bottom, and one from each medium group keeping in mind boy/girl, ethnicity and racial ratio. You'll have to use your own judgement about personality factors. Two possible teams are:
Team A:
#1 Juana; #2 Karen; #3 Bob; #4 Rich
Team B:
#1 Gerry; #2 Jason; #3 Lin; #4 Vickie

PAIR 4 CHECK HELP
(adapted from Team Assisted Instruction (TAI) originally called Team Assisted Individualization (TAI Mathematics) by Robert Slavin, Marshall Leavey and Nancy Madden, at the Johns Hopkins University. 1982.)

The original TAI Mathematics was developed to be used with a set of prepackaged math materials (grades 3 - 8 available from the Johns Hopkins University) and it was designed to combine the best features of two instructional methods: individualized instruction and cooperative learning. The TAI model solved the problem of individualization by having students work in small heterogeneous groups, within which pairs and/or triads were formed. Each student, however, was to work on an instructional unit at his or her own skill level as in programmed instruction. A series of skillsheets, checkout sheets, and final tests with answer sheets are provided in the TAI Mathematics model.

The following is our adaptation which is extended to any knowledge-level material such as math, history or science for grades 3 - 12 (and adult in some areas). We call this approach:

Pair 4 Check Help
(1985)

This approach recognizes that students are at different levels of skill, knowledge, and ability but that they can help each other and that they can learn advanced thinking processes through teaming to learn.

COMPONENTS:

1. Pretest
2. Establish pairs within heterogeneous groups of four students
3. Class Instruction
4. Homogeneous group instruction by teacher
5. Team study and practice
6. Homework
7. Individual quiz
8. Team member check
9. Team help
10. Teacher monitor and help
11. Individual quizzes, team help, teacher help
12. Post-Test
13. Student profile
14. Team Score
15. Team Reward
16. Regroup

Appendix IV: Cooperative Student Study Teams

B. Preparing to use Pair 4 Check Help
   You need:
   1. Pretest for unit
   2. Lesson Plan
   3. Skill sheets at different skill levels <u>or</u> use textbook
   4. Student folders for completed worksheets and quizzes.
   5. Individual Quizzes congruent with worksheets <u>or</u> textbook assignment
   6. Team score sheet
   7. Post-Test

C. Steps: (Remember, this approach is for knowledge level material only, i.e., must have only one correct answer.)

1. Pretest class - Be sure students understand this is a **survey** and <u>not</u> a graded test.
2. Group Students in teams of four. Teams should be heterogeneous relative to boy/girl, race and ethnicity represented in class as a whole. Also, use your own judgement relative to student personality. Assign groups to work area. Be sure they understand they will be together for the entire unit and they will receive a team score.
3. Teacher provides an instructional overview on unit material (a unit might take one to four weeks to cover.)
4. Teacher separates class into 3 groups; each group of students will be within a range of skill level. Teacher then provides direct instruction to one group at a time on the underlying concepts of these students' skill sheets. The rest of the class are in their teams practicing with skill sheets.
5. Students get skill sheets at their level of ability:
   - Students work through material (allow appropriate amount of time)
   - Pairs within groups check each other's work. We suggest that students complete 2 - 3 problems on a given worksheet and have a team member check their answers before going on. If the answers are correct, the student continues and completes the worksheet. If incorrect, team members "teach" student the skills associated with that content. If no one on the team knows the correct process, they can ask another team or the teacher may be called on for help.

6. Homework is given as often as appropriate for the content. This might be as seldom as once or twice weekly or as often as daily. Pairs are also provided with answer sheets for homework assignments and check each other's work. Homework scores are recorded on the student's profile.

7. Individual Practice Quiz:
   a. As appropriate but at least weekly, students take a quiz on the unit material covered thus far.
   b. Again, answer sheets are provided and pairs score each other's quiz.
   c. Scores are recorded on student profile.
   d. Incorrect answers are discussed by all team members with teacher help, as needed.

8. Teacher "homogeneous" group instruction continues on a weekly basis.

9. Post-Test - at the end of the unit, a post-test is administered.
   a. Individual scores can be used in grade book.
   b. Individual scores of each team are totaled and averaged (i.d., total team members individual scores and divide by number of team members for Team Average Score.)
   c. Record Team averages on Team Score Sheet.

10. Team Recognition Ideas
    a. Use team averages for bonus points
    b. Give certificate for each team with a team average at or above 80%.

c. Give rewards to teams with team average at or above 80%
d. Give rewards to teams who worked especially well together based on your observations.

11. Regroup pairs and teams for next unit based on post-test scores.

D. *What to do if.......*

1. **Team members are not helping each other...**
   a.) go back and review communication, group member responsibilities, problem solving and the advantages of cooperative approaches. (Introduction & Chapters 2, 3, 4)
   b.) refer students back to team members when they ask you a question or when their answer is incorrect.
   c. offer rewards agreed upon by the teacher and group for cooperating and helping each other. (see Chapter 8)

2. **Students don't want to work with someone.........**
   Reread Chapter 6.

3. **Absences**...Remind them of interdependence and group member responsibilities. (Excessive absences require parent contact.) If some students are routinely absent we do one of two things: group the habitually absent together (this has a better chance of teaching responsibility) or double-up within group, in other words, if you have groups of 4, an habitually absent student would become the 5th member of that group and would be working on the same material as one of the other members thus the group would not suffer as a result of that student's absence. This, however, does not help the student to learn responsibility.

If you establish a cooperative classroom, taking the time to teach the critical social skills and if you have a meaningful reward system, you should experience few absences.

GLOSSARY

Advanced Facilitator: Individual who helps group fulfill its objective; concerned more with group process than product.

Advanced Recorder: Individual who writes, on large sheets of paper that are placed in full view of all participants, the key phrases of a discussion, decisions made by the group, and the future plans of the group.

Autocratic Decision: One person unilaterally makes decision for all.

Beginning Recorder: Student who writes group's responses to submit to teacher.

Behavior: An action that is tangible and quantifiable.

Brainstorming: Generating ideas, without evaluation, usually allowing a very short period of time (3 - 7 minutes).

Checker: Has answer key and checks accuracy of group's answers; to be used when studying content areas where there is one correct answer such as math and spelling.

Checking Out Perceptions: Asking speaker if what you think he is feeling is accurate.

Congruence: Verbal and nonverbal messages are saying the same thing.

Consensus Decision: Group as a whole makes decision; final decision may not be each individual's favorite but all agree they can support the decision.

Democratic Decision: Decision made through some type of voting.

Dyad: Two individuals; a pair.

Energizer Activities: Brief activities that help students regain energy, usually an activity which is very different than the present task; intended to "cure" glazed eyes, inability to attend to task, etc.

Facilitator as Monitor: Similar to the old monitor role; gets and distributes papers and other resources group needs to complete assignment; turns work in to teacher.

Frame of Reference: The sum total of our knowledge and experiences.

Getting Acquainted Activities: Short activities designed to help students know each other and the teacher.

The Nurturing Classroom

Goal: The expected outcome of a behavior or activity.

Goal Structure: The process through which the expected goal will be accomplished.

Three goal structures have been identified:

1. Individualistic - students work alone

2. Competitive - students work against each other to gain a limited number of rewards

3. Cooperative - students must work with each other to accomplish the goal.

Heterogeneous Group: A student grouping that includes high, middle, and low performers, as well as a ratio of girl/boy, ethnic, and racial identical or nearly identical to the ratio in the entire class population.

Homogeneous Group: Group where all members are of a similar performance level.

Internal Dialogue: Talking to ourselves within our mind.

Mediated Learning Experience: (MLE) Exposure to alternative thinking paths, or ways of thinking about different situations.

Metacognition: Thinking about thinking, an attribute of effective thinkers.

Nonverbal Message: All parts of message except spoken words, includes tone, tempo, volume, eye movement, facial expressions, gestures, gutteral sounds, etc.

Observer: Using an observation form, conducts frequency count of specific predetermined behavior(s); observations may be of each individual group member, small cooperative groups, or the entire class. Observer provides quantitative report, without evaluation or judgment of any kind.

Paraphrasing: Saying, in your own words, your understanding of the speaker's message.

Simple Cooperation: An instructional methodology that focuses on teaching social skills while maintaining an emphasis on academic skills. Students are assigned to heterogeneous or homogeneous groups for social and academic skills learning activities. Can be used with "Effective Teaching" and other instructional models.

Successful Communication: Transference of ideas, thoughts, attitudes and opinions from a sender, speaker, to a receiver, listener, with the receiver understanding the message in the same manner as sender intended. Transference of meaning.

Thinking Paths: A way of thinking about something; a thinking strategy.

Transition Activity: A brief activity that provides a mind-set for the activity to follow - it helps refocus individual thoughts back to the group. Transition is conducted between major activities, after recess or lunch, at the beginning of the class period.

Triad: A group of three.

Wrap-Up: A brief activity immediately following a cooperative lesson. The activity focuses on either the social skill objective or the academic objective and provides students an opportunity to enhance thinking and communication skills. The Wrap-Up provides closure by asking students to analyze their use of specific social skills or what they learned from the academic content.

REFERENCES

&

RESOURCES

References & Resources

Ackoff, Russel. *The Art of Problem Solving*. New York: John Wiley and Sons, 1978.

Aronson, E.; Blaney N.; Stephan, C.; Sikes, J. and Snapp, M. *The Jigsaw Classroom*. Beverly Hills, CA: Sage Publications, 1978.

Baron, Joan Boykoff and Sternberg, Robert J., ed. *Teaching Thinking Skills: Theory and Practice*. NY: W.H. Freeman and Company. 1987.

Bloom, Benjamin and Broder, L.J. *Problem Solving Processes of College Students*. Chicago: University of Chicago Press. 1950.

Bloom, Benjamin, and others. *Taxonomy of Educational Objectives: Cognitive and Affective Domains*. NJ: Longman, 1969.

Byer, Barry. *Developing a Thinking Skills Program: Practical Strategies for Teachers*. Allyn Bacon. 1988.

Canfield, Jack and Wells, Harold C.. *100 Ways to Enhance Self-Concept in the Classroom*. Englewood Cliffs, N.J.: Prentice-Hall, 1976.

Cathcart, Robert S.. *Small Group Communciation*. Dubuque, Iowa: Wm. C. Brown Company Publishers, 1979.

Center for Multisensory Learning, University of California, Berkeley. *SAVI/SELPH*. Lawrence Hall of Science, 1976. (Note: This is a Science program based on small group instruction; lesson plans are included.)

Cetron, Marvin. *Schools of the Future*. New York: McGraw Hill, 1985.

Chance, Paul. *Thinking in theClassroom: A Summary of Programs*. Teachers College Press. 1986.

Christinson, Mary Ann and Bassano, Sharron. *Look Who's Talking: A Guide to the Development of Successful Conversation Groups in Intermediate and Advanced ESL Classrooms*. 2nd. ed. Hayward, CA: Alemany Press. 1981.

Chuska, Kenneth R. *Teaching the Process of Thinking, K-12*. Bloomington, Indiana: Phi Delta Kappa Educational Foundation. 1986.

Co-operative College of Canada. *Co-operation and Community Life*, 1983. Order from: Co-operative College of Canada, 141-105 Street West, Saskatoon, Saskatchewan S7N 1N3.

_____ . *Co-operative Outlooks*. 1983. Order from Co-operative College of Canada.

Cornell, Joseph. *Sharing Nature With Children.* Order from: Ananda Publications, 14618 Tyler Foote Rd., Nevada City, CA 95959.

Costa, Arthur L. "Mediating the Metacognitive." *Educational Leadership,* November 1984, pp. 57 - 62.

_____. *Developing Minds: A Resource Book for Teaching Thinking.* VA. Association for Supervision & Curriculum Development. 1985.

Costa, Arthur and Lowery, W. *Issues in Teaching Thinking.* Midwest Publishers. 1988.

de Bono, Edward. de Bono's Thinking Course. NY: Facts on File Publications. 1985

Dillon, J.T. *Teaching and The Art of Questioning.* Bloomington, Indiana: Phi Delta Kappa Educational Foundation. 1983.

Dishon, Dee and O'Leary, Pat Wilson. *A Guidebook for Cooperative Learning: A Technique for Creating More Effective Schools.* Holmes Beach, Florida: Learning Publications, Inc.1984.

Doyle, Michael and Straus, David. *How to Make Meetings Work.* New York: Playboy Paperbacks, 1976.

Educators for Social Responsibility. *Perspectives.* Cambridge, MA: Educators for Social Responsibility, 1983.

Feingold, Norman S. and Miller, Norma Reno . *Emerging Careers*: New Occupations for the Year 2000 and Beyond. Maryland: Garrett Park Press.

Feuerstein, Reuven. *The Dynamic Assessment of Retarded Performers.* Baltimore, MD: University Park Press, 1979.

_____. *Instrumental Enrichment.* Baltimore, MD: University Park Press, 1980.

Fluegelman, Andrew. *The New Games Book.* NY: Doubleday, 1976.

_____. ed. *More New Games.* NY: Doubleday. 1981.

Gall, Meredith. Synthesis of Research on Teachers' Questioning. *Educational Leadership.* November 1984, 40 - 47.

Gibbs, Jeanne. *Tribes: A Process for Social Development and Cooperative Learning.* 1987. Order from: Center Source Publications, P.O. Box 436, Santa Rosa, CA 94502.

References & Resources

Gordon, Dr. Thomas. *Leader Effectiveness Training*. Wynden Books, 1977.

_____.___. *Parent Effectiveness Training in Action*. New York: G.P. Putnam and Sons, 1976.

_____ *Teacher Effectiveness Training*. NY: Longman, Inc., 1974.

Grinder, John and Bandler, Richard. *The Structure of Magic II*. Santa Clara, CA: Science and Behavior Books, Inc., 1976.

Healy, Mary K. *Using Student Writing Response Groups in the Classroom*. Berkeley: University of California, Berkeley Bay Area Writing Project, 1980.

Hill, Wm. Fawcett. *Learning Through Discussion*. Beverly Hills, CA: Sage Publications, 1977.

Johnson, David W. *Reaching Out*. Englewood Cliffs, NJ: Prentice-Hall, 1981.

Johnson, David W. and Johnson, Frank P.. *Joining Together: Group Theory and Group Skills*. 4th ed. Englewood Cliffs, NJ: Prentice-Hall, Inc. 1987.

Johnson, David and Johnson, Frank. *Joining Together*. Englewood Cliffs, NJ: Prentice-Hall, 1982.

Johnson, David W. and Johnson, Roger T.. *Learning Together and Alone: Cooperative, Competitive and Individualistic Learning*. 4th ed. Englewood Cliffs, NJ: Prentice-Hall, Inc., 1987.

Johnson, David; Johnson, Roger T.; Holubec, Edythe Johnson; and Roy, Patricia. *Circles of Learning*. ASCD Publications, 1984.

Johnson, Roger T.; Johnson, David W. and Holubec; and Edythe Johnson, ed. *Structuring Cooperative Learning: Lesson Plans for Teachers*. 1987. Order from: Interaction Book Company, 7208 Cornelia Drive, Edina, MN 55435.

Johnson, David. *Creative Conflict*. MN: Interaction Book Company. 1988.

Judson, Stephanie. *A Manual on Nonviolence and Children*. Order from: Nonviolence and Children Program, Friends Peace Committee, 1515 Cherry St. Philadelphia, PA 19102

Kaplan, Phyllis G.; Crawford, Susan K.; and Nelson, Shelley L.. *Nice Nifty Innovations for Creative Expression*. Denver, CO: Love Publishing Co., 1977.

Kagan, Spencer. *Cooperative Learning Resources for Teachers*. 1985. Order from: Professor Spencer Kagan, School of Education, University of California, Riverside, CA 92521.

Kaufman, Roger. *Identifying and Solving Problems: A System Approach*. San Diego, CA: University Associates, Inc., 1979.

Knapp, Clifford and Goodman, Joel. *Humanizing Environmental Education*. Order from: American Camping Association, Bradford Woods, Martinsville, IN 46151-7902

Kreidler, William. *Creative Conflict Resolution: More Than 200 Activities for Keeping Peace in the Classroom*. Glenview, IL: Scott, Foresman and Co., 1984.

Lewis, David and Greene, James. *Thinking Better*. NY: Rawson, Wade Publishers, Inc., 1982.

Lipman, Matthew and others. "The New Jersey Task Force Taxonomy of Thinking Skills." *Educational Leadership*. September 1984, p. 73.

Male, Mary, Johnson, D., Johnson, R. and Anderson, M. *Cooperative Learning and Computers: An Activity Guide for Teachers*. CA: Educational-Apple-Cations. 1987.

Marzano, Robert, et. al. *Dimensions of Thinking*. VA: Association for Supervision and Curriculum Development. 1988.

McCabe, Margaret E. *The Public High School in the Year 2010: A National Delphi Study*. Dissertation, University of La Verne, La Verne, CA. 1983.

McCabe, Margaret E. and Rhoades, Jacqueline. *Cooperative Meeting Management*. Willits, CA: ITA Publications, 1985.

McCabe, Margaret E. and Rhoades, Jacqueline. *How to Say What You Mean*. CA: ITA Publications, 1985.

Martinelli, Kenneth J.. "Thinking Straight About Thinking." *The School Administrator* 44 (January 1987): pp. 21 - 23.

Meichenbaum, Donald. *Cognitive Behavior Modification*. NY: Plenum Press, 1979.

Moorman, Chick and Dishon, Dee. *Our Classroom: We Can Learn Together*. MI: The Institute for Personal Power, 1983.

Moskowitz, Gertrude. *Caring and Sharing in the Foreign Language Class*. Rowley, MA: Newbury House Publishers, 1978.

Naisbitt, John. *Megatrends*. NJ: Warner Books, 1982.

Nierenberg, Gerard and Calero, Henry H. . *Meta Talk*. NJ: Pocket Books, 1975.

Olson, Carol Booth. "Fostering Critical Thinking Skills Through Writing." *Educational Leadership*, November 1984, pp. 28 - 39.

Orlick, Terry. The *Second Cooperative Sports and Games Book*. NY: Pantheon Books, 1981.

Prutzman, Priscilla and Leonard, M. . *The Friendly Classroom for a Small Planet*. 1978. Order from: Children's Creative Response to Conflict, 15 Rutherford Place, New York, NY 10003.

Raths, Louis E. and others. *Teaching for Thinking: Theories, Strategies, and Activities for the Classroom*. New York: Teachers College Press. 1986

Reid, JoAnne; Forrestal, Peter; and Cook, Jonathon. *Small Group Work in the Classroom*. 1982. Order from: The Manager, Education Supplies Branch, 23 Miles Rd., Kewdale 6105, Western Australia.

Rhoades, Jacqueline and McCabe, Margaret. *Simple Cooperation in the Classroom*. CA: ITA Publications. 1985.

Samson, Richard W.. *Thinking Skills: A Guide to Logic and Comprehension*. Stamford, Conneticut: Innovative Sciences, Inc. 1981.

Saskatchewan Department of Co-Operation and Co-operative Development. *Working Together, Learning Together*. 1983. Order from: The Steward Resource Centre, STF, Box 1108, Saskatoon, Saskatchewan S7K 3N3

Schmuck, Richard and Schmuck, Patricia . *A Humanistic Psychology of Education: Making the School Everybody's House*. Palo Alto, CA: Mayfield Publishing Co., 1974.

_____. *Group Process in the Classroom*. 4th ed. IA: Wm. C. Brown Co., 1983.

Schneiderwind, Nancy and Davidson, Ellen. *Open Minds to Equity: A Sourcebook of Learning Activities to Promote Race, Sex, Class and Age Equity*. NJ: Prentice-Hall, 1983.

_____. *Cooperative Learning - Cooperative Lives: A Sourcebook of Learning Activities for Building a Peaceful World*. Dubuque, IA: Wm. C. Brown Co., 1987.

Sexton, Thomas G. and Poling, Donald R. *Can Intelligence Be Taught*? Bloomingdale, Indiana: Phi Delta Kappa Educational Foundation 1973,

Sharan, Shlomo and Sharan, Yael. *Small Group Teaching*. NJ: Educational Publications, 1976.

Sharan, Shlomo; Hare, Paul; Clark, D.; and Hertz-Lazarowitz, Rachel. *Cooperation in Education*. Provo, Utah, Brigham Young University Press, 1979.

Slavin, Robert E. *Cooperative Learning: Student Teams*. Washington, D.C.: National Education Association, 1982.

_____. *Using Student Team Learning*. 3rd. ed. 1986. Order from: Center for Research on Elementary and Middle Schools, The Johns Hopkins University, 3505 North Charles St., Baltimore, MD 21218.

_____. *Cooperative Learning*. NY: Longman, Inc., 1983

Slavin, Robert; Sharan, Shlomo; Kagan, Spencer; Hertz-Lazarowitz, Rachel; Webb, Clark; and Schmuck, Richard. *Learning to Cooperate, Cooperating to Learn*. NY: Plenum Press, 1985.

Solomon, Letitia Ursa. *The Rotten Chicken*. Ukiah, CA: Henchanted Books, 1984.

Sternberg, Robert J. "How Can We Teach Intelligence?" *Educational Leadership*, September 1984, pp. 38 - 47.

_____. *Intelligence Applied: Understanding and Increasing Your Intellectual Skills*. San Diego: Harcourt, Brace, Jovanovich. 1986.

_____ "Teaching Critical Thinking: Eight Easy Ways to Fail Before You Begin." *Phi Delta Kappan* 68 (February 1987): pp. 456 - 459.

Wassermann, Selma. "Teaching for Thinking: Louis E. Raths Revisited." *Phi Delta Kappan* 68 (February 1987): pp. 460 -465.

Whimbey, Arthur and Whimbey, Linda Shaw. *Intelligence Can Be Taught*. NY: Bantam Books, 1976.

Whimby, Arthur. Students Can Learn to be Better Problem Solvers." *Educational Leadership*. Vol. 37, #7. April 1980.

Winter, M.D., Arthur and Winter, Ruth. *Build Your Brain Power*. NY: St. Martin's, 1986.

Worsham, Antoinette M. and Stockton, Anita J.. *A Model for Teaching Thinking Skills: The Inclusion Process*. Bloomingdale, Indiana: Phi Delta Kappa Educational Foundation. 1986. (This PDK "Fastback" includes instructions for four thinking skills lessons.)

INDEX

Index

3 C's 54
    Practice 74
Academic Achievement x, 12
Academic Components 237
Academic Groups 154
    Duration 154
Academic Learning 24
Academic Lessons 165
Academic Progress 169
Acceptance and Understanding 21
Active Listening 65, 78
Advanced Facilitator 138
    and Communication Skills 138
    Responsibilities 138
Advanced Recorder 135, 136
    Techniques 136
Agreement
    Written 102
Anger 56
    Expressing 57
Anxiety 26, 27
Appreciation Forms 128
Aronson, Elliot x
ASCD 229
Asking Questions 20, 60
    and Looking Dumb 52
Assignments 188
Attitudes 50
Autocratic 103
Autocratic Decisions 107
Beginning Recorder
    Responsibilities 124
Behavior
    Defined 131
Behavior vs Attitude
    Teaching 131
Behaviors
    and Feelings 131
Birthday Line 160
Bloom, Benjamin 213
Bloom's Taxonomy 213, 224, 225, 227
Body Language 62
Bonus Points 191
Brainstorming 102
    Activities 109
    Rules 102
    Techniques 102
Breaking Up 26, 27
Breaking Up Activities 9
Check Perceptions 62
    Checker 130, 138,
    Introducing 276

Checking Perceptions 65, 76
Claiming Thoughts 54
Clarifying 59
Classroom
    Getting their attention techniques 74
Classroom Environment 3, 7, 17, 29
    and Conflict 27
    Safe 68
Color Spectrum 163
Comfort Zone 65
Communication 19, 49, 50, 174
    and Simple Cooperation 49
    Complex Process 52
    Components 69, 70
    Continuum 70
    Definition 50
    Misinterpretation 52
    Nonverbal 49
    Self-Examination 50
    Speaker 53
    Teaching 69
    Why Study 49
Communication Skills 6
Communicaton
    Nonverbal 53, 62, 86
Communicaton Loop 51
Completing the Task 6, 25
Compliments 125, 126
Conflict 9, 27, 28, 57, 97
    and Direct Intervention 98
    and Problem Solving 99
    as Learning Experiences 98
    Cooperative Groups 152
    Defined 97
    Learned Approach 97
Congruence 66, 67
Congruence Activities
    How to be a Good Listener 91, 92
    On Becoming a Poet 91
    On Becoming an Actor 92
Consensus Decisions 24, 107
    Advantages 107
Continuums xvi
Cooperation
    and Research xv, 6
    Introducing to Students 254
Cooperative Activities
    Benefit of 11
Cooperative Classroom
    Explaining to Students 254, 261
Cooperative Group Assignments
    Signatures 124

Cooperative Groups 7, 151-159
Cooperative Learning xv
    Formal Beginning xv
Counting Off 159
DeBono, Edward 228
Decision Making 103-108
    Consensus 24, 107
    Democratic 107
Dependability 121
Designing Lessons 236-150
    to Promote Higher Level Thinking 213, 214
Deutsch, Morton x
Dewey, John xv
Direct Instruction 4, 255, 256
Direct Intervention
    Messages it gives 98
Effective Thinking 210
    Attributes 210-212
Employers 46
Energizer Activities 41-43
Energizers 22-23
    Aardvarks and Antelopes 42
    Applause 46
    Bees 46
    Guess That Number 45
    WHIP 41
Expressing & Naming Feelings
    Literature and Feelings 85
Expressing & Naming Feelings Activities
    Find the Feeling 84
    Identify the Feeling 84
    Music is my Business 84
Eye Contact 54, 65, 69
Facilitator
    Advanced 138, 139
Facilitator as Monitor
    Responsibilities 123
Fear
    Rejection 67
    Feedback 51, 52, 63
    Rules 70
Feelings 21, 56
    Hiding 66
Feuerstein, Reuven 204, 228
Following Directions Activity
    Unknown Design 82
Frame of Reference 52, 57, 202
Future 6
Getting Acquainted 9, 21
Getting Acquainted Activities
    Focus Worksheet 43
    Getting Acquainted Cards 39
    Guess That Number 45

Guess That Person 38
    Importance of 33
    One Fact 40
    Self-Description 37
    Similarities and Differences 36
    What We Have in Common 39
    Introductions 36
    Memory Game 37
"Give 'em three" 68
Gordon, Thomas 58, 65
Gordon, Thomas 57
Grades 13
    and Cooperation 187
    Group 13, 187, 190
    Group Examples 191
    Individual 10, 190
Group Development 7, 17, 29
    Process 17, 19
Group Grades 190-192
    Definition 190
    Examples 191
Group Growth 28
Group Identity 153
Group Maturity 26
Group Member 120
    Responsibilities 121-122
Group Rewards
    Examples 189
Group Roles 7, 10, 119-140
    Advantages 119
    Combining 142
    Continuum 120
    Elementary School 145
    Implementation Activities 145
    Introducing to Students 151
    Reader 142
    Rotate 121, 139, 140
    Rotating 121
    Secondary 145
    Skills 9
    Teaching 121
Group Roles Continuum 120, 244
Group Selection
    Academic 154
    and Objectives 154
    Teacher Selection Techniques 155-158
Grouping Students 151
Group Member
    Responsibilities 122
    Teaching 121-122
Groups 151
    Academic 154
    Cohesive 17, 19, 22

Index

Groups (con't)
    Cooperative 5
    Duration 152
    Forming 17
    Heterogeneous 154
    Homogeneous 154
    Random Selection Techniques 158
    Size 153
    Teacher-Selected 155
    Team Name 153
Guess That Person 38
Heterogeneous Groups 154
    and Thinking Skills 155
High Achievers 14
    and Thinking Skills 206
    Parents 13
How to Organize for Success 229
I-Messages 58
    Practice 76, 77
Implementation Plan Sample 260
Incentives 187
Incongruence 66, 67
Initiative
    Develop 19
Intelligence 204
Internal Dialogue 207, 220
    and Mediation 207, 220
Johns Hopkins University x
Johnson, David xv, 4, 7
Johnson, Frank xv
Johnson, Roger xv, 4, 7
Leader 143
Leadership
    Laissez-Faire 19
Leadership Development 5, 23, 24
Learning How to Learn 201
Learning Time
    Engaged 25
Lesson
    Simple Cooperation 12, 236, 239, 240
Lesson Activities
    and Objectives 241
Lesson Design
    and Internal Dialogue 208
    Aspects 237
    Planning 241
    to Enhance Thinking Skills 204, 213
Lesson Plan 245-250
    and Social Skills 237
    Sample Format 245
    Samples 247-250, 281-317
Lewin, Kurt xv
Lipman, Matthew 229

Listener/Receiver 58
    Active Listening 68
    Asking Questions 60
    Aspects of good listener 68, 69
    Becoming a good 77, 78
    Checking Perceptions 62
    Clarify 59, 60
    Eye Contact 54, 69
    Feedback 69, 70
    Nonverbal Signals 62, 63
    Paraphrasing 61
    Techniques 59, 60
Listening
    Powerful 68, 69
    Teaching Clarifying 272
Listening & Speaking Activities
    News Reporter 81
    Verbal Map 82
Listening Activities
    Asking Questions 79
    Paraphrasing Student Writing 80
    Paraphrasing Verbal Messages 79, 80
    Paraphrasing Written Messages 80
Mainstreaming 7
Mead, George Herbert xv
Mediated Learning Experience 204
Mediation 204
    Sample Activities 217
Mediation and Internal Dialogue
    Explaining to Students 217, 219
Meeker, Mary 229
Meetings 119
    Agenda 119
    and Group Roles 119, 120
    Cooperative Groups 119
    Defined 119
    Successful 119
Metacognition 207, 208
    Defined 207
Motivation 187
Multi-Modality 12
Mystery Envelopes 157, 159
Name Tags 155
Nonverbal Messages 52
    and Observer Role 132
    Aspects of 62
    Definition 53, 62
    Misunderstood 63
    Proximity 64, 65
    Watching Yourself 63
Nonverbal Messages Activities
    Becoming Aware 88
    Expression 87

Nonverbal Messages Activities (con't)
    Giving Directions 88
    Mirroring 86
    Music Interpretation 87
Objectives 11, 151, 154, 239, 240, 241, 243
    and Lesson Activities 241
    Life Cycle 243
Observation
    and Developing Thinking Skills 222
    and Thinking Skills 209
    Teacher 169-209
Observations
    Explaining to Students 266
Observer 130, 131, 143
    Assigning 133
    Demonstrate 132
    Forms 133
    Points to Remember 133
    Teaching 132
Observer vs Praiser 130, 143
Opening Activities 22, 33
    Focus Worksheet 43, 44
    Guess That Number 45
    WHIP 41
Organize for Success Worksheet 230-232
Paraphrasing 61
    Example 61
Parents
    Meeting with 13
    of High Achievers 14
Participatory Decisions 107
Perception-Checking Activities 91-92
Praiser 125-129
    Assigning 127
    Teaching Elementary 125
    Teaching Secondary 125
Praiser vs Observer 130, 143
Praising
    Give Cues 126
    Modeling 126
    Sample Behavior List for 127
    Teaching 125-129, 270
    Written 128, 129
Primary-age children 135, 143
Principal 17

Problem Solving 99
    Steps 99-102
Productivity 24
Proximity
    Eye Level 69
Questioning Strategies Self-Analysis 227

Rath, Louis E. 210
Reader 142
Recorder
    Advanced 135-137
    Advanced, Responsibilities 137
    Advanced Techniques 137
    Beginning 124
    Making Corrections 136
Research Studies xv, 4, 6
Respect 17
Responsibility 5, 6, 17, 20, **188**
    Developing 119
    Group 189
    Individual 21, 187
    Social 5, 21
Restating 61
Rewards 10
    and Cooperation 187
    Examples 189, 190
    Group 10, 187, 188
    Individual 10, 190
    Selecting 188
Ridiculing 68
Role Playing 126
    and Thinking 217
Room Arrangement 235, **236**
Self-Concept xv
Self-Esteem 5
Self-Grouping 159
Self-Talking 204
Sharan, Shlomo xv
Simple Cooperation
    and Communication Skills 50-72
    as a "model" xvi
    Definition 3
Slavin, Robert xv, 7
Social Responsibility 17
Social Skill Progress
    Monitoring Techniques 169
Social Skills 6, 7, 261
    as part of the Curriculum 3
    Continuums 237, 238
Solution Finding 99
Speaker/Receiver
    Restating 75, 76
Speaker/Sender 53, **54**, 70
    Congruence 66, 67
    Restating 61
    Techniques 53-56
Special Education **Students 7**
Standards 7, 9, 67
    as Social Skills 19

Standards (con't)
    Explaining to Students 261
    Positive Phrasing 19-32
    Process for Establishing 32
    Sample List 20, 21
    Students Setting 6, 23-25
    Teacher Set 17
Students
    New 18
Subject Area Selection 162
Sullivan, Harry Stack xv
Teacher
    as Communicator 49
Teacher Observation
    and Objectives 178
    Class 170
    Cooperative Groups 170, 172
    Individual 170, 172
    Purpose 172
    Report 170, 172
    Report Rules 172, 173
Teacher Observation Form 171
Teachers
    and Conflict 9, 98
    and Listening Skills 50
    as Facilitators 11
    Elementary 12
    Exceptional 17
    Get Attention of Class 74
    Group Selection Techniques 155-162
    Laissez-Faire 19
    Observation 169
    Secondary 12
    Set Standards 17-19
The Rotten Chicken 85
Thinking
    Defined 202
    Effective 209, 210
Thinking "Bank" 203, 205
Thinking Paths 203, 205, 207
Thinking Skills 11, 200
    and Group Process 207, 215
    and Internal Dialogue 207, 220
    and Observation 209. 222
    and Research 201
    and Wrap-Up 208
    Development of 206
    Higher Order Tasks 213
    Infusing Higher Level Questions Guide 225
    Organize for Success Worksheet 230-232
    Published Programs 215, 228, 229
    Questioning Strategies 224
    Teaching 206

Thinking Skills Activities
    Alternative Solutions 220
    Qualities 217
    Reinforce Internal Dialogue 223
    Writing Higher-Level Questions 225, 226
Thinking Skills Programs
    California Writing Project 228
    CoRT 228
    Philosophy for Children 229
    Project Impact 229
    Structure of the Intellect 229
    Tactics For Thinking 229
Thinking Strategies
    and Achievement 204, 206
    Self-Analysis 227
Thinking Tasks
    Higher Order 206
Time-Keeper 129, 130, 142
    Teaching 129, 130
Transition Activities 9, 23, 34
    Elementary 22
    Focus Worksheet 44
    Getting Acquainted Cards 39
    One Fact 40
    Secondary 22
    WHIP 41
University of California, Irvine 228
Verbal Message
    Definition 53
Verbal/Nonverbal Congruence 66-68
Wall Charts 156
    Sample 156
Whimbey, Art 208
Wrap-Up 173
    Factors to Consider 174, 175
    How to Conduct 173
    Importance of 175
    Purposes 173
    Sample Activities 178-184
    Techniques 174
Wrap-Up Activities 180-184
    and Thinking Skills 208, 221

NOTES

NOTES

NOTES